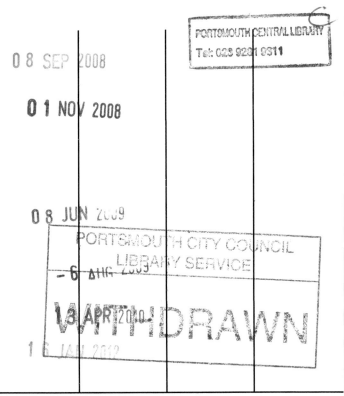

Belonging

Belonging

SAMEEM ALI

WITH

HUMPHREY PRICE

JOHN MURRAY

First published in Great Britain in 2008 by John Murray (Publishers)
An Hachette Livre UK company

4

© Sameem Ali and Humphrey Price 2008

The right of Sameem Ali and Humphrey Price to be identified
as the Authors of the Work has been asserted by them in
accordance with the Copyright, Designs and Patents Act 1988.

A CIP catalogue record for this title is available from the British Library

Hardback ISBN 978-0-7195-6460-4
Trade paperback ISBN 978-0-7195-6461-1

Typeset in Bembo by Hewer Text UK Ltd, Edinburgh
Printed and bound by Clays Ltd, St Ives plc

John Murray policy is to use papers that are natural, renewable
and recyclable products and made from wood grown in sustainable forests.
The logging and manufacturing processes are expected to conform
to the environmental regulations of the country of origin.

John Murray (Publishers)
338 Euston Road
London NW1 3BH

www.johnmurray.co.uk

Prologue

There are many things about my past I find it hard to recall; to this day I cry when I remember all the things that were done and said to me. My memories are not a comfort to me, a place to retreat to; they are a curse.

My mother was everything to me, and I spent my childhood determined to give her no cause to think me anything other than her most dutiful, best behaved, hardworking daughter. A daughter worthy of calling her own, one she could properly cherish. A daughter who deserved her love.

Some years ago, when I finally told someone about my past, and she'd got over her astonishment, she said, 'You must have been adopted. There simply can't be any other reason; no mother would treat her own daughter that way. Why don't we track down your social services file, find out who your real mother was, see what we can find out about your background?'

It seemed so simple, so right. Of course that was what must have happened; why had I never thought of it before? It would explain so much, and answer all my questions. I took up the idea eagerly, and so it was that the two of us found ourselves a few weeks later, in an office, tears pouring down my face as I looked through a file that had just been handed to me that explained that, no, I wasn't adopted, that I'd been taken in by the social services when my family couldn't cope and returned to the family some years later when they wanted me once more. I'd wanted so much to be happy about my childhood and I'd thought this was going to be the way to reclaim those years; instead I felt as if I'd been mugged by my own past. It was my own flesh and blood who had hit me, beat me, whipped me, abducted me, forced me into marriage, scarred me, ignored me, humiliated me, and, worst of all, failed to love me. I could get over almost everything but not this: I was a little girl, and I wanted the one thing they wouldn't give me. I deserved love.

I

I had been taken from my father and placed in a children's home when I was six months old. My mother was ill after I was born, and returned to Pakistan with my brothers and sisters, but why I was left behind, and why my father didn't travel with her, I don't know. I had been taken from my father's house when the neighbours heard me crying all day and night. My father, I read in my file, suffered from mental illness, and was not considered capable of looking after a tiny baby on his own. When my mother returned, with the rest of the family, I remained in care.

Living in the children's home was the best period of my childhood; I felt a happiness there I wasn't to know again until I became an adult.

My memories of the home are frustrating; while I can hazily recall my routine there, I don't remember much about the people I was with, or my nursery school. Days and weeks are a blur; I can remember seasons, like it being cold and snowing in winter, and hot and bright in summer, but that's all. Sometimes the recollections steal up on me: when I was reading one night, I had a flashback to a time when someone read the same story to me – I could hear the person's voice speaking the words just ahead of mine. As no one had ever read to me in our family when I went to live with them, the voice I heard was probably that of Auntie Peggy, the woman who looked after me in the children's home.

The clearest memory I have of being in the children's home was the Christmas I got a Sindy doll. I was six, and I was in the big sitting room with the other five or six children and a mound of presents, the excitement building as we waited for our gifts to be handed out to us. First for me was a box wrapped in red shiny paper: a Sindy. A fierce feeling of delight surged through me as I unwrapped the box. I loved that Sindy doll, but when I left the children's home to live with my family, I left her behind. I suppose I remember that Christmas because, later on, I missed that doll.

I never felt short of love in the children's home. Auntie Peggy, who was a small, chubby lady with a round face and friendly eyes, and who smelled of soap, flowers and warm bread, gave me love. She wore her hair short; in the winter she'd tuck it under a scarf and there'd be a little bit of fringe that poked out, waving in the stiff breeze that came off Cannock Chase.

Walking, or rather running about on Cannock Chase was also something that I remember vividly. There was a large black Labrador at the home, Jet, and he would come for walks with us on the Chase; running everywhere, chasing sticks or birds or just the air, he would return so fast as to send us giddy with laughter and excitement. I loved burying my face into the thick fur at the back of his neck, and patting him on his sleek head.

Inside the house, I can remember only the dining room, where we ate, and the kitchen, the big sitting room, where we watched TV, and my bedroom. In the kitchen I would sit on the counter, spoon in hand, scraping out the bowl after helping to bake cakes. I had to be careful not to get dirty, though, and always wore my apron when I was in the kitchen. All our aprons hung on pegs by the doors; mine was blue.

My bedroom had three single beds and was decorated with posters of David Cassidy and the Bay City Rollers – my favourite was the singer, Les McKeown. By my bed was a cabinet on which I kept the things I treasured: Sindy, a little china dolphin I'd bought in a shop in Rhyl (my souvenir from our trip to the seaside), a book borrowed from the playroom, and pine cones, collected from the nearby wood. If I lay down on my pillow, and the curtains were a little open, I could see all these items just before I drifted off to sleep.

One of the other beds was Amanda's. She'd been in the home as far back as I could remember, although she was six months younger. Amanda and I were inseparable, and did everything together, as best friends should. We were in the same class at school and when we were

4

This is a true story, although some identities have been disguised.

I want to dedicate this book to my family, Osghar, Azmier and Asim in the playroom at the end of the corridor, and the two boys in the room next door to us tried to pinch our toys,we stuck up for one another. The two boys would get found out and they'd argue with the staff and say rude things to them; as punishment they'd have to miss TV on a Saturday morning.

We loved the huge garden at the back of the house, and played out there every chance we got. Even in winter, when Amanda and I would have to have help pulling on – and off – the rubber boots we had to wear, it was where we longed to be most of all. We had slides and swings and grass to roll about on, bushes to hide in, secret corners where Amanda and I would take our dolls for games in the afternoons. In the summertime, we never wanted to come in at all.

During the week, for school, I wore a skirt that came to my knees and a cardigan that had little red buttons on it; when I was very young, Auntie Peggy had to do up the buttons for me. It was only a small school, I realise now, and the playground was tiny, but to me it seemed like the whole world.

We would be woken up at half past seven every morning by Auntie Peggy, and we would wash and get dressed – I could manage without any help by then – before coming downstairs for breakfast, where the cereal bowls and plates for toast were already laid out on the table, with little glasses for juice next to each place. Amanda had trouble telling the time, but I'd learned and I was very proud to be able to tell her – if we woke a little early – when Auntie Peggy would come to wake us up.

At school I was teased about my stutter. I had to learn to speak more slowly, to let my brain finish thinking of all the words I was going to say before I spoke. Auntie Peggy used to make me laugh, saying that my brain was running ahead of me, and I'd giggle as I pictured my brain running down the road. With time and a lot of practice, learning to take a breath at the right moments, or singing through the difficult sounds, I managed to get my stutter under control and in due course it didn't bother me any more.

A further problem showed up: my feet. I was born with a problem that had to be corrected, and I had operations on my feet into my teens. I can only vaguely remember this but my file spells it out: 'Still walking with feet well apart . . . if necessary [Sam will need] plastic splints. Her feet have gone over at the ankles.'

As I was a bit older than Amanda, I was allowed to stay up a little later in the evenings. Although I'd be almost asleep, lying on the settee watching *Crossroads*, I would protest if anyone tried to tell me to go to bed. When I went up to our bedroom, I learned not to wake Amanda by closing the door properly, turning the handle so that the lock didn't bang, just like Auntie Peggy had shown me.

At the weekends we slept in, although we were always ready to come downstairs long before the staff were ready for us. We didn't have to get dressed until it was time for lunch, so we could sit in front of the TV and play with Jet.

In the afternoons we'd put on our boots and coats and a member of staff would take us round the corner to the sweet shop, where we could spend our pocket money. Then we'd walk on to Cannock Chase, where we would stay for the rest of the afternoon, as long as it wasn't too wet.

The Chase was where I was at my happiest during my childhood. Mile upon mile of woods and open land, it seemed like a magical place to Amanda and me; it seemed to us that it went on for ever and ever. There were little muddy streams to lie beside and stare into; tiny dips in the ground where we could hide and stare at the clouds rushing past over our heads. It seemed to have its own colours and its own smell, which I've never found anywhere else, and it was the perfect place for us to run about, playing chasing games and hide-and-seek and our very own games, like spot the goblin, which we'd play sitting down in the trees and which was really about us screaming loudly with excitement.

Jet also loved the Chase and he'd run along with us, and when we were tired out he'd sit down next to us and pant as loudly as we did. We'd throw sticks for him and he'd run and bring them back to us, every time.

When we eventually came home we'd be very hungry for our tea. We'd have to wash our hands and we always had lovely teas on a Saturday – burgers and chips, with ice cream for pudding, perhaps. Sometimes it was banana sandwiches, which I hated, so I was given cucumber sandwiches instead. Other times we were treated to bacon sandwiches. I always loved the puddings and cakes.

On Sundays, we'd dress nicely and go to church. Afterwards we'd stay behind for Sunday school, which I enjoyed; the tunes we sang stuck in my mind and I'd often sing them on the way home: 'Morning Has Broken', or 'All Things Bright And Beautiful'.

I remember one special day when we were allowed to help ring the bells. At the back of the old church was a tower, and we were carefully led up the steep stairs to the long ropes that were connected to the bells high above. The grown-ups showed us how they pulled on the ropes, and how there was a soft bit for them to hold on to so that their hands didn't get sore. They tied string to the ropes and explained how we could pull the string to make the cord come down, and that we had to let it run through our hands when the string was pulled back up so that it wouldn't make our fingers sore. When we pulled the cords, we weren't doing much; the grown-ups standing beside us pulled the ropes at the same time. But we made the bells ring, and the noise when they started was so much louder than when we were outside the church, that Amanda and I clamped our hands to our ears and shrieked with delight.

I felt safe, and well looked after: food was ready at lunch-time, my best friend sat beside me at school, Jet always brought the stick back when it was thrown across the Chase. Every morning Auntie Peggy would wake me, every evening she'd check on me after my bath, make sure I was tucked in, and give me a kiss goodnight. If I fell, she picked me up; if I grazed my knee, she cleaned it and put a plaster on it. She was so good to me I was sure she must be my mother, as mothers were always good to their children in the stories we read. She laughed when I said this to her one day and told me, 'No, I'm your Auntie, Sam, just like I am to all the children here.'

Once I was outside playing tag with Amanda, who was chasing me and although I ran as fast as my legs could carry me, I fell and grazed my knee. It hurt and I started to cry. I hobbled inside to tell Auntie Peggy.

'Brave girls don't cry, shh, stop crying, blow on your knee, and watch all the pain disappear.'

I didn't want to stop crying but I did as she told me.

'That's a brave girl; see, all the pain's gone now.'

I beamed at her; I liked being the brave one.

Every now and again my dad would come to visit me in the home. Him coming and then going didn't seem weird to me at all; he would arrive, speak to the staff in the office, come out and ruffle my hair, and hand me some sweets from of his pocket before heading off. Dad was taller than anyone else in the home, but he was always smiling, and his teeth gleamed white against his dark skin. I have no memory of what he said to me; I only remember the treats, really. He'd put his arm round me, and speak sweetly to me, and I'd pull sweets and chocolates out of his pockets – which we both laughed at – that I would keep for later to share with Amanda. He would talk to Auntie Peggy for a while, and they'd both look at me as they said things I didn't listen to, but to me he was a distant figure; he had nothing to do with my life there. He was my dad – that's about all I can remember of his visits. As I never knew when to expect them, they weren't something I looked forward to, or dreaded, or anything of that sort. It seemed the way of things to me: you fell, and you scraped your knee; dads arrived, sweets in their pockets.

There was one exception to my routine: sometimes, when I came back from playing outside, the third bed, next to my own, would be made up with sheets and blankets. I would rush downstairs, and knock on the office door, where Auntie Peggy would be waiting for me with my sister. Having Mena to stay was more exciting than anything in my life – more than Christmas, more than the seaside. I had someone of my very own to be with, and it made me feel special.

The first time she came to stay, I was puzzled by the changes in my room and wondered who this strange girl with Auntie Peggy was. She seemed so different to me; she was smaller, and wore a sort of long dress over a pair of baggy trousers. Her hair, though dark like mine, was pulled back into a long pigtail, and her eyes were wide open; she clung to Auntie Peggy as though she were about to be set adrift in an open sea. I was very happy to see another girl to play with but she seemed so shy.

'Sam, this is your sister Mena,' said Auntie Peggy. 'She's come to stay with us for a little while. Come and say hello to her.'

My *sister*? Of course I knew what that meant but I didn't know anything about her. I smiled at Mena, who stared warily back at me. I reached out and held her hand. 'Hello,' I said. She continued to stare back at me.

'Why don't you take Mena up to show her where she's going to sleep?' said Auntie Peggy. 'We've put some clothes into the bottom drawer in your room. Why don't you help Mena to get changed? She might like to play and won't want to get her nice home clothes dirty.'

What did she mean, her home clothes? She was home, surely? But grown-ups said funny things sometimes, so I turned and, keeping hold of Mena's hand, took off up the stairs.

I was so *proud*. My sister – my own sister. Nobody else in the home had a sister staying with them. I was lucky to have her here with me, and I felt very excited. First I would show her my room, show her off to Amanda, and then we would go outside and play on the swings. Perhaps she knew things to do in the woods that I didn't.

We went upstairs, and she sat down on the bed and let me get some clothes out for her, telling me what she would and wouldn't wear. We settled on some trousers, because she didn't want to show her legs, and a bright top with long sleeves. Amanda came in and stood by the door, so I told her to come and say hello to my sister. Then we ran downstairs and out into the garden, my heart almost bursting with excitement and pride. I showed her the swings, and she climbed carefully into one. Mena didn't know how to swing her legs to make it move, so I stood behind and pushed. 'Not too hard! Not too hard!' she shrieked, frightened by the speed and the height. I wanted to sit in the seat next to her and swing too, but she couldn't make it move on her own and didn't want anyone else pushing her.

'Come on,' I said, running across the grass, 'Let's play hide-and-seek.' Amanda had to look for us together as Mena didn't want to hide on her own. Even playing tag with her was difficult because when she was 'it', I had to run slowly to let her tag me because she wasn't a fast runner. But I didn't care; she was my sister, and I knew I had to look after her here, where she was a stranger.

I never asked why she was here; where she came from; and whether or not she'd known she had a sister before today. This was my home, my world, and she'd come to stay with me. Just like Dad came to see me and brought sweets, so Mena came and stayed in my room with me.

Mena was older than me, a whole two years older, but I felt that I had to show her everything, and teach her everything. She seemed shy to me, and not at all brave; Amanda and I liked to tell stories about the goblins on Cannock Chase when we were in bed, but Mena was frightened by them and made us close the window, so we learned not to tell those kinds of stories when she was around. She came, perhaps, twice a year; I don't know for sure how long she stayed but it might have been for a few days or a whole summer.

Living in the home had made me brave, because I knew of nothing to fear. I was never cold; I was never hungry. My clothes were always clean and the welcome I received, when I came home from school, was always warm. My life was perfect.

Until the day I met my mother.

2

It must have been in the holidays: I wasn't at school, and Mena was staying with me. It was her last day before she went away again and we knew Dad had driven up to collect her, so we both went down to the office when it was time for her to go. This time, though, Dad wasn't alone, and he didn't bend down to rub my cheek and give me a sweet as he usually did; instead he lifted up my hand and pressed it against the palm of the woman who was with him. She was thinner and a little shorter than my dad, and she wasn't smiling at me but instead seemed to be studying me intently. She wore the same sort of funny clothes that Mena had on when she arrived at the home, before she changed into jeans. She also had a scarf wrapped around her hair. I thought she looked very serious and smart. 'Sameem,' said my dad, 'this is your mother. Say hello.'

My mother made no move to draw me towards her for a hug; her hand held mine in a thin grip, and I looked up at her. 'Hello,' I said politely. Was this the right thing to do? I had no idea. The stories we were read all had mothers in them, but they were with their children, and they hugged and kissed them goodnight, like Auntie Peggy did with me. My mother didn't seem to want to hug or kiss me, and instead was simply looking at me. Suddenly she turned to my father and garbled out some noises — it sounded harsh and strange and a bit frightening, so I backed away a little. Mena was right behind me and as I moved I bumped into her; she didn't seem to want to come in front and hug Mother either. Mother's hand held mine more tightly, and she turned back to me and spoke more soothingly. Her other hand reached out towards me, and, with Mena pushing me from behind, I stepped forward to hold that one too. She spoke again to my father, who then smiled at me and said, 'She says you look so different to how she remembers. You look all grown-up and big.' I smiled warily at her; what was she going to do next?

She looked over my head and spoke some more of those strange words, saying something to Mena. Mena stepped around me, and spoke back to her, then turned and went upstairs. I would have gone with her but my mother kept hold of my hand. I remember that more than anything else, and a new sensation swept through me; that was the moment when I felt different. I had a mother, I'd never had one before, and she had come to see *me*. I looked up at the woman again, and she looked down and – for the first time – smiled at me. I smiled back. When she spoke this time, it didn't sound harsh or strange; it was Mother speaking, so how could it? I replied, 'Okay,' as I didn't understand anything she'd just said, but it seemed the right thing to do. Before I knew it, Mena was beside me, once again dressed in her away clothes, and they were gone. I didn't mind them going – after all, this was my home; but from then on, my mother was the most important visitor I had. Amanda's mother never visited her at all. Having my sister visit me made me feel like a princess; having my mother come to where I lived made me feel like a queen. So I idolised her; and when she came to visit, I was always happy to go and sit next to her and hold her hand.

That my mother only came when Mena had to leave didn't trouble me at all; it was my dad who came to see me alone. All those years Dad came and visited almost every week, but Mother only came when Mena was going home.

It would work this way: I would go and stand by her, and hold her hand, and Mother would look down at me, bend her head towards me, and say, 'You all right?' I'd say, 'Yes,' and that would be the extent of our conversation. Dad would smile encouragingly at me. Once Mena had changed her clothes, the three of them would be gone. I never wondered why they always left me behind, because here was where I was supposed to be.

When I was seven, Mother started coming to see me more often, when Mena wasn't there, and so I saw her on my own. Because these visits were just for me and made me feel different to everyone else in the home, I thought Mother was perfect. The funny spicy smell I noticed when I hugged her didn't bother me; the fact that we couldn't say more to each other than 'You all right?' and 'Yes,' didn't bother me. She was Mother and could do no wrong. I'd sit beside her on the large settee – '*Beja beja*', she'd say, and I'd know that meant 'Sit here' – and I'd hold her hand and smile.

The stories I'd read in books told me what a mother was, and they always seemed perfect. Auntie Peggy was perfect already, as far as I was concerned, so my Mother must be even better. I'd already decided that I adored her, and loved her, so never mind that everything about her seemed different; I just accepted those differences. Having a mother, and loving her, seemed like the most natural thing in the world.

Just as it seemed natural that I would be going home in a few months' time.

'Sam,' said Auntie Peggy one day, 'I have something important to talk to you about.' She had found me playing in the playroom and taken me back to my bedroom to talk to me. She sat on the bed next to me and took my hands in hers. There was something unusual about the way she was speaking, her voice was all shaky, but I didn't know why. 'You're going home,' she continued.

'Home? But I'm home now.'

Auntie Peggy smiled. 'No, I mean your family's home. You're going home to live with your family.'

'My family?' I wondered what she meant.

'Yes. You have three brothers, and another sister as well as Mena.'

I just stared at her. A whole family! But I'd be leaving here – what would that mean? I blinked quickly as my eyes filled with tears. 'Will Mena be there?' I asked. She nodded. 'Will we all be coming back here? Will you come and see me?'

She chuckled. 'No, silly. You're going home for good. I have to stay here with Amanda and all the other children.'

I didn't know what 'for good' meant, but having a family – and going to live with them – was the most exciting thing that had ever happened to me. I remembered when another girl in the home, older than me, had gone back to her family, and how happy it had made her. Over the next few days, I imagined I was her, and that I was as happy as her, while I made plans for all the things I'd do with my family.

I'd lie in bed at night and talk to Amanda about the games we'd play together. 'I hope your brothers aren't like the boys next door,' Amanda said.

No, I told her, we'd be a family, and get along and be happy like in all the books I'd read. And in all the images in my mind of the games we'd play, and the lovely big house we'd live in to fit all my brothers and sisters, Amanda was always there, because my best friend would have to come and visit. 'And I'll come and stay with you, here,' I said, 'so you'll have to keep my bed tidy and ready for me.'

When the day I was to leave came round I was ready, with a case packed with my clothes. I had a bath and I put on my best dress, to look smart. Auntie Peggy made a special effort with my hair; then I went downstairs to wait.

After what seemed an eternity, a car drove up and Mother stepped out. There was a grown-up with her I didn't recognise, driving the car. Mother spoke to Auntie Peggy for a moment or two, then reached out a hand to me and said something in the language I didn't understand. But I put out my hand to hold hers and let her lead me to the car.

The grown-up got out of the car and put my small case in the boot. He was thin, with hair down to his shoulders and a thick, curly moustache. 'I'm Manz,' he said to me. 'I'm your brother. Into the car with you.'

My brother seemed so old – I couldn't imagine playing games with him. I shyly murmured, 'Good morning,' as I'd been taught to do. What had seemed exciting the night before began to feel strange and a little scary. Suddenly I felt very small, and then I heard a voice behind me say, 'Goodbye, Sam.' Auntie Peggy stood by the front door, with Amanda beside her.

I pulled my hand from Mother's grip and ran back to them both. I was confused. I should be happy yet I'd got a knot in my stomach and tears filled my eyes. I was happy to be going to my family, but I hadn't realised how sad it would make me to go away from Amanda and my home. I reached up to hug Auntie Peggy. I heard her say, 'I want you to be a good girl,' and I whispered back, 'I will, I promise,' not knowing what that promise would cost me.

Next I hugged Amanda, and she was crying as much as me.

'Don't cry,' I said, 'I'll come back and visit you.'

Then the man who put my case in the boot said snappily, 'Come on, we have to leave now.' Mother took my shoulders and pulled me away from Amanda. With a sad look back, I followed Mother down the path to the car.

The man held open the back door on the passenger side and motioned impatiently at me. I hesitated and, taking a deep breath, got into the car. I knelt on the seat and looked out of the window at Auntie Peggy and Amanda, and waved really hard as we drove off. We turned the corner and they were nearly out of sight, but I kept looking back and waving.

3

Mother and my brother Manz took me home with them to Walsall. I had never been so far out of the children's home without a grown-up I knew beside me, but I wasn't worried as I had Mother sitting there in front of me.

We drove for some time. Mother and Manz didn't speak to me on the way back to the house, but instead talked to each other in their own language. I was too uneasy to ask questions, so instead I sat and stared out of the window as we travelled along. Sometimes I sang a little, to myself, quietly. Leaving the home had been such a shock – even though I'd known it was coming, of course I hadn't known how I'd feel – that I was happy to sit waiting till I was spoken to; it all seemed too much to me.

The car slowed down as the traffic built up. 'We're nearly there,' said Manz from the front, without looking round at me. The houses around us changed, the people changed. Everything seemed smaller, less tidy, although it was more colourful. In fact there was more of everything, except grass and trees. Shops spilled out on to the pavement, and the people forced their way past each other to get from one to another. At their feet were little children; I pressed my face up to the window of the car – perhaps they would all be my friends.

The car stopped outside the smallest, messiest house. The garden was overgrown and full of weeds; I couldn't see into the house as the curtains were closed across the windows. I knew I shouldn't be, but a little bit of me was disappointed. I stepped out of the car and faced the house. The front door was a sickly green colour, with paint peeling off in places, revealing the wood underneath. Mother started walking up the garden path, while Manz pulled my case out of the car. I followed her. Mena was there, hovering like a ghost by the door, dressed in her dress and baggy trousers. She seemed thinner than I remembered, and although from her smile I could tell she was pleased to see me she didn't run out to greet me, to welcome me to this house. It wasn't my home; not yet. But I so wanted it to be my home, and in my excitement and nervousness I reached up with my hand to clutch Mother's. 'Ami,' I began.

'*Chalander*,' she said, brushing off my hand. I was shocked – not at what she said, as I had no idea what the word meant, but more at how she said it. Nobody had ever spoken to me like that; no adult at the home would have spoken to a child that way. But there was so much going on around me, with Manz barging past me with my case, and Mother heading through the door, that I was rushing to say hello to Mena before I could think about Mother's abrupt change of mood.

Mena flung her arms around me; I hugged her back. It was a relief to have someone to be nice to me, and I felt a warm glow beginning to melt the knot inside my stomach. We pulled apart and smiled broadly at each other. I was just about to say something to her when Mother again said something I didn't understand in her new, sharp voice. Mena jerked back from me and pulled me towards her, into the house.

Mother walked down the dark hallway and through a doorway into the room beyond. Mena walked slowly after her, and I went with her, noticing the gloom all around. The room we went into was almost bare of furniture; there was no carpet. Along one wall was a low leather settee, tattered and frayed in places; on it sat a stranger, an older girl in the same kind of clothes as Mena. By the window – with the curtains drawn across, blocking out the light from the street – stood a small wooden table. I was puzzled by everything: why was no one nice, why was it so smelly, dark and dirty? But I wanted to fit in, so I thought it better that I didn't ask.

Mother sat down on the settee next to a little boy, and didn't look to see what I was doing, or show me to my room, or anything. She said something to the other girl, who turned and spoke to me; at least, she looked at me as she said something, but I didn't understand a word. I looked at Mena questioningly. The girl on the sofa sighed heavily, and stood up; walking over to me, she looked down and said, 'My name is Tara, I'm your eldest sister. You're to call me Baji,' she said. 'You must go and change; we don't wear clothes like *that*' – she gestured dismissively at my smartest dress, which I had been so proud to put on that morning, and I felt a sudden wave of shame pass over me as I looked down at my dress – 'here. We don't like to show our legs. You'll have to try to fit in better.'

And she turned and walked back to the sofa, where she sat and stared at me in an unfriendly way, which made me feel worse. My face started to burn with the humiliation I felt, and I thought, I must have done something wrong, but I don't know what. I was torn in two: I wanted to know what I'd done, but didn't want to be snapped at by Mother like she had just done at the door.

Luckily Mena came to the rescue. She tugged my arm, and said, 'Come on, I'll take you upstairs and get you changed.'

Then another, slightly older lady came in. She looked at me and said something to Tara – Baji – who replied, gesturing towards me carelessly. 'Okay,' I said, wondering what else Tara expected. The lady walked over to me, and I did as I knew I should: 'Hello,' I said, hoping I didn't sound as upset as I felt. She was wearing the same sort of clothes as everyone else in the room, but she had a scarf around her head as well, and her hair was tied in a thick plait round the side. She smiled at me, the first person to do so since Mena welcomed me in. She said something to me that I didn't understand.

Tara spoke from the sofa: 'This is Hanif. She is married to Paji, and you're to call her Bhabi.'

I just smiled at Hanif, puzzled and anxious. I didn't know what Tara meant. Who was Paji? Was Hanif another sister? No one in my family was as I'd imagined them to be: they were all so much older than me, none of them had noticed the nice dress I'd worn specially for the day, and – apart from Mena – no one had spoken a friendly word to me.

At that moment Mena reminded me, 'Come on, time to change.'

I wanted to tell her how glad I was that she was here, that this time I was the one feeling a little less brave, but she walked out of the room ahead of me and went quickly up the steep stairs. I followed her; there were three doors, one facing us, one to the left and one to the right. It was dark as the doors were shut and there was no window. Mena went ahead into the room on the left. It wasn't as smelly as downstairs, because the window was open, and I saw that there were two large beds, a wardrobe, and a dark, threadbare carpet on the floor. The walls had nothing on them but greenish-looking patches by the ceiling.

I said, 'What's wrong? Why's everyone so cross?' but Mena ignored me.

Instead she pointed to the bed next to the window and said, 'You'll be sharing with me. Baji sleeps in the other one.'

There was no sheet on the mattress; instead there was a pile of old blankets heaped at the foot of the bed. There was one pillow, which looked grey and covered with stains. I didn't even want to sit on the bed, let alone sleep in it. I wondered if I could go back to the home and get some sheets and my nice blankets to sleep in. And my posters to put up on the walls, so that the place seemed less bare.

The excitement of the journey here had worn off, and instead I felt like crying; it was all so different to what I'd expected. Also, I didn't want to share a room with Tara, who seemed scary, and old, to me at least. 'How old's Tara, Baji, I mean? And who sleeps in the other rooms?' I asked; perhaps there would be a nicer bed I could sleep in somewhere else.

'Baji's nearly twelve. Saber sleeps in the room next door. But don't go in there; he hates people going into his room. And Hanif and Paji sleep in the other room.'

That name again. 'Who's Paji? And where does Mother sleep? And who's that little boy downstairs?'

Mena laughed. 'Hey, slow down; don't worry, I'll explain everything. Mother sleeps downstairs. She gets out of breath walking upstairs so she sleeps on the sofa with Salim.'

I didn't understand, and just shook my head.

Mena came and put her arm around me. 'Don't look sad,' she said, trying to sound comforting. 'I'm glad you're here to talk to. I know you don't understand the language, so I'll teach you, and if you're good, you'll be fine.'

The echoes of what Auntie Peggy had said to me before I left came to mind: *be a good girl*. I gave Mena a small smile.

'Look, sit down,' she said. I sat as gingerly as I could on the revolting bed. '*Baji* means "elder sister", so that's what we call Tara,' Mena carried on. '*Paji* means "older brother", and that's Manz, who drove you here. Hanif is his wife, so she's our sister-in-law, and that's what *Babhi* means.'

'Why doesn't anyone like the way I dress? What's wrong with this?' I touched my best dress, which now I just felt rotten about.

'It's because we're Muslim, Sam. Muslims dress like this – like me,' said Mena. She could see I looked even more confused, and sighed. 'Okay, I forgot you don't know this. Muslims are like Christians in that they believe in God, but they believe different things, and one of those is how we dress. You'll have to find out the others later.'

I remembered what we said in Sunday school: 'I believe in one God, one Church,' and I felt a sense of relief. At least something made sense. 'But I'm Christian,' I said, and was about to add that that meant I could wear my dress, but Mena interrupted hurriedly.

'Shh, Sam, don't say that.' Mena grabbed my shoulders and gave me a tiny shake. 'Keep your voice down! If anyone hears you say that, they'll be angry and they'll hit you.'

'What?' Surely she must be joking. 'They hit you? Why?'

She looked towards the closed door, then leaned closer, almost whispering. 'Once, I didn't clean the floor properly and Mother hit me, and then Baji beat me after that. I just keep out of everyone's way now.'

I stared at her. I'd been hit, once, at school; a boy had pulled my hair, which I hated, so I'd turned round and slapped his face. He had punched me back before a teacher came and stopped us; we both missed swimming class that week. But that was a boy of my age; a grown-up hitting me was something I couldn't imagine. But before I could reply, Tara called up from downstairs. 'Mena, bring Salim downstairs when you come to eat.'

'Who's Salim?' I asked Mena.

'He's our youngest brother. He's starting nursery this summer.'

Mena pointed out of the door. 'He'll be next door. Let's get you changed and then we'll take him down.'

'Next door? Saber's room, right?'

She nodded.

'So how old is he?'

'He's twelve, two years older than me,' she said, standing and picking up some clothes left at the foot of the bed. 'Come on then, I'll help you get changed.'

I took off my dress and folded it up before putting it on the bed, and then with Mena's help dressed in clothes she held out to me. I'd never worn an outfit quite like this before, and I felt peculiar; they looked like dressing-up clothes – a bright orange long dress with matching trousers. Mena tied a scarf over my hair. There was a mirror on the wardrobe door, and I looked at myself in it. Was that really me? I looked a little bit more like my mother and sisters, and that made me feel more at home. But the scratchy fabric itched and the long sleeves and long trousers were uncomfortable.

'Is that okay?' Mena smiled hesitantly at me, as if she wanted me to like the clothes for her sake.

'It's all right, I suppose,' and I managed a weak smile back.

She headed out of the room and opened the door of the other bedroom, and brought out Salim, the little boy I'd seen downstairs. 'This is your sister, Sam,' said Mena, and Salim looked at me, without saying anything.

'Hello,' I said, smiling, and he smiled a little back at me. Mena ruffled his hair and they turned to go down the stairs and I followed, walking down the stairs carefully, as the dress was so long I thought I'd trip on it.

When we got to the kitchen, I asked Mena where the bathroom was. She pointed to the back door. 'Out there.'

A toilet outside? I was horrified. In the garden where everyone can see you? Mena noticed my reaction, and took me outside; I stumbled on the doorstep, but, to my immense relief, Mena pointed to a door next to the one we'd just come through.

'There,' she said. 'Be quick, dinner's ready.'

I cautiously pushed the door, which creaked scarily as it swung open, and peered inside. It was dark and smelly, and I could make out a toilet near the back wall. I stepped into the cold room and tried to find the light switch by patting my hand on the wall. Immediately I snatched it away, as the wall was damp and sticky. 'Come on, hurry up,' urged Mena. There was a faint ray of light coming from a small window; that would have to do.

When I'd done my business, I closed the door behind me and shivered – but not just from the cold. 'Where do I wash my hands?'

'In here,' replied Mena. Back in the warm kitchen, I ran my hands under the cold water; Hanif, busy with plates and cutlery, looked me up and down and then said something to Mena. I wished she'd spoken in English so that I could understand her, but Mena translated. 'She said you look nice now.' They both smiled at me.

I didn't feel nice. There was no soap for my hands to wash off that sticky feeling from the walls, and the trousers were loose at the top so that I kept having to hitch them up. I felt very uncomfortable.

Mena was talking to Hanif, so I searched for something to dry my hands on. There didn't seem to be anything, so I quickly brushed them over my clothes. I looked around the kitchen; there was no table, just a worktop covered with flour, jars and bowls. The stove was on, and some large saucepans were steaming away, but the top was thick with burned-on food.

'Right,' said Mena. 'Time to eat.' And she handed me a plate. 'Do what I do,' she said. First she took what looked like a pancake off a pile by the side of the stove, and then Hanif scooped something out of one of the pans. 'That's chicken,' explained Mena. I did the same, politely saying, 'Thank you,' to Hanif when she'd served me, which made her laugh.

The two of us went into the room that I'd not been in to yet. As we walked in, a powerful smell hit me, one I didn't recognise. The closest I could think of was the smell of Jet's fur on rainy days, or the piles of wet leaves we ran through on the Chase, and I wanted to turn round and go out. But Mena walked on in and, as I hadn't had any lunch when we were driving from the home and so was very hungry, I went in too.

The room was almost as cold as the toilet outside, but at least there was a light that Mena turned on. We sat down on the only thing in the room, a black settee that was very spongy, and balanced the plates our knees. We always ate at the table at the home so I wasn't sure I could manage this well enough, and I waited to see what Mena did.

Mena put her plate on her lap, broke off a piece of the pancake, dipped it into the sauce, and ate it. 'What are you waiting for?' she mumbled, her mouth full.

'What do I do?' I said. 'Where are the knives and forks?'

'Just pick up the *roti* with your hands, break some off, and use it to scoop up the food. Look, like this.' And she put another mouthful of food, heaped on to the pancake, into her mouth. 'Hmm,' she said appreciatively.

I picked up the *roti*, tore some off as Mena had done, and dipped it into the chicken on top, and into my mouth.

Ouch! It was like putting a fire in my mouth. My whole face suddenly flooded with heat, and I wanted to get rid of this awful taste, but because I was trying to be good I didn't spit it out. I flapped my hands furiously and Mena saw, jumped up, said, 'I'll get you some water,' and rushed out. I had just managed to swallow when she came back with a cup in her hand, and I grabbed the water from her and downed it all.

'Ew!' I said. 'What was that? I can't eat *that*.'

I heard laughter; Tara and Hanif had followed Mena to see what the fuss was, and were chuckling at me.

'It's curry,' said Mena.

I'd never eaten anything like it. I was used to the food we all ate in the home, like sausages, or stew. And chips – I loved chips.

Hanif and Tara said something to each other, and then went back to the kitchen. 'What did they say?' I asked Mena. I hated not knowing what was being said – I imagined it was about me.

I was right. Mena looked at her knees, and said, 'They said they don't know what else to cook for you so you'll have to get used to it.'

'But I don't like it! Isn't there anything else?' My lips seemed to be boiling, I touched them carefully.

'No, there is nothing else. I know you don't like it,' she said, then sighed. 'Look, just eat the plain *roti*; don't put any curry on it.'

I tore a piece off the *roti* that didn't have anything on it, and put it carefully in my mouth. Without the curry, it tasted better, a bit like dry toast. 'I can manage this,' I said.

'You'll have to get used to it, you know, Sam. Don't worry, it's not so hard to eat when there's rice,' she added, when I pulled a face. 'Tonight, though, I'll eat the rest for you, okay?' Mena offered.

I handed it to her, and wondered why there wasn't more to eat, while she cleaned my plate. At the home, there were always slices of bread and butter when we'd finished what was on our plates. I didn't ask if there was any pudding; it wasn't polite to do so. I was cold, and being hungry didn't help; I wondered if I might be having a nice hot bath, later, as that would make me feel better, but I hadn't seen a bathroom yet and I didn't want to find out that it, too, was outside in the dark. After Mena finished, we went through to the kitchen to put our plates in the sink.

Tara shouted from the room where she was sitting with Mother, 'Wash up.'

'Okay,' said Mena. Auntie Peggy never asked us to do that, nor did she let us speak so bossily to each other; she said it wasn't polite. Mena washed up and placed the dishes on the drainer, while I stood beside her, watching. I needed her to explain everything that was going on around us so that it wouldn't seem so daunting. Besides which I kept drinking water to ease the burning in my mouth, which was finally fading away. When she'd finished washing the dishes, she shook the water from her hands and then wiped them on her dress.

At the home I was used to knowing the time, with clocks both upstairs and downstairs. It helped me know what I should be doing next. I hadn't seen one anywhere in the house yet, so I asked Mena, 'What's the time?'

'I don't know,' Mena said with a shrug. 'It's not bedtime yet because Manz hasn't come home.'

'Isn't there a clock?'

'We don't need to know what time it is.'

I wanted to ask her why, but I had so many questions. I hadn't seen my brother Saber at all yet, for instance. Where had Salim gone? Where did he eat? Why didn't the family all eat together? Mena and I went into the room where we'd eaten and she explained more about the comings and goings in the house. I asked her loads of questions but she could only answer some of them.

Above all, I wondered why Mother hadn't come to see that we'd eaten properly, just as Auntie Peggy checked on us in the home to make sure we'd cleared our plates.

Then Manz came in. Hanif went into the kitchen and dished up a plate of food for him, and said to us that as Manz was home, it was time for bed. 'Where do we brush our teeth?' I asked, wondering if we'd have to go outside to use the bathroom.

'Follow me,' said Mena. She went to the kitchen sink and took the salt bowl, dipped her finger in it, and started rubbing her teeth with the salt, then spat it out in the sink and rinsed her mouth with tap water. I watched in horror. 'Don't you use a toothbrush? Or toothpaste?'

'No,' Mena said. 'There isn't any. Just do as I did.'

I tried it, but almost gagged from the taste of the salt in my throat. Then we went upstairs to find that Tara had come up to bed already and had her back turned towards us. Mena climbed on to the bed and started pulling the blankets up around her.

'I have to change before I go to bed,' I whispered, not wanting to wake up Tara. 'Where's my case?'

'I don't know. Just sleep in the clothes you have on. That's what I do.'

'No, I want to change into my pyjamas,' I insisted. 'Where did my case go?'

Mena sat up and said grumpily, 'Just sleep in the clothes you have on and we'll find it tomorrow, all right?' She lay back down again and pulled the covers up to her head.

I wanted to get changed; I always did at night-time. The more I did things as I always did, in the home, the better I'd feel, I knew that. So I didn't care what Mena said now; I had to find my case. I decided it must still be downstairs. 'I need to go to the toilet. Will you come with me?' I asked Mena, planning to look for the case while I was downstairs.

'Are you crazy?' she hissed, looking up at me again. 'It's dark! I'm not going outside and you better not, either. The bogey-man will get you.'

I remembered how easily Mena had been scared by the stories Amanda and I told in the home, so I just said, 'There's no such thing as the bogey-man.'

She paused, then said, 'Mother will shout at you if you make a noise.'

'Does she sleep downstairs?'

'Yes. I told you before. She gets very tired when she walks upstairs.'

'Oh, Mena, please come with me.'

But she refused, so I summoned up my courage and went on my own. The house was quiet but there were lights still on so I could see where I was going. I went as quietly as I could downstairs and through the kitchen without making a sound. I couldn't see my case anywhere. I opened the back door and left it open; it was dark outside, and silent apart from the distant noises of cars. I didn't feel so brave now. I left the toilet door open as I went as quickly as possible, then dashed back inside, locking the kitchen door; something made me shiver, and I ran quietly up to bed.

'The bogey-man didn't get you then,' Mena said as I got in next to her. I was grateful for the company in bed that night, because my day had been so strange.

'No, I told you there's no such thing,' I said, hoping I sounded braver than I felt.

I lay as still as I could, trying not to think about what the mattress had looked like in the light, while Mena tossed and turned, and prayed I'd fall asleep. My first day with my family was not what I'd hoped for – perhaps tomorrow would be better. I thought about Auntie Peggy, and what she'd said; I would be a good girl. Then they would love me.

4

That night I had a dream, an odd dream in which I'd walked on to the Chase and got lost. I was in a damp part of the woods, though it was light and all I could do was stand there and wonder how to get home, while this smell filled my nostrils. Then Mena moved beside me, and I woke with a start; the smell was still there but instead of being in my nice comfortable bed, with smiling faces of pop stars looking down at me, I was in this filthy room in this strange house. I had no idea what time it was, but it was light outside. I lay there for a while; but there were no sounds elsewhere in the house, so I closed my eyes again and went back to sleep.

When I next woke up, I was squashed in by Mena, who lay curled up beside me, fast asleep, and I didn't want to wake her. In the light coming through the thin curtains, I could see how horrible the bed was, how grubby the walls seemed. I was still excited to be with my family, but I was disappointed by the shabbiness of their home; I had imagined that they lived in a much nicer place, and this – even more than the greeting I'd received yesterday – made me miserable.

I remembered it was Sunday, and I wondered if I'd be going to church today. It didn't seem like it because no one was awake yet. What about in the street, or the houses opposite? I manoeuvred my feet carefully around Mena, slipped out of bed, and peeped through the curtains. All the curtains I could see were still drawn. Didn't anyone around here go to church?

I heard a sound behind me, as one of the other bedroom doors opened. No one came into the room to tell us to get up and have a wash, but the footsteps carried on downstairs, so I was about to follow when Mena raised her head from the pillow and asked, 'Where are you going?'

'Downstairs. I need to use the toilet.'

She moaned, 'Don't go down yet. If you do, I'll have to get up, too.'

Why didn't she want to get up? Another mystery. I got back into bed, and lay down next to her. 'What time is it?'

'No idea. Early. Look, if the curtains opposite are open, then I get up. Are they?'

'No, not yet.'

'Then go back to sleep.'

'I can't.' I sat up again, and was just about to ask Mena why I couldn't go downstairs, when Tara shouted from underneath her covers.

'Shut up, you two, I'm trying to sleep!'

I looked at Mena, who raised her eyebrows at me, and then rolled over to go back to sleep.

I sat there, bored, looking through the crack in the curtains until the ones opposite were drawn.

I jumped up. 'The curtains are open at last, time to get up!'

Mena groaned again. Tara snapped, 'What's your problem? Go back to sleep. Why are you in such a rush to get up?'

'I need to go to the toilet.' I didn't care what either of them said, as I went to the bedroom door. 'I'm going downstairs now.'

Downstairs I found Mother sitting on the settee, Salim next to her. She looked up and I said a cheerful good morning to her, but she didn't acknowledge me at all, so I carried on out back. Outside the floor of the small toilet was cold, and made me shiver. As I sat there, I looked about me and saw how grimy it was; it was still gloomy in there even in daylight. I hoped I'd find my case and get my slippers out, because the floor was horrible. I opened the door to go back into the kitchen.

Tara elbowed past me, saying, 'About time you finished.'

'I just went in,' I started to say, but she'd slammed the door shut and didn't reply. I tiptoed back into the warm kitchen, and wiped the dirt off the soles of my feet.

Hanif was standing at the stove and cooking the round pancakes – *roti*, I corrected myself – on the open flame of the cooker. I watched her turn the *roti* over and over, her hands covered in flour; she kept snatching her hands away from the flame. My stomach grumbled, but I didn't know how to ask her if I could have some. There were no bowls about and no cereal that I could see for me to point to; and I knew that even if I asked her very politely she wouldn't understand so I waited for Tara to come back and then said to her, 'Excuse me, may I please have some breakfast? I'm really hungry.'

'What?' she said.

'I'm hungry.'

Hanif said something, and Tara replied, before turning back to me. 'Want some toast?'

'Yes, please.'

'There's the bread.' Tara pointed to a shelf. 'Pass it over.' There was a packet of white sliced bread and I gave it to her. 'Open it, then. I ain't doing everything for you,' she said.

I'd never had to open a packet of bread and didn't know how, so stood there fumbling for a moment. 'Oh, can't you do anything?' Tara snapped. 'Just give it to me.'

Hanif spoke again, and Tara smiled and gave the bread back to me and said, 'She says that you've got to learn to do things for yourself, so until you can open it you're not getting any.'

I still couldn't see how to open it, and, as I was getting frustrated and hungry, I tore the plastic wrapping and yanked out some bread.

'What did you do that for, you stupid girl!' cried Tara, snatching the loaf away. 'Now it'll all go stale.'

'I just want something to eat.'

'You do it the way you're told. I'm not making anything for you now.'

I was hungry, and I was fed up with this; why did she have to make everything so difficult? Couldn't I just have some toast?

'Now give me back that bread,' she said, pointing to the slices in my hand.

I shoved one of the pieces into my mouth; anything was better than nothing.

Tara grabbed me. 'Spit it out!'

I wouldn't; instead I swallowed it. Tara cursed and pushed me away from her, and I bounced off the fridge on to the floor. I started crying, when Mother walked in. I didn't want to get into trouble so said immediately, 'Mother,' I started to say, 'It's her fault, she—'

Mother didn't even look at me. She said something to Hanif, who gave her a plate of leftovers from the previous night, glanced at Tara, and walked back out of the room, all without taking any notice of me at all. Tara looked back at me, her eyes gleaming, and she spoke to Hanif, who laughed. The two of them helped themselves to food – after Tara had put the loaf of bread back on the shelf – and left the room, following Mother. I stayed lying on the floor, tears pouring down my face. I couldn't believe anyone could be so mean, least of all my own sister.

Mena came in and knelt down beside me, wiping my eyes with the sleeve of her top. 'What are you doing down here?' she said, speaking in the way I did when I wanted to stop Amanda from crying, like I'd been foolish or something.

'Tara wouldn't give me breakfast, she wouldn't get the bread out. I tore the bag open and she snatched it away and pushed me over. Mother came in but didn't say anything,' I sobbed.

'I told you to stay upstairs. You've got to wait until everyone's out of the kitchen,' she said. 'That's what I do.' I wanted to say, Well, now I know, you could have told me; but I didn't. She helped me up. 'Shall we make some toast, then?' she asked.

'Yes, please.'

Mena explained that we always had fresh bread because Manz – who worked in a bakery – brought loaves home every night. She showed me how to open the packet by untying the top, and where the grill pan was and how to light it. I felt a bit better as she did all this, sitting on a stool while I watched, as she kept looking over at me and smiling encouragingly. I was glad Mena was there, being nice to me; no one else seemed to be bothered at all, and Mother hadn't spoken to me once since we'd come from the home.

When the toast was ready Mena took a tub of margarine out of the fridge, and spread it with the handle of a spoon.

'Let's eat in the kitchen,' she said, 'because if we go in with the others, Mother will start finding things for us to do.'

So we stood in the kitchen and ate.

When I'd finished, I felt better and started to get curious again. 'I wonder what happened to my case. Did it go behind here?'

There was a curtain across part of the end wall of the kitchen. I got up and looked behind it; there was a switch on the wall and I turned it on.

'Is it there?' said Mena.

'No, there's no case. What is this stuff, though?' I asked. The area behind the curtain was plain – there was nothing on the concrete floor or the bare walls, apart from a boiler – and all that stood in the middle was a very large tin bucket-thing, rather like a water trough on a farm for the animals, and a couple of low stools.

'Oh, that's where we have a bath and wash the clothes,' Mena said.

'You're joking.'

'No, once a week it's bath night, and clothes get washed on Sundays.'

Once a week? No more than that? At the home, I'd have a lovely warm bubble bath every other night.

After our plain breakfast, we went back upstairs to our bedroom. I could hear, from the noises coming through the open window, that the area had woken up, and that children were outside playing.

'Let's go and play.'

Mena quickly said, 'No.'

'Why not?'

'Because I don't want to.'

'But why not?'

'Those boys are horrible. They kick me, and if they catch me going to the shops to buy some eggs or anything, they steal my money. I don't go to the shops any more.'

'All right,' I said, 'but let's go into the back garden then.'

Mena thought for a moment, said, 'Okay, let's ask,' and we ran back downstairs, into the kitchen. Hanif was there and Mena spoke to her; she said something back, and walked away into the room where Mother was. Mena turned to me: 'It's okay, she says we can take Salim too.'

It was a sunny summer's morning, and the sun was nice and warm when the three of us stepped outside. The garden was as big as the one at the children's home, but nowhere near as tidy. An overgrown lawn stretched as far as the back wall; the grass was, in places, as tall as me. There was a paved area with weeds growing out of the cracks, and in the middle of the garden a tall tree with a piece of rope hanging from a branch, with a tyre tied to the end of it.

'A swing!' I was pleased to see something familiar.

'Saber made that,' Mena said.

I started swinging, while Salim had found a burst football and was happily kicking it around. He chucked it into the tall grass and was about to dive in and collect it when Mena said, '*Nahi Salim ider ow.*' Salim stopped and Mena stepped into the grass to retrieve the ball. She tossed it to him. '*Ider ow,*' she said again and led Salim to the paved area.

'What did you just say?' I asked, curious, as I let the swing stop.

'What?'

'Just then, I think it was *ider ow.*'

'Oh, that. It means "come here". *Ow* means "come", and *ider* means "here".'

'*Ider ow*, Mena, *ider ow!*' I said and she laughed. 'How do you say "no"?'

'*Nahi.*'

'And how do you say "yes"?'

'*Ji.*'

'*Ji, nahi, ider ow, Ji, nahi, ider ow.*; I chanted it a few more times as I kicked my legs back and forth to see how high I could swing.

Mena took a tiny step closer to me. 'Don't swing too high. The rope might break.'

Her worrying began to irritate me. 'How do you say "it won't"?'

'Just say *nahi.*'

'*Nahi*, Mena, *nahi!*' I laughed.

After a while I stopped, though, as I could see how much it bothered Mena. So instead I decided to climb the tree. I'd always climbed the trees on Cannock Chase, and I was quite good at it. But my sister panicked.

'Sam! Get down!' Mena cried. 'Please. You're going to fall.'

I wanted to say it was all right, nothing was going to happen, but I thought today I'd do as she said; there were plenty more days to climb as high as I liked.

I wandered into the long grass. I could lie down here, and no one would even know I was there, the grass was so high. It was nice and dry in the warm sun and I spread my arms and legs wide, making a pattern in the grass. Salim came and lay down next to me, doing the same thing. We both laughed as he copied me, the grass tickling us as we lay there.

'We've been out here long enough,' said Mena, who'd stayed back on the paved part of the garden. 'We must get back inside.'

Mena's nervousness was beginning to frustrate me, but I said nothing to her. Instead I picked up Salim and tickled him, and then chased him back to the house.

I needed to use the toilet again. I had noticed earlier that there wasn't any toilet roll, and, as I was desperate to go, I asked Mena where the toilet roll was kept. She asked why I needed it, so I told her. She said, 'We Muslims don't use that. We wash ourselves; there's a *lota* in the toilet.' I looked puzzled at the word, and Mena explained it was a plastic jug with a spout. 'Fill up the *lota* with water and take it in with you.' So I filled it up with water and took it in with me but as I didn't know how to wash myself I ended up tearing strips off some newspaper that I found on the windowsill. It was some weeks later before I eventually discovered how to use the toilet the way that Mena and everyone else did, as, when I was going into the toilet one day, I saw Mother washing herself, using the *lota*. She had left the toilet door wide open, and I could see what she was doing, and so I learned how to do it myself.

Inside, I started to look properly around my new home. Mother refused to open the curtains, so we lived in semi-darkness and had to move around with just the weedy light from an overhead bulb to guide us. I didn't understand why at first, it took me a long time to get used to it.

I went with Mena into Mother's room. This had a small cupboard, with a television and video player on it, taking up the wall facing the settee, and there was a doorway (leading into the room where Mena and I had eaten) on the same side. The walls were a gooey brown colour, and the floor was covered in dirty grey vinyl – at least, as far as I could see. The dirt didn't seem to matter to Salim who immediately sat down and began playing with a red and white car.

How he could play with the noise in there, I don't know, as Mother and Hanif were working at something on a wooden table, which I learned to call the bench. I wandered over to see what they were doing; maybe this was some kind of toy or game they were making for us to play with. Tara was sitting on the floor beside them.

Mother said something to Mena, gesturing to both of us. 'Sit down next to me,' said Mena. Tara huffed at me and turned her head away; I had to squeeze in next to Mena, wedged up against the wall. 'We've got to help,' Mena explained.

I watched as Mena and Tara picked up objects out of bags in front of them. There were fierce-looking pieces of metal, as long as my fingers and with jagged edges, coming out of one bag, and screws out of another. I recognised screws, as Auntie Peggy had once fixed a plug in front of me in the home, and I had been fascinated to watch it disappear into its plastic hole and firmly grip the plug so that I couldn't take it apart at all. But I didn't know what the claws were for.

'Here, this is what we do,' said Mena. She took two of the claws and fitted them together at the base, then slid the screw into the hole they made, joining them together. When they were ready, she handed it up on to the bench. Hanif took one and fiddled a spring into the base of the claw, then passed it to Mother who placed the claw into the machine, and lowered a long handle down on to it. There was a grinding noise and Mother lifted the long handle and took the claw out, placing it into a bag on her right-hand side.

'Now you try,' said Tara, eyeing me up. I felt that she was waiting for me to make a mistake so that she could laugh at me and tell Mother, and so it proved.

'Look, that's not how you do it,' Tara snapped. 'You're hopeless. Can't you do it just like you were shown?'

'I didn't have time to see what you were doing properly,' I said. 'Show me again.'

Her fingers moved quickly once more and I couldn't keep up. Mena nudged me, and I watched her instead. She moved more slowly, so I could follow what she did, and, although Tara *tssked* at us both, I managed to put one together that didn't get pushed back at me to do again. It was an unfamiliar feeling in my hands and I moved more slowly than the other two, so that I had only completed about ten when Mother said something to Mena, who looked at me and said, 'We'll just finish these ones we're working on and go and serve the dinner.'

I was a bit surprised that we had to do this as in the home the children didn't have to do anything for the evening meal, but said nothing until we were able to stand up and walk out into the kitchen. I was glad someone had mentioned food as I'd been hungry all afternoon. 'Do you always have to work?' I asked Mena, once we were out of the room. 'Do you have to do the cooking?'

'No, mostly Hanif and Tara do it. I'm expected to serve it for Mother and the others, though, so it'll be nice to have someone to help me in the kitchen.' She smiled.

We chattered away as Mena explained what she was doing, taking plates from the cupboard. She lifted rice from a large pan, and shared it out on to the plates. Then she took each plate and ladled some of that spicy sauce I hadn't liked from the night before on top of the rice.

'What were we making in there?' I asked.

'They're for something called jump leads. A car has a battery to start it, and sometimes the battery doesn't work. Then you put the claws on the battery and on another battery to start the car, although,' Mena added, 'I've never seen that. Once the claws are picked up the wires are put on them to make them work.'

I asked Mena why we were making them here, in the house, and she said that Mother earned money for every bag she filled, and we all had to help. 'So we have to do this every day?' I was astonished. No, Mena told me, not when we were at school. And she said that we mustn't let anyone know that Mother was earning money this way.

Making the claws became our job, Mena's and mine. We would fix the claw together, fit the screw into the claw, and then hand it to Mother. She and Hanif would then fit the spring into the claw, using the machine in front of them, and place the finished object into a bag. I soon learned that every other day someone would come to the door and take the filled bag away. Tara would sit with Mena and me, but she wouldn't do any work, she'd just tell us what we were doing wrong. 'Do it like this, not like that,' she'd say, and we would. We were happy to help Mother so it didn't feel strange to be working this way – it was just another oddity about my family's house. The clips that didn't work properly we kept, and used as clothes pegs to hang the washing out in the garden.

Mena explained why we had to keep the curtains drawn against people looking in: Mother was earning money, making these claws, while claiming benefits for us; not only did she fear being caught and having to pay the money back, but she was also worried about her status as an immigrant. She might be sent back to Pakistan.

When Mena had finished serving the food, keeping plenty back for Manz, I helped her carry the plates through to the others. We ate in the kitchen. I again tasted the sauce that Mena put out but I found it so strong and bitter, burning my mouth, that I had to drink a couple of glasses of water just to cool my mouth down. Once more I ate nothing for dinner except for the dry *roti* – that was all I could manage.

When we had eaten, Mena and I wandered back into Mother's room. We sat down on the filthy floor to join Tara, Hanif and Mother in watching TV. I had hoped we could watch some of the TV programmes that I'd loved at the home, but no such luck; it was a film that involved a lot of singing and dancing, and I couldn't understand a word. I asked Mena to tell me what was going on, but was immediately shouted at by Tara for making too much noise, so I gave up and just watched the pictures and listened to the music. I didn't really like it, but it seemed to make everyone else happy.

As we lay on that floor, I heard a noise behind me. It was a horrible hawking sound, and although Mena didn't move, I instantly turned my head to see what was going on. Mother was turned to the wall and clearing her throat. Horrified, I watched her spit, and thick greeny-grey phlegm hit the wall at her side of the settee. I stared, mesmerised, as it slid down the wall and gathered on the skirting board that was – I quickly realised – stained from her previous efforts at clearing her throat. I looked at the others in the room; no one seemed to take any notice of this at all. I wanted to ask Mother if she was all right, but as she turned and carried on watching the film as if nothing had happened, I knew that what she'd done was her normal behaviour.

When the film finished, I watched as Mother stood up and said something to Tara. I couldn't understand her words, but when she had finished talking, Tara pulled up the seat of the settee and took out a duvet and some pillows. Then she pushed down the back, and the settee became flat like a bed. Mother took the pillows and the duvet and lay down to sleep. Although the TV was in here, this was very much Mother's room, and when she wanted to sleep we all had to leave. There was nothing to do except go up to bed, and sleep. There were no books to read. We had no pyjamas to change into, and we didn't need to worry about clean underwear because we never wore any anyway.

The next day was the same. We didn't go out, except to the back garden to play, and only if we took Salim with us. Then we had to work beside Mother while she made the claw-clips; and dish out the food that Hanif and Tara had made earlier. Tara continued to boss me around, and Hanif didn't speak to me at all, because she didn't know any English. Mother mostly ignored me. I finally met my brother, Saber, only he never seemed to be around. I don't what he got up to. Manz was gone by the time we got up and was always back late, so I never got to speak to him, as when he was at home we had to be careful not to annoy him – not to disturb his rest, or bother him while he was eating. If it hadn't been for Mena and Salim, I'd have been the loneliest I'd ever been in my life.

In another dream. I was back in Cannock Chase again – only it was different from how I remembered it, somehow nicer, and I was lying asleep on some thick grass, sheltered by trees. Then I realised that the slope I was on the edge of was not a gentle grassy bank but a cliff and that I was about to roll off, down into whatever lay below. I felt an arm reach out and shake me, and it was Auntie Peggy smiling down at me, and she told me that I shouldn't lie there as I could have an accident. As I was holding out my hand to her I felt a jolt and this time

SAMEEM ALI

I really did wake up, to find myself being kicked in the back by Mena, moving about in her sleep in our little bedroom in Walsall.

One day when I'd carried my plate back to the kitchen Tara had said, rudely, 'Wash up,' and so I found myself clearing up after everyone in the house. Mena would help me with this task as it seemed to be hers to dish up the dinner, which we'd both serve to the others. I could just about reach over the top of the sink to the brush and soap behind, but soon I learned how to clean and dry plates, cutlery and glasses; I used to hate having to wash out each of the heavy cooking pans, though.

I didn't really understand what was going on in that house. No one, for instance, ever said anything about Dad. He was never there, so I don't know where he lived. Once I mentioned him to Mena but she looked around, checked it was okay to speak, and told me not to talk about him around the others. I had been craving chocolate, which Mother never gave us, and I thought Dad would bring some when he came to visit. I didn't find it strange that he didn't live with us because I was used to seeing him only every so often anyway. But it seemed like a long time since I had last seen him. 'Dad doesn't come often,' explained Mena, 'because Mother shouts at him.' Well, I knew how that felt because I didn't like to be shouted at either, so I stopped wondering why he didn't come to visit. As a child, I accepted so many things that later puzzled me as an adult; why didn't I question that? I'd think, but I didn't.

I still couldn't eat much of the food that all the others ate, and so I ate a lot of the bread that Manz brought back. Over the next few weeks I grew thin and tired. Luckily for me it wasn't too long before we were due to start school – and that meant I'd get to eat one meal a day, at least.

The night before the first day of school, I was about to get into bed when Tara came in. 'You'll need some other clothes for school. There're some I don't need any more in here,' she said and rummaged in the wardrobe. 'Here, you can wear these tomorrow. They don't fit me any more.'

38

'Thanks,' I said, wishing I had some clothes all of my own and didn't have to share them with anyone else, or be given hand-me-downs like these.

We all got into bed, but I didn't get to sleep until long after it was dark; I couldn't help hoping that my new school would be a nice place to go, and that I'd make friends there. Slowly I was becoming used to my strange new home, with rules that I didn't understand and nobody, except Mena it seemed, being nice to me. I lay there and wished that my promise to Auntie Peggy – that I'd be good – would finally work out, and people – my new school friends, my family, my mother – would like me.

5

Manz was always the first to leave the house, for his job, so the following morning he banged on our door as he went past. 'Time to get up,' he yelled.

I was eager to start the day and so jumped out of bed; Tara continued to lie under her blanket, moaning about the noise and the early hour. Mena sat up in bed, stretching and yawning, but not budging. Nothing, though, could alter my mood today; I was going to school, and I would meet new people, and make friends, so, when I went downstairs and opened the back door to go to the toilet, it seemed only right that there was a nice warm breeze to greet me. Mother was in the kitchen when I came back in, with her back turned to me, so I crept past her as quietly as I could.

Tara passed me on the way downstairs, and I went into our room to change. Mena now got up and went downstairs to use the toilet, while I put on the shalwar-kameez, the tunic and pyjama-style trousers that we all wore.

When Mena came back, I asked her, 'When are we leaving?'

'Have Tara and Saber left?'

'I don't know. Do we have to go later than them?'

Mena pointed out of the window. 'See, there they go now, up to the shop.'

I looked out and saw my older brother and sister walking up the road. 'Yes, I see them,' I said.

'Okay, now we don't go until the bus comes.'

I didn't understand. 'What?'

'See the bus stop on the main road?' Mena said, gesturing to the corner that Saber and Tara had just turned round. 'The man in the suit? When the bus comes for him, that's when it's time to go to school.'

Why, oh, why didn't they have clocks in the house like everyone else? 'What shall we do till then? Eat some breakfast?'

'I'm not going downstairs till it's time to leave,' Mena said vehemently. 'Mother will tell us to make her breakfast and then we'll be late for school.'

So we stayed watching out of the window, until the bus came for the man in the suit, and then Mena ushered me down the stairs as fast as she could, and through the front door before Mother had a chance to call out to us.

I wasn't used to leaving the house without a grown-up saying goodbye to me, and certainly not to walking all the way to school without an adult alongside me. Mena and I had to cross busy main roads all by ourselves, and I found myself holding on tight to her as we did so. Mena suddenly seemed like the older sister she really was.

At the school, the playground was full of children of all ages and sizes, some with their parents, some on their own like us. But one thing struck me immediately; at the school I'd been to in Cannock Chase, most of the children were white. Here, almost all of them were brown girls and boys, like me, with dark hair.

'Let's find someone to play with,' I said to Mena, excitedly, but she said no.

'We have to go and find your teacher so you know where you need to go to today, first.'

Inside, we walked down a long corridor, past classrooms with little windows in the doors so that grown-ups could look through, and stopped outside one that had a name on the door. Mrs Young, it said, and there was a child's painting of a group of children stuck underneath. The children were all brown and wearing bright clothes, like me.

Mena knocked, and a woman answered, 'Come in.'

We went in. A smartly dressed woman was sitting behind the desk, and she smiled when she saw who it was. 'Hello, Mena, did you have a nice holiday?' She had a pleasant voice.

Mena didn't reply, though, merely nodded, and, taking me by the elbow, pulled me in front of her.

'Ah, you must be Mena's sister Sameem,' beamed the lady. 'I'm your teacher, Mrs Young.'

A bell rang out in the corridor and I heard the sounds of dozens of children milling up and down, some coming into the classroom. Mrs Young busied herself sorting out seats for everyone, including me. Mena waved goodbye, and mouthed and pointed to let me know I should meet her outside the classroom when it was time for break.

Mrs Young took out a large book from the drawer in her desk and told us she would be calling out our names, and that we should all answer by saying politely, 'Here, Mrs Young.' Most of the children seemed to know each other and nobody spoke to me; they all turned to look at me when Mrs Young called my name, but no one smiled. 'I'm sure you'll make friends soon,' she said, and carried on with the register.

The first lesson was reading. Mrs Young said, 'Come on, Sameem, you can read first since you're new. Come up here so everyone can see you as you read.'

I walked slowly to the front of the class, being careful not to trip on my clothes or do anything else to make myself look foolish, and stood next to her as she sat down in her chair. She handed me a book – I can't remember now what it was, but I knew straight away that it wasn't going to be any trouble for me to read – and asked me to start. I read the first couple of pages with ease.

'That's enough, Sameem.' Mrs Young stopped me. 'Let's try something harder; you can manage that one fine, can't you.' She chose another book from the pile on her desk and handed it to me. This was a little harder, as, although I read it fairly easily, I stumbled on a few words.

'Very good, you can stop there.' Mrs Young seemed pleased. 'Go back to your seat now, but take the book with you.'

I walked back to my desk, looking at some faces as I did so, but no one looked encouragingly at me; it seemed that it would take me a while to make friends after all.

And so the morning passed, until the bell rang for break. 'Line up, everyone,' Mrs Young said.

We all formed a crocodile line. As my seat was near the back, I was last in line, so I could see Mena waiting for me as we filed out. She didn't ask how my morning had been, didn't say anything in fact, but instead walked off to the playground so I followed her.

Outside, children swarmed over the climbing frame, played skipping games, and ran about shouting at each other as they did so. I itched to join them and was ready to run off, but Mena held on to my arm. 'Over here,' she said, and we stood by the side of the doors, near the grown-up on duty, and didn't move all through playtime. It seemed Mena had no friends, and no desire to run about with the other children. We just stood and watched everyone else having fun.

I loved the food at lunchtime, although everyone else hated it, or at least said so. It was the first meal I'd been able to eat in ages, so I devoured whatever was put in front of me. I even enjoyed the pudding, semolina, and asked for seconds. One of the other children on my table said, 'Yuk, I don't know how you can eat that.'

Afternoon school seemed to go just as the morning had; no one spoke to me in class, and Mena was there to meet me at the end of the day. 'See you tomorrow, Sameem,' said Mrs Young with a smile as I left.

We walked home, and still Mena barely spoke. I realised that she didn't like school, didn't enjoy it the way I always had at Cannock Chase, and so I didn't try to talk to her about my day. 'Tomorrow Salim starts nursery,' she said, 'and we'll be walking him to school with us.'

'Okay,' I replied, and that was all the conversation we had on the way home.

When we came in, I expected Mother to greet us at the door, to ask how our day had been, but she was lying down. 'There you are,' she said. 'Get me some tea.' In the kitchen, the dishes from breakfast and lunch were sitting in the sink, waiting to be washed up. Mena seemed to cheer up a little with a task to do, and we worked together to tidy the kitchen.

Hanif cooked dinner; she made rice and something called dahl, which looked like soup but didn't taste anything like it. If anything, it was worse than the curry, so I just ate some rice. When I went to bed that night, I was still hungry.

The next morning Salim came with us to school, dressed in a smart new pair of trousers and T-shirt that Mother had bought him. I thought with a pang how nice it would have been to have had my own new clothes when I started school, but Salim was so excited to be going to school, talking all the way there, that I couldn't think about it too much.

I did well in lessons again that day, although Mena still wanted to stand by the wall and watch the other children at breaktime, so it wasn't as good a day as I would have liked. We were walking out of the playground after school when suddenly I said, 'Mena – Salim!' We'd forgotten our little brother. Laughing, we rushed back to the nursery, to find he was waiting there with his teacher, beaming over his first day.

I discovered, over the next few days, that I didn't have to stand beside Mena at playtime. Children who didn't want to play outside were allowed to sit in the library and read, and that's what I did. I didn't make friends sitting there, but I wasn't bothered about that because the books were all the friends I needed. Mena came to look for me the first time I went there, and asked me if I was going to come out and play.

'No. I like this book I'm reading, so I think I'll stay here.'

It hadn't taken me long to realise why Mena had no friends at school, and why no one was being very nice to me. Our clothes were handed down, and we were laughed at for that. And because I was no longer the little girl who had run freely across Cannock Chase, I was no use to anyone in their games at playtime. Worse, though, for me, was that my stutter was easily mocked; and it had returned.

It reappeared soon after we'd come home from school, and I'd washed up the dishes left during the day. We were sitting down, eating the meal Hanif had prepared. Mother was sitting in her usual place, and Mena and I were on the floor, resting our backs against her settee. Hanif had doled out the food in the kitchen and Mena had brought my plate through; normally I managed by just eating the dry *roti* and leaving the spicy food for Mena. This time, though, Hanif had piled the curry on top of the *roti*, and although I tried to take a bite, it was just too much for me. Even a little bit made my eyes water and my mouth burn.

I put my plate down. 'Mena, I can't eat this, you'll have to eat it for me.' Tara looked over at me and then said something to Mother. Out of the blue I felt a tremendous thump on my back and I fell forward, shrieking with surprise and fright.

I looked behind me. Mother was glaring at me, and she said something. It was her – my own mother had just hit me. I couldn't understand why. I started crying, looking around at the other faces, seeing Hanif looking sternly at me, Tara smirking, and Mena looking down at her plate. 'Mena . . . what?' I managed to croak out.

'Just eat your food. Don't be a waster,' she said, avoiding my gaze.

I turned back. Mother was eating again, ignoring me. I wanted to say to her, please, I'm not wasting food, I just can't eat it, it's too hot for me. I started to say something, but all that happened was I stuttered. 'M-m-m-m-m-' was all that came out.

Mother looked at me in surprise. Tara laughed. None of them knew I stuttered, because I'd learned how to deal with it, but the shock of being hit by my own mother brought it on again.

Eventually they left the room and Mena finished my food for me, but that was it now; I couldn't speak easily around them, and of course the stutter appeared at the worst times at school as well. None of the things I'd learned to do to control my stutter in the children's home worked any more, and although it didn't seem bad when it was just Mena and me on our own, around the others it was a torment.

Mother decided she could fix my stutter by cutting the skin under my tongue, which she told me was pulling my tongue down in the wrong way. She shouted angrily at Hanif to help her, and the two of them laid me down on the kitchen floor, and told me to open my mouth. I was confused but did as I was told. In Mother's hand was a razor blade, the kind found in an old-fashioned razor. I stared at it in horror; 'Mother, what—' I started to say, but Hanif pulled me back down to lie flat.

'Now hold still, Sameem,' Mother said, Tara translating for her, while Hanif held my arms down with her knees and my mouth open with her hands. Mother leaned forward with the razor and I had to watch as the blade came closer; I wanted to close my mouth, to shut my eyes, but I couldn't. I tried to pull myself into the floor as Mother's dirty fingers forced their way into my mouth and I tried not to retch. Then I felt a sharp tearing pain under my tongue as she flicked the blade backwards and forwards through the tag of skin that held my tongue to the floor of my mouth. I wanted to scream, I wanted to pull away. Why was she doing this to me? She kept saying, 'Hold still, child. If I cut this the stutter will disappear and you'll be able to speak properly. If you muck about then I'll cut your mouth by mistake,' and I tried very hard to keep still after that but my legs kept twisting and turning under her; the pain and revulsion of the taste of my own blood in my mouth was too great. She pinched me to keep me still and, finally, sat back. 'There, finished,' she said, as if somehow I'd asked her to do this for me and she had accomplished a task. Hanif let go of my head and I turned to the side and spat out the blood into a bowl.

To this day, the skin underneath my tongue hasn't grown back; where she cut me is clearly visible.

Mother seemed satisfied with her work. 'There, now you'll be able to move your tongue properly and that stutter will disappear.'

I sat there on the floor and sobbed in shock, but it wasn't the throbbing pain that upset me the most, it was Mother's lack of care for me, the way she seemed to see me as an object to boss about, to ridicule, to hurt. Whatever I was to her, I wasn't her daughter. And as I longed to be her much loved daughter, more than anything, I would do whatever she wanted in an effort to make her love me. Even lie down and let her mutilate me. Of course the stutter didn't go away.

Dad was the only grown-up face I felt safe around, and so when he did come over on his infrequent visits I would look to him for comfort. He'd take Mena and me to the park, but when we got back Mother would shout at him about one thing or another, so he stopped taking us out. At first I didn't know what was being said, but then, once I'd started to learn the language, I began to understand; Mother would ask him for money and when he said he didn't have any she would tell him to get lost. He just walked off.

What I didn't understand, though, and what did trouble me at nights sometimes when I'd had a really bad day, was why Dad didn't take me away to live with him; he must know Mother shouted at me as much as she did at him, so why did he leave me here with her?

Of course when he did visit it wasn't easy for all of us. For a start, Dad smoked, which Mother hated because of her asthma. Indeed everyone seemed to mind, apart from me. Dad was different to the rest of my family. He was calm, and nothing seemed to bother him, unlike Mother who always seemed to have things on her mind. Mother never appeared to smile, but, even though he didn't say anything to me, Dad would always smile warmly at me, and that smile was only for me.

Hanif did most of the cooking when I first came to the house, and it was a year before I had my first cookery lesson. I was eager to try to help, of course, and thought that cooking might give me a little more to eat – as well as a taste for the curry I still disliked – and I didn't notice that neither Tara nor Mena was expected to learn from Hanif as I was.

I had to learn to speak the language that Mother and Tara used to exclude me. Mena helped, teaching me things in the kitchen. 'What's this?' she'd say, holding up a pot or a plate or a spoon, and I'd have to tell her the Punjabi word; but the best way I found of learning the language was to look at the films that we all sat around to watch.

We never seemed to watch normal television, and most evenings Tara would stick a tape into the machine and it would be films with titles like *Songs from Indian Movies*. I'd lie on the floor, my chin cupped in my hands, and I'd look longingly at these cheerful, happy families; they'd be laughing (and singing and dancing, which I always found silly) and doing everything together. Just like my family, the girl the son married came to live with his family; but there the similarities stopped. Hanif didn't look after her mother-in-law, as the women in the films did; it seemed to be my job to cook, clean and help with the washing. Why should Hanif make the effort, when she had a slave – me – to do it all for her?

I'd sneak into the room when Mother wasn't around, and play the tapes again and again, trying the words out, until I understood what was being said around me, and what to say in reply. The only thing I never learned from the films were the awful words Mother would use against me, as the films were too polite to include such swearing.

Hanif was the only one in the house who refused to learn English. Mother used it when she had to, but Hanif wouldn't learn any. When she wanted my help, she'd tell Mena, who'd translate; when I had learned enough Punjabi, she'd sometimes say nice things to me after I'd been beaten by Mother, although what she usually said was, 'Try not to upset her so, Sameem, you know she doesn't like to be upset,' as if somehow Mother's being upset was worse than the cuts and bruises I bore.

(I realised much later on why Hanif was nice to me: she wanted me to marry a cousin of hers, so that he could come over to England. That would have meant I'd have to live with her and work for her all the time. Mother, however, chose not to go along with Hanif's plans after there was some dispute over land ownership back in Pakistan, which meant Mother stopped speaking to her for a time.)

Hanif was at her most patient in the kitchen, perhaps because she wasn't watched over by Mother. So it was easy for me to ask questions and not get told off for talking too much, or for saying the wrong thing or asking something stupid.

I had watched Hanif peel onions so she gave me one to do on my own. I started by pulling the skin off, but she sighed and reached over to help me.

'Put it down and cut it; here's a knife.'

I had watched her chopping before, the blade slicing through the vegetables on the board, but was surprised at how hard it was when I tried. I pushed the knife down into the onion flesh, but it wouldn't cut right through. Hanif was standing next to me, watching, so she took hold of my hand and held it at the edge of the onion. 'Try and cut a bit off at a time,' she said. 'Now turn it on to the part you just cut and cut it again.'

Tears started in my eyes which I wiped away before I cut again; it got easier each time I cut the onion.

'Now cut the big pieces into small pieces and put them in the pot.'

Once I'd finished I looked up at her and saw that she was actually smiling at me. 'See, you can cut an onion, that's good.'

I wanted to cut another onion, I wanted to cook a curry, I wanted to see her smile again, I wanted to feel I had pleased her. I felt good when I was being taught, I was getting attention and praise. Hanif then showed me how to make *rotis*, and that's when I burned my fingers cooking them over the naked flame. Next she taught me how to fry the onions, and how much chilli powder and spices to use.

Within a week or two the curry one night was all my own work, and within about six months I was preparing and cooking everything that my family ate. I was pleased and proud to cook for my family; I didn't mind that I was expected to cook for everyone when I came home from school. I didn't even seem to notice that no one thanked me. Over the weeks and months, I was taught to cook the spicy foods they all ate; I learned to serve everyone else first, and always to leave enough for Manz when he came home, so although I had hoped to eat well I never had enough.

Mena helped me when I got stuck. 'Do you remember how many spoons of chilli to use in vegetable curry?' Or 'How much water should I put in the rice?'

Mena always knew the answer, even though it was always me cooking. I don't know what I would have done without her. We did a lot of things together: I would cook, she would watch, and talk to me as I did so; I would wash the dishes and she would put them in the cupboard; I would brush the floor and she would hold the shovel at the end so I could sweep the dirt into it, and when I hung up the clothes on the line she would hold the other end.

We used to play word games while we were cooking, or washing-up. In one you had to make the other person say a certain word, such as 'Yes'.

'You have to answer quickly,' Mena said.

'Okay.'

'What are you cooking?'

'Vegetables.'

'Do you like them?'

'No.'

'Do you like me?'

I nodded.

'You can't nod, you said yes,' she said delightedly.

'No, I didn't.'

I liked playing these games with Mena but I missed not having other things to play with, like colouring pencils and pens, colouring books, dot-to-dot books and jigsaw puzzles.

Walking home from school one day, Mena tried to teach me to whistle. I couldn't. I tried and tried but I couldn't get it. I'd purse my lips together and blow; all that came out was air, no sound.

I tried all the way home, a twenty-minute walk; I tried while I was cooking; I tried under the covers at bedtime. Then on the way to school the following morning I blew gently, and there was a slight whistle right at the end of the blow.

'You did it,' said Mena excitedly.

I tried again. Nothing.

'I can't do it while I'm smiling,' I said.

I forced my face to be still and serious, and tried again; this time there was a proper whistle, a long shrill note.

'I can whistle, I can whistle.' I was so happy I almost danced all the rest of the way to school. I whistled whenever I got the chance that day. I whistled when I got home, I whistled while I washed the dishes. But there was a noise behind me, and I looked round; Mena had gone to the toilet, and Hanif was standing there.

'Where have you learned that from?'

'Nowhere.'

'Did you learn that from school?'

'No, I just learned it.'

'Men whistle at girls; if I hear it again, I'll tell your brother, okay?'

I nodded and she walked out of the door.

When Mena came back I told her what Hanif had said . 'She's only jealous because she can't whistle,' she commented. We both smiled at each other.

I didn't whistle in the house again, or anywhere near where Hanif or Manz might hear me, but I whistled to my heart's content when we were away from the house.

Cleaning was the job I hated most. The house was always dusty and there was no vacuum cleaner to help me with the job; I had to sweep everything up with a brush and mop the floor to try to keep the dust down as I did so. The worst part, though, was cleaning the wall next to where Mother sat. I'd already seen how she hawked up phlegm and spat it out against the wall, where it slid down the surface; now I had to be the one to wipe the wall down with a cloth, and try to mop the thick goo off the floor. Some of it always got on my fingers and I would have to stop myself from retching because to do so in front of Mother, when I was supposed to be helping her, would just have brought a blow to my head. It was disgusting. She claimed her asthma made her spit like this, and as there was always dust everywhere perhaps this was so; but I didn't really believe her. Why the wall? Why not a bucket, or something easy to keep clean? It was revolting, and little Salim was told to keep away, while I, of course, had to clean this up. Mena couldn't – wouldn't – come near, as she said it made her sick just to look at the mess.

Worse, though, came when Mother needed to pee. Again she claimed she had to do this here, in the room in front of us, because she wasn't well enough to make it outside in time, so she kept a potty under the sofa. We children – not Saber or Manz, she'd never do it in front of them, it would be just us girls and Salim – would be watching TV when she would suddenly pull out the potty, draw a blanket over her middle, and squat down to pee. We'd lie there trying not to listen, but when she finished she'd call me over. 'Sameem! Sameem!' And it was me who had to take the potty she'd just filled and carry it out to empty down the toilet. Mena almost vomited if she was asked to do this, so it was always my job, even though it made me heave as well.

★   ★   ★

Tara's bullying became worse than before. I was her slave. I was expected to do everything for her – fetch her glasses of water, get her food, make her bed, take her clothes off the line, carry her dirty dishes back to the kitchen – and she never lifted a finger.I don't know how she managed before I came along. She would speak Punjabi in front of me, although all I could make out was my name, and the grown-ups would laugh, looking at me as they did so.

Tara always seemed especially pleased when she got others to laugh at me; I started to think of her as a spoiled princess. And I got my revenge, putting her clothes down as instructed, but not bothering to remove the schoolbook from the chair so that she would panic when she couldn't find it.

One day, Tara called out. 'Sam, go to the shop and get some milk.' Mena came with me and we were walking down the road when two boys – Carl and Luke, the two who had taken money from Mena before – came up to us. The two boys came close, so that I backed towards the wall, where Mena slid behind me.

'What are you doing out of the house?' said Carl.

'Have you got money?' said Luke.

They stood so close to us I could feel their breath on me. Mena was shaking, and it made me feel a bit scared too. 'Leave us alone,' I said.

Carl laughed. 'Give us your money,' he said.

'Why?' I hoped I sounded less scared than I felt.

'If you don't, I'll punch you.'

Luke smirked at this.

'Just give him the money, Sam,' Mena pleaded from behind me.

This boy was just like the boy who'd lived in the room next door to me in the home, and I wasn't going to give in to him. I was sick of being bullied. 'No,' I said.

He raised his hand to hit me, and in doing so turned his head a little towards me. So I reached out and grabbed his hair, the short ones just above the ear. I pulled hard. It'd worked before, and it worked now.

'Owwwwww!' he screamed.

I didn't see why these two horrible boys should think they could bully me like everyone else too. I pulled a little harder, and he screamed louder. Luke backed away, a scared look on his face.

Mena was now eagerly leaning over me, yelling, 'Pull it harder! Pull it harder!'

'NO! No, don't. Please don't!' Carl said, tears running down his face.

I kept hold of him, and stepped right up close. 'You're going to leave Mena and me alone from now on, aren't you? Do you understand?'

'Yes, yes. We'll leave you alone. Just lemme go,' he begged.

To make sure, I gave one last tug, which made him cry even louder, then pushed him away from me. He backed away fast, his hand clasped to his ear. Luke ran off after him.

Mena was bouncing, she was so excited. 'You should have pulled it harder!'

'No, that was enough,' I said. 'C'mon, let's get the milk.' I felt I'd done something great, giving a bully a taste of his own medicine. At least I knew I could still stand up for myself when I had to.

Funnily enough, from then on Carl and Luke used to smile to us in the street when we passed, and never tried to bother us ever again.

Tara moved downstairs when we started going to school. There was a space under the stairs that had a single bed squeezed into it, and Tara slept down there. I moved into Tara's bed, and so – bliss – had my own bed to sleep in again. With Tara gone from our room, we could talk as we pleased, and – when I'd completed all my chores – our room became a little retreat from the world. Only when it wasn't too cold, as we didn't have any heating there, of course. Mother never came upstairs, so we were safe – mostly. Some nights, though, Tara came back up to sleep with us – if her bed was dirty (she wouldn't let Salim on it as he sometimes peed on the bed and she'd shout at him before coming upstairs) then she'd come up and kick me out – so that I had to climb in with Mena again.

Reading was everything to me. Because I kept myself to myself, I never had any friends at school. I would hide away in the library, reading thrilling stories about children getting together to prove that adults were wrong. The Famous Five, Nancy Drew, the Hardy Boys and the Secret Seven were my favourite characters and I read as many of these books as the library held. Sometimes I solved the mystery before the end and I would whisper to myself, *I knew it.* These books were an escape from the horrible world I lived in. I didn't feel that I belonged, either at home or at school. No one made an effort to welcome me, no one helped me fit in. The way I learned to cope was by not having expectations, although if I hadn't had my books to read, I don't know how I would have survived life at home.

6

Once we were at school, Mena told me that we would have to start going to the local mosque. I looked forward to this, expecting it to be a bit like Sunday school because Mena told me we'd be studying a religious book. But it turned out that I was wrong; it was more like being at home. In fact, it was even in a home.

When we got back from school, we went upstairs to fetch our scarves off the hook behind the bedroom door. Mena showed me how to wrap mine tightly around my head. On our way out, Mother ordered us, 'You come straight home after the mosque.'

The mosque was about the same distance from home as school, only in the opposite direction. As we walked along, I saw some open ground, mostly made up of little hills. Mena said they were called the monkey hills.

'Why do you call them that?'

'I don't know, but that's what Saber calls them.' Mena looked a bit cross. 'He should come to the mosque with us but instead he goes out and plays on the hills with his friends.'

As we walked on, I kept looking back over my shoulder, hoping to see Saber up on the hills, but I couldn't catch sight of him at all.

The mosque was a big house where about thirty children went to learn the Quran. The girls, who all looked alike with their white scarves, were put in the big front room, the boys in another. We all sat on the floor, and it was cold. We sat there waiting for the religious teacher – the *molvi* – to arrive, and while we waited some of the girls adjusted their scarves, tucking every last strand of hair away. I couldn't see why they were so obsessed about this.

The *molvi* appeared, and as we sat quietly, waiting to start, he walked among us, and came to a stop behind me. Suddenly I felt a blow on my shoulder.

I cried out in shock and pain and looked up; why had he hit me? He didn't say anything, but pointed to my hair. Mena leaned over and tucked a few strands that had come loose back under my scarf. I couldn't understand why the *molvi* had hit me, instead of telling me so that I could do something about it. The tears I wept were as much in fury at this injustice as they were of pain. The other girls stared down into their Qurans, careful not to make eye contact with me.

When we left, I asked Mena how often we were going to have to go to this horrible house. She said we were to be taught Islam by reading the Quran, which is the way most people learn. We would go every day, after school. We started with the *Qaida,* a thirty-page booklet. On the first page is the Arabic alphabet and we were taught a line each day (there are about six lines per page); afterwards we learned what each letter would sound like if there's a dash or a particular symbol above or below the letter. Then we were taught what the letters would sound like if you joined them up. There would be words of four letters long, then on the next page they would be six letters long and so on.

All the time we were being taught how to read the *Qaida* the *molvi* would say 'Hurry, you are nearly ready to read the Quran.' All the girls in the room who were just beginning to learn would smile from ear to ear at his words. He had a way of making it sound magical and mysterious, and I wanted to start reading it as soon as possible, as we all did. We didn't understand what we were reading, we were just told to read it this way; we would sit there reciting the teachings of that day over and over again so we didn't forget them. If we didn't remember the previous day's teachings we were shouted at or even hit.

When I could read nine letters joined up, the *molvi* said I was ready to read the Quran. It took me about a year or so; once I knew how to read the Quran, when I was nine, I didn't have to go to the mosque again, as I wasn't taught to write Arabic, only to read it. Once we could read the Quran we knew all we had to about Islam.

★   ★   ★

As the summer changed into autumn, each time we walked past the monkey hills I would look longingly over, imagining myself lost in them. One time, as we were walking to the mosque, I said to Mena, 'I'm not going to the mosque today. I'm going to look for Saber.'

'What are you doing, Sam?' Mena, as ever, was nervous about what mother would say, and do, if she found out we'd skipped our class.

'Mother won't find out, Mena. It's only for one week.' And I strode ahead. After a moment's hesitation, she followed.

I didn't tell her why I was heading up there; I wanted to see what it was like, sure, but I also wanted to see what Saber was doing. My older brother was a mystery to me; he hardly ever seemed to be at home, and he never had to do any chores when he was around. He wasn't mean to me, like Tara or Manz, but he wasn't quite my friend, like Mena. He was a puzzle. Besides, I also wanted someone to look after me, and maybe Saber – the big brother I read about in the books I loved – would do that.

Mena and I set off up the first hill, and when we reached the top we looked down saw was a group of boys. I strained to see who they were, and Mena said, 'Is that Saber? I can't tell.'

'There's only one way to find out,' I said. 'Saber! Saber!' I shouted down to them.

One of the boys looked up, and walked away from the others towards us.

'That must be him – let's go down.' And I led the way.

But he wasn't pleased to see us when we got there. 'What are you two doing? Why are you here? Why aren't you at the mosque?'

'We can come here if we like; and why aren't you at the mosque, then?'

He looked crossly at me for a bit, but then he ducked his head and looked up at us both with a small guilty smile on his face. 'Yeah, you got me. I don't like going 'cos I don't learn the words, and then I get hit for not knowing.'

'I was hit too,' I said, but if I expected any sympathy I got none.

'But you've got to go, both of you, because if you don't then Mother will get to hear about it and we'll all be in trouble.'

I wanted to say, Why don't you go? Why should we? But I'd already started to think like everyone else in my family – which was, let the men get their way. So instead I said, 'Okay, but not this week, yeah? We're here now, we'll go next week, but just this week let us stay, okay?'

Saber looked thoughtful for a moment. 'Okay, you can stay. We're fixing this bike; just don't get in our way or say anything stupid, right?'

So we sat down near the boys while they fiddled about with the bike's chain and the gears. The grease was getting everywhere, but none of the boys seemed to care; I wondered how Saber was going to clean that off before he got home.

After a while sitting there, I grew fidgety. I looked up at the next hill: 'I wonder what's over there?'

Mena – who'd been silent up till now, as if saying nothing would mean she wouldn't be noticed – said, 'I don't know, I've never been here before.'

I stood up, and Saber straightened up too. 'Where are you going?' he asked.

'I'm going to go up that hill and see what's over there,' I said. 'Mena, you coming with me?'

Mena stood up too. 'Yeah, I'll go.'

Saber glanced back at his friends and then called, 'Don't go off too far. You'll have to be home in half an hour or Mother will be suspicious.'

'Okay,' we called back over our shoulders. And we walked up the hill. To my surprise, Mena was suddenly excited. 'I've never been this far. How far do you think it goes, Sam?'

'I don't know, let's see when we get to the top,' I said.

We reached the top of the hill, both of us panting a little with the effort, and stared into the distance. Another hill, and then another. But we had a great view of the streets around us, as we were high up and in the evening sunlight. 'I don't ever want to go home,' I said.

'Me too,' said Mena. Then she sighed. 'But we have to, and soon. If we're not back when Mother expects us we'll be in trouble.'

'Let's just stay up here for a little.'

So we sat on the grass for a few minutes, leaning against each other as we enjoyed the peace and calm of the evening. This was the closest I'd been to the Chase, this open landscape; the huge sky above, teeming with birds as they flew about in the warm air, calling me. I wanted their freedom, the ease with which they could slip away from everything here to their own playground.

As the sun sank lower, and the shadows lengthened, Mena stood up and dusted down her clothes. 'Come on, you,' she said, 'it's time we went home.'

At the bottom of the hill, Saber's mood had darkened as well. 'Don't come here again, right? I'll come home when I want to.' And he turned his back on us and walked over to his friends.

Why had he suddenly changed? I felt no closer to him, but perhaps he too daydreamed about getting away, only for Mena and me to come along and remind him of reality.

I never went up those hills again, although I always loved looking up into the sky, seeing the birds darting about and imagining them settling there, resting as we had. It wasn't just because I loved the open light and air; I also loved the exercise. Cooped up either in school or in that house all day, I felt tired and lethargic; walking up those hills reminded me of the days spent racing across the Chase with Amanda.

It was only when I was out of the house – walking to and from school, or going to and from the mosque, or doing a routine trip to the corner shop – that I was able to think about home, and how I felt puzzled there all the time. I found everything strange there, and although I tried my hardest to do what they asked of me – or more usually expected of me, without explaining why, or what it was they wanted – I never seemed to get it right. But although I struggled to fit in, I kept trying; I started enjoying the food because it was all I was given to eat and I wanted more than anything to be liked, to feel wanted by my brothers and sisters. I wanted Mother to love me, and if I did anything wrong and she shouted at me or hit me then I felt it was my fault, that I had provoked her. It was trying hard, and loving them, but only getting abuse and slaps back that I found so hard to understand.

And Mother in particular was not what I'd expected. I'd never met anyone like her before. All the people I'd met – like Auntie Peggy, my father, the vicar at the church, the cook who made us cakes and let us lick the bowl – were kind and caring. I had never been yelled at and I had certainly never been hit by anyone. Mother smelled of masala and, when she wasn't lying down, sat cross-legged on the settee. Her eyes were kind-looking and with her jet-black hair neatly tied in a pony tail or plaited, she never looked scary.

But from the very first week I was there, home was a frightening place to live. Mother didn't speak much to me, or indeed to Mena or anyone else, but yelled a lot. All Mother's mouth did was yell and spit, the revolting yellow phlegm she'd cough up and then spit out against the wall. I never wanted to kiss Mother or her me; her kiss would never feel like Auntie Peggy's gentle goodnight kiss. Her hands weren't gentle to hold, like Aunty Peggy's soft hands. Auntie Peggy would hold my hand when she had to put a thermometer in my mouth, and play 'round and round the garden' when I was done to make me smile again; she'd hold my hand when I was little and had to walk to school with a grown-up. Since I'd left the home, Mother never, ever offered me her hand, or held mine; the only time she touched me was to hit me. I thought if Mother ever held my hand she would squeeze it so tightly it would hurt.

Almost all the time I was around Mother at home I felt not so much fear as puzzlement. What had I done wrong? What was it about me that made her so angry? Why was it always me that she was so evil-tempered with? I wished I knew.

I couldn't let on how scared I felt, walking in from school. Mother would be sitting there on the settee, and fear rushed through me as I sensed her waiting to yell as soon as I entered the room.

'It's about time you were back, what have you been doing on the way home, idle child? Clean the floor,' she'd shout. Scared to open my mouth in case nothing came out – I'd get a smack there and then if that happened – I'd nod and do as I was told.

Sometimes it would be 'Clean the table,' or, 'Make me a cup of tea,' but every day there was something to be done the minute I got in, always the same: 'Sam, do this' or 'Sam, do that.' It took a few months for my mind to adjust to my new life.

I didn't know why my mother wouldn't treat me like the mothers I had read about. I knew from books what a mother was: kind, welcoming, safe, a warm and generous person to be cuddled by. My dream mother would sing me to sleep, cradling my head in the palm of her hand as she did so. But in some fairy tales there were wicked mothers and stepmothers, sending their children or their husband's children off to the woods to die. Perhaps that was the story I was in, I sometimes thought. My real mother ignored me, if I was lucky; if I bothered her at all – and I had still to find out what it was I did that inflamed her anger; that remained a mystery – she would reach out with her hand and slap me. Hard enough to bruise me.

Was this how families behaved? I didn't know because I hadn't had one before, which was why I accepted it. In the space of a few short weeks, I became a very wise seven-year-old. I knew that being in my own home wasn't safe, wasn't the cheery place I had imagined it to be, in my foolish, childish way. I knew that being with my sisters and brothers wasn't going to make me happy. I was afraid of Mother.

(In later life I'd be told that understanding something, knowing about it, took the fear away. Try telling that to a seven-year-old girl who knows she is about to be struck by her own mother, her brother, her sister. Try explaining that.)

It began in the kitchen.

'Sameem, *haramdee*, what is this? Did I not tell you about this last week?'

But even as I was turning round to see what it was I'd done wrong, I felt a sudden sharp pain in my back. I fell forward, partly from surprise and partly from the force of the blow. Tara laughed. I looked round. What had happened? I expected Mother to look as shocked as I did, wondering who had pushed me over.

But Mother simply leaned down towards me, pushing her finger into my face. 'If you don't try harder, then you'll get worse. It's up to you,' and she turned back to her food.

Mena whispered in my ear as we went up the stairs. 'You had better be careful,' she said. 'They've always said that if I didn't do as I was told I'd get a slap, but she didn't even bother to warn you. Don't provoke them.'

I stared at her in amazement. How had I just provoked Mother into hitting me? What had I done? Nothing, apart from slave over the stove for her, as I did every night? I knew that she wouldn't hit me again – it must have been a mistake.

I was wrong about Mother. And not just her, either; my sister and brother, too. It was as if Tara and Manz had been waiting for this to happen: Tara was almost gleeful that Mother hit me. But it was worse: I could sense some sort of relief in them.

It took me a long time to realise this, and in truth it's maybe something I've come to understand only in the last few years, but my older brothers and sister, no matter how cruel towards me they may have been, lived in fear of my mother and her moods and rages, so much so that when I became her target, they were glad – glad it wasn't them. Lying in bed one evening, my back pressed up against Mena's, I remembered once being stung by a bee when I was in the children's home, and how Auntie Peggy had told me that the bee was only doing what came naturally to it and that my getting in its way simply made the bee react: it didn't know what it was doing, it was behaving in the only way it knew to protect itself, and wasn't aware of the consequences to its sting. I imagined my family were like bees, protecting what they had, acting instinctively against the outsider, the interloper – me. What they did to me, how I felt, didn't seem to matter to them. Why I was an outsider, and not one of the family – I couldn't figure that out at all. I never did.

The violence depended not so much on me as on my mother; whatever I did or didn't do was less important than how she felt at the time. Food not served exactly as she liked it – even if that wasn't the way she'd liked it last time – or noise at the wrong moment, or mess of any sort, might set her off; but I could also set her off just by being in the room, lying on the floor watching the Bollywood films that everyone else liked to see. At first, watching her hug Salim, I wanted her to cuddle me too, reaching out to her: 'Ami,' I begged, 'please . . .' but I got no further because she pulled her hand away from mine or turned away from me.

The beatings grew worse. A slap to the back of my head, a punch to the shoulders, a pinch on the arm, a kick to the leg; all the time being told off for something or other. 'I told you not to do that,' or, 'Don't you speak to me that way,' or 'Didn't I say you weren't supposed to do that.' Then it was her shoe; if I was within reach, she'd slip off her sandal, a thin flat shoe, and swipe at me. When she was really angry with me, she'd flip the shoe over and beat me with the heel end, so as to hurt me more.

Why I didn't run up the stairs, away from her, where with her asthma she couldn't easily follow, I can't answer, except by saying that I always thought she had a reason, and that if I did as she wanted then she'd stop. That if I was a 'good' daughter then she wouldn't have cause to beat me, and that her rage would die as swiftly and incomprehensibly as it had been born, so that the sweet and loving mother hidden underneath could emerge. That foolish delusion even survived the day she beat me with her stick.

Her *pika*, as she called it, though I didn't know what the word meant, lay under her bed. It was used only on me; none of my brothers or sisters was touched. The stick was about two feet long, and as thick as my thumb. It fell on my arms, my back, my legs, as I screamed and cowered beneath her.

Mena comforted me afterwards, when it was safe to do so; that is, when she would not suffer the way I had done. Nobody else came near me. Nobody cleaned or bathed my cuts and bruises, there were no plasters or cream in our house for such things. I sobbed as quietly as I could, fearing my mother, not understanding what I had done to be treated so – less well than a dog. But every time things were the same: my mother acted as if nothing had happened, the others ignored me, and I was left alone in my pain and fear.

I was hit most days; usually it was just a shove or a slap on the back to urge me to hurry up with a chore I was doing. If I took too much time washing the dishes Mother shouted at me to hurry up and then Hanif, who didn't often hit me and instead mostly just shouted at me, might give me a light slap; or if I didn't put some clothes away before going to school I got a smack with the sole of Mother's sandal when I came home. What I'd done wrong determined what I was beaten with.

It took me a while to become Auntie Peggy's 'brave one' again: a few months of beatings and abuse, a few months for my body to get used to the pain. Although it was my mother who did this – she'd actually say, after she'd hit me, 'She's used to it now,' – I still wanted to please her. I guess I wanted her to give me a chocolate biscuit, like Auntie Peggy used to when I was brave.

I forgot to put salt in the curry once. I was about ten years old and had finished cooking the curry and boiling some rice. Mother, sitting cross-legged on the settee as usual, shouted that she wanted some food. I ladled some out of the pan and took it to her, then returned to the kitchen to get her some water. I had just placed the glass of water on the floor when she grabbed me by the hair and jerked my head back. 'Who's going to put salt in the curry? Is your grandma going to come back from her grave and do it for you?' she screamed as she pushed me over. She told me to fix the food before Manz came home or else he would beat me with the *pika* – the stick.

I didn't get beaten with it much, really. I was shown it as a threat more often than I was beaten with it.

Over time, being hit did something weird to me. I started to feel that I deserved it; that there must have been something wrong with *me*, that it was *my* fault Mother didn't love me. I knew – even then I knew – it was a kind of madness, but I couldn't stop myself from feeling this way. So, when one day I bled after being hit, instead of fearing the sight of my own blood, I welcomed it. Mother's blow had landed just on the inside of my wrist and her bangle caught on my skin. The skin tore and blood gushed out, the sight gripping me. At last I could see something physical, a sign of my pain that up till now had been hidden; I could *see* as well as *feel* my arm hurting, and it felt good to know this. It was a release – and it caused a change within me. I found a broken glass bangle of Hanif's and hid it away under my bed.

One day, when my head was ringing with the shouting and the slaps I'd received, with the hatred I felt for myself for failing to please them all yet again, I took the bangle, hid away in the outside toilet and scraped it along the top of my arm, from the elbow downwards. It was a sensation unlike anything I'd known before because it should have hurt me, but it didn't; the blood welled up, pooling on my arm. Some dark secret was leaking out of me, and as it did, I felt better. It was about showing something to myself: it felt more real to me, and at least I could see it. I dabbed at the easily wipeable trickles of blood, and when the flow stopped I quickly pulled my sleeves down to cover the wounds and returned to the kitchen. No one was any the wiser about what I'd done, and the secret I carried thrilled me.

I cut myself again and again, scraping but not gouging the skin. I was in control: I told myself when to start and when to stop. Sometimes I scoured the top of my skin with Manz's razor; but what I liked to use best was the stolen broken bangle. Somehow it made the whole process right. There was a reason for the flowers of blood that bloomed on my arm when I scratched at my skin with the bangle; I was cutting myself, and the blows that fell upon me were washed away in the trickle of my own blood.

I didn't dig deep enough to make the blood ooze, it was just a trickle that I could wipe. But I didn't do it to hurt myself, it was to experience the feeling. I had got so used to getting beaten, I just wanted to feel pain – that was the sensation that I wanted. It was a liberation, like when I had a horrible spot that I would pop; it hurt, but it was a release too.

Being beaten was the only physical contact I had with my family. So my behaviour wasn't harming me, it was showing love. I was loving myself by cutting myself.

I only did it about ten or twelve times, over some eighteen months, starting when I was eleven. I only did it when things were very bad, and I was pushed towards it. I'd be beaten, but I thought I didn't get beaten enough. I'd do something wrong, but they wouldn't even say it was wrong and hit me, so I had to cut myself to show that they cared enough for me to be hurt for my misdemeanour. I did it in silence. Speaking made no difference. But the feeling was good. I started answering back because I wanted to be beaten, I wanted the physical contact with my family. I would answer back even more, and when that didn't work, I'd go and harm myself. In the toilet no one would bother me, and I'd cut and I'd cry, I felt sorry for myself and lonely. I wanted someone to take away my pain. I felt hopeless, I wasn't worth anything, I didn't feel part of my family and I had nowhere else to go, although I felt trapped as well. The only way for me to give vent to these feelings was to scrape the top of my arm or leg and watch the skin change colour when the blood trickled on to it.

It was my cry for help, but who was going to hear me?

As a child I was very accepting; this was my family, I must fit in. As much as I hated the abuse hurled at me, the slaps and punches and kicks, as much as I wished for some of the comforts I'd had back in the children's home, as much as I longed for someone to put their arms around me, and just let me cuddle up against them, as much as I wished for someone else to do the chores that always seemed to be mine, I still woke up each morning – came home each day from school – eager to make this day different. This would be the day I'd speak Punjabi better, I'd tell myself; this would be the day I would cook something so that Mother would look up at me after her first bite, smile, and say, this is good, well done. Of course it never happened. But I kept on trying.

I had no choice but to try; I had only Mena on my side. At night, or in the kitchen, after I'd been hit, she'd ask me if my arm hurt. I'd never admit that it did; even if moving it sent a burning pain up my arm, I never told her how much it really hurt. Sometimes my back would hurt as I sat down; I'd flinch but never say anything. The only way to get rid of it was to cry, but, with Mena by my side, I rarely got the chance to do that. Sometimes I could cry outside in the toilet, sometimes silently when we walked to school and the cold breeze hit my face. My eyes would water and I would open them wide, to make them water more, so that I could release my fear and sadness without Mena knowing. I suppose I wanted to protect her, although I couldn't protect myself.

I wanted so much. I wanted to help around the house, I wanted to clean, I wanted to cook the food, I even wanted to take mother's pee-pot to the toilet, because I thought I was pleasing them. I thought this was the way things were done. I didn't feel like my sisters and brothers, I felt different; I tried so hard but I still doubted myself. I told myself that I didn't know everything. I was told to get used to the food because it was what they ate, I was told to wear the clothes I was given because that was what they wore. I was shown once how to do something and was called good when I learned, but afterwards I was expected to do it right and if I didn't I got shouted at or even hit. And I accepted it all; I even welcomed it. I wanted to be one of the family, I wanted them to treat me like their sister, and I thought the only way I could do this would be to please them. I wanted so much, so very, very, much, for Mother to love me, and for her to think I'd done well. I wanted her to look at me, to see *me*, rather than stare past me as she always did. I did everything for her, and nothing was ever good enough.

7

Lying in bed at night, in my daytime clothes, was my only opportunity to think properly, when I was in the house. At all other times I was being told to do this or that, and was always wary that someone was about to say – or do – something to me. So it was at night that I could let my imagination go. In these daydreams, I'd be living freely somewhere, perhaps on the Chase, perhaps in the park or the hills near home. I was always with other children, but they were never my family, or anyone from school. These were children who befriended me, and we shared everything, whether it was something we'd brought with us or found in the woods.

I was a little girl still, and I wanted to play, but with Mother around there was never any time to play. Even if I'd been able to, though, there was nothing for Mena and I to play with, as the case I'd brought from the children's home never showed up and there were no dressing-up clothes or toys, except for Salim's toys.

Saturday mornings, however, when Mother and Hanif went shopping in town, provided one small outlet. Mena and I watched television, laughing at Chris Tarrant and Sally James and Lenny Henry on *Tiswas*. After that, we'd change channels and watch cartoons; lying there on the floor, I almost felt as if I was a little girl in the home again, waiting for my lunch in the dining room. Only I was, of course, just a little girl and I had Tara to remind me of this. She'd come in and tell us that she was going to turn off the TV, and she'd threaten to tell Mother if we didn't; but we'd ignore her because we knew that she'd sit down and watch it with us too. She was only young herself, after all.

If we were lucky, when Mother was out, we'd be able to see other programmes, like *Charlie's Angels*. We all loved it and Mena and I used to pretend we were the girls in the programme, and sometimes we could persuade Tara to play with us too. When she got older, that stopped, but for a time it was easy to get her to come out with us. I'd tell them both I'd hidden something in the garden – a hairbrush, say – and pretend it was a gun; they'd have to come out and find it. I always wanted to be Sabrina, the one with the long black hair. As Tara grew older, and more reluctant to play, I'd hide her homework book, so she had to come out and look for it with Mena if only to get her work done.

But as soon as we heard Mother and Hanif coming back into the front garden, and their voices by the front door, we'd rush to turn off the TV or tear back into the kitchen. I'd stand by the sink and pretend I'd been getting their lunch ready all morning.

Saturday mornings were usually fun, then, but Sunday mornings were the opposite. Hanif would get me out of bed and I'd have to wash the clothes with her.

'Sam, get all the clothes, it's wash day,' she'd say as she shook me awake. I'd have to knock on the bedroom doors – 'Go away!' Saber would yell – and collect the clothes from everyone, take them all downstairs and pile them up by the tin basin in the little annexe room next to the kitchen.

Hanif meanwhile filled the basin with water, and she would wash each item by hand and then pass it to me. I had to rinse all the soap out, using the cold tap next to the boiler (the water in the tin bath was hot), and then dry them. This meant an arm-aching time of wringing the clothes again and again until they were ready to hang up. Because the water was cold, by the time I was done my hands were rubbed raw and numb; even my shoulders ached from the cold. If it was fine, then I'd take the clothes outside and hang them up; if it was wet, then they'd have to go on a clothes-line stretched about the boiler so that they could dry there.

As the weeks and months went by, I kept hoping that someone in my family would notice how good I was being, how hard I'd been working. I did resent them for not showing me any affection, but more than anything I still wanted them to accept me.

Feeling like an outsider meant that I never had any clothes of my own – I always had Tara's hand-me-downs, and I wasn't allowed to put my clothes away properly in the wardrobe but only to heap them at the bottom; I had to pull them out and pile them all back again when I'd found a matching set for my shalwar-kameez. I had old, scuffed shoes, which pinched.

And I talked to myself sometimes, pretending I had a friend; she would cuddle me after I'd been hit and kiss me better when the bruises hurt too much.

That winter Mena, Saber and I were walking back from the mosque, past the monkey hills, talking about the things we really wanted. I missed not being able to go and buy sweeties and chocolates, so I said, 'That's what I want, right now. In fact . . .' And I turned to look at them as an idea came to me that moment. 'Why don't we go carol singing, get some money, and buy some sweets?' The two of them looked at me as if I were mad. I explained: Christian children went round people's houses at this time of year, singing songs called carols, and people gave them money. We'd done it as little children in the home, though the money went to charity and not into our pockets. Saber thought it was a great idea; Mena, of course, was a little worried. But they both made the same point: 'We don't know any carols, we can't sing.' I said I'd do the singing, they should just hum along. We practised while walking down to the estate of smart new houses, where we knew no Asian people lived (so Mother wouldn't get to hear about it), and sang – or I did, anyway – 'Away In A Manger' outside six or seven of them. We must have been awful but we made enough to have ten pence each. I spent my ten pence on a packet of Snaps, and loads and loads of blackjacks and fruit salads – four for a penny, we ate all the way home. It made up for not having a birthday treat that year, savouring the delicious taste of the sweets, made all the more exciting because we'd got them ourselves, without Mother knowing.

This year, I was in a new class at school and my teacher, Mr Rowe, was responsible for the Christmas play; he got very involved, and even painted the backdrops himself. We were going to perform the story of Noah's Ark, and I was very excited to be chosen as one of the animals to be led on by Noah, while we all sang, 'The animals went in two by two, hurrah, hurrah!'.

I gave the letter to Mother, inviting her to come and see the play. She didn't read it – she never read any letters in English – so I had to read it to her. And, because it needed a signature at the bottom, I signed it as well. At school, the time came for our performance. We all went out on to the stage, and the hall was full of parents beaming at their children. Although Mr Rowe had told us not to, everyone in my class searched the room to find their family and then waved madly at them. Camera flashes went off, and everyone smiled.

Except me. Try as I might, and even though Mother hadn't said anything about coming, I was devastated that no one from my family had come along to watch. I thought I must be the only child there whose family had stayed away. Worse still, along with my crushing sense of humiliation was the sick feeling building up inside me as I realised that Mother had forgotten that I was going to be late home today, because of the play, and I'd get beaten for that, too.

My tenth birthday passed like any other day, I had to cook and clean as usual, and no one said anything to me about it. As I was wiping the kitchen floor, that evening, I thought sadly about what it would have been like if I'd been back in the home. My 'special day', as it was called, would have meant that I had to do nothing – a treat for the birthday boy or girl. I hadn't felt like eating curry and *rotis* that evening, I wanted a huge birthday cake with candles so I could make a wish as I blew them out.

Mena came into the kitchen and sat down on the stool.

'It's my birthday today,' I said, after a moment's silence. I wanted someone to say 'Happy Birthday' to me.

Mena smiled sadly. 'Happy birthday,' she said. 'Do you know what I do when it's my birthday?'

I stopped what I was doing; although I knew Mena had birthdays like me, I'd never known when hers was and she'd never mentioned it to me. 'No, what?'

'When it's bedtime, shut your eyes tight and make a wish. Keep it to yourself, and don't tell anyone or it won't come true. That's what you have to do.'

I thought of Mena, lying in bed next to me, doing this on her birthday while I slept, and it made me sadder still. We both looked at each other, and although no words were spoken, we didn't need them to know what the other was thinking.

We had stopped making the claws for jump leads within a few months of my coming to the house. Mother and Hanif, instead, went out to work, which was both good and bad: we had some peace in the house, but when they came home they were always tired and demanded food immediately. 'Get the food. Is the meal ready? Hope the dinner's ready, we're starving, we've been working all day.' That's all I heard when they came in – never a please or thank you.

Then they stopped going to work; the Social stopped their money so they must have been found out, and had to rely on Manz's earnings instead. I was still expected to cook, however. It was like that in our house; everyone else seemed to live differently from me. Eid, the Muslim festival that takes place twice a year, was just another time for me to work; and while everyone else got to wear new clothes, I was given the ones that Tara had had last year, and I would get into trouble if I spilled food on them while I was cooking.

The only rest I had was during Ramadan, when all Muslims have to fast from dawn to dusk. That meant no cooking, of course, which made it enough of a holiday for me; but Mother also bought food that she didn't normally give us, like fruit and salad – perhaps this was because we couldn't drink during the day either. So we'd eat apples, bananas and oranges by the handful. Ramadan seemed to relax Mother too – it was the only time she didn't shout at me for not doing things. Of course the fasting was hard, especially if it fell during the summer, when it would be light from three in the morning till ten at night.

During Ramadan, when I was ten, I picked up a penny on my way to school, and was so pleased that I went straight into a sweet shop and bought something tasty. When I got to school, chewing away, one of the other girls said to me, 'Aren't you supposed to be fasting?' and I had to spit it out, quickly.

★   ★   ★

Tara was too old to play games with us now but we could still – sometimes – have fun with her. We were in the kitchen one day when Tara stubbed her toe on the table leg. She swore, loudly, and Mena and I laughed. She swore again, calling us names, but she had a smile on her face this time. Mena swore back and I joined in, the three of us using the worst words we could think of to say to each other. I won the game in the end; the others said I knew the worst words, but I was only repeating what Mother said to me.

Tara relaxed when Mother was out of the house. Once, the pair of us sat at the table while she plaited my hair, patiently teaching me how to do it myself. My hair was getting longer, and reached below my shoulders, but it was nowhere near as long as Mena's or Tara's. At the time I thought this was something of a breakthrough between the two of us, but as soon as Mother returned Tara went back to bossing me about.

Saber was different; he was still mostly absent, and he'd turn up to eat and sleep but go missing for hours at a time, and Mother never asked him where he'd been. He never seemed to let her bother him. One night we heard him come in – Mena and I were upstairs, staying out of everyone's way – and Mother shouted, 'Don't you dare make a mess with that. What do you want that for?'

'Nothing, it's for school,' Saber shouted back as his footsteps moved upstairs. He came in to see us, grinning, with an empty cardboard box in his hand.

'What's that for?' I asked.

'Do you want to play a game?'

I looked at him; the only games he liked were 'help me clean my bike' or 'can you give me some food.' So I was suspicious. 'What kind of game?'

'It's a good game, it's called draughts. Who's got a pen or a pencil?'

'Me,' I said, intrigued. I liked the sound of something new that I'd have to learn. In the wardrobe, underneath all my clothes, was the assortment of Biros and pencils I had collected. I pulled one out and handed it to him.

Saber started to tear the box. It was difficult but finally he ripped out a piece and shaped it into two squares; he passed one to me and told me to tear it into twelve little pieces and he handed Mena the other with the same instruction.

'Then colour yours in.'

Next he took a straight piece of card and used it as a ruler and drew lines across and then down the large piece of cardboard remaining. 'It looks like a chess board,' I said, and Saber looked up and smiled at me.

'Okay, have you finished?'

I was eager to play. He placed the board on the bed in front of him, and held out both hands. We put our coloured squares into his palms.

'Who wants to play first?' he asked.

'Me!' I shouted with excitement.

'Shh, keep your voice down,' both Saber and Mena said. 'We don't want Mother to hear.'

'Sorry.'

Saber placed the counters on the board, missing a square in between each; one side had my counters on and the other had Saber's.

'I have to get my counters from this end to your end, and you have to stop me and I'll do the same; you can only move diagonally and if your counter is next to mine, like this, I can jump it, the person who takes all the other person's counters is the winner. Okay?'

'Hmm, I'll pick up the rules as we go,' I said, a little confused.

I watched intently as he made his way to my end of the board. I just moved my counters wherever I liked; I didn't know you had to use strategy at that time, so needless to say Saber won.

'Oh, and when I get to your end you put one of my counters on top and crown me, that means I can move up and down now.'

I turned to my sister. She was sitting there looking nervous. 'Mena, your turn.'

'I don't want to play, I don't get it,' she said.

'Okay, I'll play again,' I quickly told Saber.

I sat there for the second time watching him move and noticed he didn't move the bottom counters until all his others had gone. I did the same on the fourth game, but he still won – although only just.

We heard Manz coming up to bed, but for some reason he didn't stick his head round the door and tell us to go to sleep although it was late.

Saber decided that that was enough. 'You're getting good. I'm going to bed now, you can keep the game. I'll play again tomorrow,' and off he went to bed.

We played again the following night, and I nearly beat him. I liked this game. I eventually won on the third night we played.

'I can't believe you won,' he said, dejected.

'I won.' I smiled. 'I beat you at your game.'

That night, I was jerked out of my sleep by some noises outside our door. I lay there for a while trying to work out what was going on, but all I could hear was footsteps going up and down the stairs. I leaned over to Mena's bed and tapped her on the shoulder until she woke up.

'What? Sam?' she said groggily.

'There's something going on,' I said. 'Someone's outside.'

I thought this might wake her properly, with her fear of the bogey-man, but instead she rolled over away from me and murmured, 'So what?'

I lay there for a while longer until I couldn't resist any more; the footsteps hadn't stopped and I could hear my mother's voice downstairs. Suddenly there was a knock at the front door.

I crept out of bed and opened our bedroom door a little way. I could hear my mother clearly now; she was at the foot of the stairs and called up, 'The ambulance is here.'

Hanif came past me, walking slowly and with her right arm stretched across her stomach. 'Is everything all right?' I said to her.

'Yes,' Hanif said, though her voice sounded as if she had to push the words out. She winced. 'I'm going into hospital to have my baby.'

'Really? A baby?'

'Go back to bed, Sam,' said Manz, who was coming up the stairs with Hanif's coat.

I watched them from my door until they were at the bottom of the stairs, then I crept after them. I crouched so that I could see out of the front door, without coming down the stairs too far. There was a man in a green uniform waiting for Hanif and he took her arm from Manz and helped her out to the waiting ambulance.

Mother was outside waving them goodbye, and, as soon as the ambulance had gone, I quietly slipped back upstairs into our room. I didn't want Mother to see me as she came indoors, as she would almost certainly ask me to make her some tea, or massage her head, or something.

I'd just got into bed when I heard another creak on the floorboards outside, and our door opened enough for Saber to slip in.

'Are you awake, Sid?' Saber called me 'Sid' sometimes, after the character on Kenny Everett's TV show, Sid Snot, because I always seemed to have a runny nose. I took it as an affectionate nickname and smiled when he used it.

'Yes,' I whispered.

He came and sat on the bed. 'What's going on?' he asked.

'Hanif's gone into hospital to have a baby,' I said.

'Ah,' he said, as if something mysterious had suddenly become clear. 'I thought she was getting fat, but figured it must be because she lies about all day and lets you do the work.'

I had no idea what getting fat had to do with hospitals and babies but I wasn't going to let on to Saber that I didn't know.

Mena stirred under her blanket. 'She's gone to get a baby?'

'That's what she said,' I told her. 'Paji has gone with her.'

'Well, since that's all it is, I'm going back to bed,' said Saber.

But when everyone else had gone back to sleep, I lay there, wondering. Why did she have to go when it was night? What had getting fat got to do with babies?

I was still asleep the following morning – a Sunday, so no one had to get up for school or for work – when Mother started shouting from downstairs, 'Sam! Sam! Come down here now!'

I pulled my head further under the blankets. Mother never came upstairs so I could hide up here a little bit longer.

Our bedroom door opened, and Salim came in. He walked up to the side of my bed and poked me. I lay there, not moving, seeing what he'd do next. He bent down and picked up one of my shoes.

'Hey,' I said, sitting up. 'What're you doing?'

'Mother said you've got to get up and help her. She said I should hit you to make you get up.' But he was smiling at me and I knew he wouldn't do it.

'All right, all right,' I said, 'I'm getting up.'

I went downstairs, and heard Mother in the kitchen so went in there to see what it was she wanted.

My heart sank; the place was a mess. It always was when Mother had been in the kitchen; she didn't care what she opened, spilled or dropped, as there was always someone else – me – to clear it up for her.

'There you are, lazy child, lying about all day when there's work to be done.' She didn't even look over her shoulder at me as she said this, but, then, Mother never did look at me.

'First take down the big pot,' she ordered, 'and put in four packets of butter. Then put it on the stove to start melting. Then go and get the pestle and mortar, and start grinding these things.'

The stuff Mother wanted me to grind was awful: hard and white, looking like runner beans. My arm started to ache very quickly but I knew I wouldn't be allowed a rest so I just had to keep going. Every time I reached what I thought was the end, and all I was left with was a fine powder, Mother took the bowl and poured its contents into the saucepan, then passed the bowl back to me with another handful of the beans. Neither of us spoke while we did this; Mother never said anything to me that wasn't an instruction of some kind, and I knew better than to ask when she expected me to be working.

Finally there was nothing left to be ground down. Mother said, 'Go wash now and get breakfast, then you can help me finish here.' I went outside to the toilet, then came back in and, after splashing some water on my face and eating a piece of toast, said, 'What are we making, Mother?'

'This is for Hanif, to help her get her strength back after getting the baby.'

I didn't ask why Hanif needed help like that, when it was me who did all the work, but I slipped away to go and wake up Mena.

★　　★　　★

We didn't see Manz until much later, when he came home to tell us that Hanif had had a little baby boy, and that they'd called him Frazand. He brought a cot with him, and he said to me, 'Sam, come upstairs and help me put this together.'

I'd never been into Manz and Hanif's bedroom. Unlike ours, it was clean and brightly decorated, with nice light wallpaper, and they even had their own TV and video set up. Most of the room was taken up with their double bed but there was space alongside one wall for us to put the cot. Manz issued instructions: 'Take this,' or 'Hang on to that while I fit this in,' but we didn't say anything to each other. I was too nervous of being alone with him in here; his rages seemed to me to be too unpredictable. As soon as the cot was ready, I went back into our room to be with Mena.

A couple of days later, Hanif came back from hospital with little Frazand wrapped up in a blanket. I look closely to see if she looked especially tired, as if she'd worked very hard like Mother had said; I did notice she seemed a lot thinner, which made me think of what Saber had said about her being fat.

Mother wanted Hanif to sit next to her on the settee, but Hanif headed straight for the stairs, saying, 'I'm tired, I want to go and lie down.'

Immediately Mother indicated ahead of her up the stairs, gesturing Hanif forward. She said, 'Yes, yes, of course. Go up and rest. Sam will bring you some food.'

No surprise there, I thought. I'd been sent to the kitchen to cook immediately I'd got back from school, to have things ready for the princess, as I'd started thinking of Hanif. Mena was already in the kitchen, eating.

'Mena, you've got to help me. I'm tired, and I still have homework to do.'

'What do you want me to do?'

'I'm going upstairs to give this food to Hanif. In the meantime can you wash up?'

I piled up some dishes with rice and curry and put them on a tray to take them up to Hanif. Once I went into her room, though, a horrible surprise greeted me. Mother was there – Mother, who never went upstairs. And all our school books were lying about on the bed next door, because Mena and I knew no one ever went in to check. Mother would throw them away – she threw anything in English away – and beat me – both of us, perhaps – if she came in and saw them. I thought fast. 'Oops! I forgot the salt and pepper.' I placed the tray down, backed out of the room, and ran into our bedroom. I quietly picked up the books and hid them under the bed, and then went downstairs to the kitchen.

Mena was already at the sink. 'You didn't hide our books!' I hissed.

'So what?' she replied. 'Mother never goes up . . .' a look of horror crossed her face.

'It's all right, I've put them under the bed for now,' I told her.

Just then Mother shouted down. 'Sam, are you dead? Has someone killed you down there? We're waiting for the salt.'

I picked up the salt and grinned at Mena. 'A lucky escape, eh?'

Back upstairs Hanif grabbed the salt crossly, as if somehow I'd insulted her by keeping her waiting for it. I thought, Huh, she's managed to get her strength back quickly enough, after all. 'Sorry, I couldn't find it at first,' I said as innocently as I could. Mother sat with her back to me and I couldn't resist: I stuck two fingers up at her when no one was looking, and I felt a little animal surge of pleasure at the gesture.

One afternoon Hanif was in the kitchen; she'd been out shopping and I was sent upstairs to try to get her son, Franz, to sleep (along with all my other chores, Hanif expected me to look after him). Her coat was hanging on a peg at the bottom of the stairs, and I knocked into it as I passed and I heard the jingle of change. I immediately remembered that I had seen children eating crisps in the playground earlier, and I'd wanted some too. So I put my hand into Hanif's coat pocket and pulled out whatever I could grab, and then ran upstairs after Franz. I picked him up and put him on the bed and started to tell him a story.

'Once upon a time there were three bears, a mummy bear, a daddy bear, and baby bear . . .'

I never had to finish his bedtime story as he would always fall asleep within a few minutes. I opened my hand and looked at how much money there was: three ten pence coins, five two pence coins, and a fifty pence coin. I thought, I don't need the fifty pence piece, that's too much, she'll notice that, but I'll keep the rest.

As I returned downstairs I dropped the fifty pence back into her pocket.

The next morning, on the way to school, I bent down as if to tie my shoelace. 'Oh, look,' I said to Mena. 'Look what I've found.' And I held one of the ten pence pieces in my hand.

'I wonder who lost it? Quickly, get up just in case he's still around.' Mena was fooled by my little game.

'What shall we get? The shop is just over there.' I'd managed to find the money in the most convenient place.

The sweets were laid out on the counter, jellies and mojos and fruit salads. The sherbet dip caught my eye; I'd missed the sensation of dipping my liquorice stick into a sherbet dip, and then – when the sherbet hit my tongue – my mouth going all funny because of the sour taste. I missed that taste.

'Can I have a sherbet dip, please. What do you want?'

'I don't know. I'll have the same as you.'

The shopkeeper handed us the dips and said, 'Six pence, please.'

I looked at the shelves again. 'Can I have eight mojos as well, please?'

He dropped them into a small paper bag and held out his hand for the money; Mena watched like a hawk as I gave him the ten pence, as if it would tell its secret when it left my hand.

I tore open the packet as soon as we got out of the shop, found the liquorice, dipped it in the sherbet and put it in my mouth. I shut my eyes tightly as my mouth got all tingly. Mena copied me and I laughed out loud as her face screwed up.

'What *is* this?' She stopped walking for a moment.

'It's sherbet, it's my favourite; do you like it?'

'I've never had anything like it before.'

'Now you have, I'm saving mine for playtime,' and I folded the top over and put it back in my pocket. Later, at playtime, Mena was waiting for me and we walked to the playground together. We both opened our dips and stood licking the tangy sherbet off the liquorice sticks.

'I really enjoyed that,' I said as I handed Mena some mojos.
'Me too.'

Over the next few weeks I'd 'find' money every day; we bought sweets, crisps and cakes; I stole money from Hanif's pocket as often as I could, so that we had sweets that we chomped as we read in bed.

But of course it couldn't last. One afteroon I came in from school and found Hanif sitting next to Mother, who held her head in her hands. She looked up when I came in.

'Come here, Sam,' Mother said as she reached down and took off her shoe. I knew what was coming. I stood there, Mena beside me, and couldn't move.

Mother shouted, 'I said come here.'

I slowly stepped towards her; she grabbed my hand as soon as I was within reach and whacked my head several times with the shoe, pulled at my hair and pushed me to the floor. I fell down, hard, and I felt my wrist twist badly as I did so.

'Did you steal money from Hanif's pocket?' Mother shouted.

'No, I found it.'

Whack! Another slap, on my face this time. I could taste blood in my mouth. She yanked my hair again. Out of the corner of my eye I saw Mena walk towards the stairs and go up.

I knew I wasn't going to get out of this as Mother whacked the shoe on my leg. I started to cry. 'Yes, I took the money,' I whispered. 'I took the money, I'm sorry, I won't do it again.'

Mother pinched my arm as hard as she could, and I shrieked. I sat on the floor sobbing, waiting for an order, waiting for them to tell me I could get up off the floor.

'Get up and get out of my sight.'

I didn't need telling twice and quickly ran upstairs. I got into bed and I cried and cried. I don't know when I stopped, or fell asleep. I woke up during the night; my arm and wrist hurt and so did my head. I lay there and cried again, staring into the dim orange glow that came through the window, wishing, praying, that somehow this nightmare would end.

The next day I put on my shoes and grabbed my coat. My wrist was still sore and it looked a little swollen. I couldn't move my hand much without it hurting. My head ached too; when I tried to comb my hair the bruises hurt too much so I just tied it back instead.

'Ready to go?' asked Mena, who'd said nothing to me so far.

'Yes.'

We left for school in silence. Halfway there Mena finally spoke. 'Are you all right?'

'I wish they would just kill me, get a knife and stab me, get it all over with,' and I started crying again. 'I get hit for no good reason. I want her to hit my head so hard I die.'

I hated being alive; I hated getting hit; I was tired of hurting.

In my last year in junior school my teacher was Mr Hastings, who was always very strict and would shout if anyone talked during his lessons. One day I was caught whispering with two of the other girls in our class, Lisa and Mandy, and Mr Hastings had obviously had enough of us.

'Off you go, you three. Take this note to the headmaster – he'll know how to deal with you.'

The one thing we all feared at school was the strap; if you were really naughty, and got sent to the head, then you'd get the strap. Children – boys and girls – who were normally very brave, would come out of the head's office in tears, and some of them cried so much that they got sent home, while the bravest would hardly cry at all.

Standing outside the head's office, waiting for him to open his door after we'd given the note to his secretary, was the worst time I could remember ever having at school. Lisa, Mandy and I were terrified: what was the strap? How bad could it be? We didn't dare look at each other in case we started crying before we'd even got in there.

After what seemed like an age, the door opened. I'd never spoken to our head teacher, Mr Marsden; he spoke from the stage at assembly, but he never came to our classes and I'd never seen him this close up before. He looked tired, and he barely glanced at us as he said, sternly, 'Come in. I have a note from your teacher. What have you to say for yourselves?'

Nobody spoke. I piped up, 'We're sorry, sir.'

He looked at me for a moment. Then he pulled open a drawer in the desk in front of him and took out a thin leather strap, about the same size as the big rulers we had for maths lessons.

So this was the infamous strap. I wasn't worried; I'd been hit by much worse than that. When he said, 'Put your left hands out,' I stuck mine out without hesitation. This wasn't going to bother me, and, sure enough, when it whacked into my palm, it didn't hurt, it just tingled a bit; it was less than the feeling left on my cheek after Mother hit me.

Mr Marsden moved on past me, and while I wondered why everyone made such a fuss about this, I heard the *whack!* sound again and Lisa burst into tears. He went on to Mandy, who pulled her hand back against her side. The head spoke again: 'I said put your left hand out!'

Mandy's arm was shaking, even I could see that. I wanted to say to him, why are you doing this? Don't hurt her, she's scared enough already. But he raised his arm, and – *whack!* – Mandy yelped in pain.

The head turned away and dismissed us, saying over his shoulder, 'Go back to class now. I don't want to see you in here again.'

The other two were clutching their hands and whimpering, so I said, 'Yes, sir,' loudly enough for all of us and followed them out.

At playtime the rest of the class huddled round us. 'What was it like? 'How big was the strap?' 'Did it hurt really badly?'

Lisa and Mandy were showing the others the red marks across their hands, but then Lisa turned to look at me. 'It didn't hurt Sam. She didn't cry or anything.'

A silence fell, and everyone stared at me. Usually people only looked at me when they were laughing and pointing, so this was different: they were looking at me in awe. Nobody, ever, had not cried when they got the strap, even the biggest and bravest of the boys.

For the rest of that summer term, nobody picked on my stutter, or laughed at my clothes.

I was nearly eleven and joined Mena at Forest Comprehensive School in Hawbush, Walsall. Before the summer holidays ended Mother took me to the flea market to buy my uniform, where there was a stall that sold clothes for the senior school. I hated these clothes because they smelled old and musty, especially as there was a stall nearby selling lovely soaps and other scented goods, which I wished we could buy instead.

School was further away now, so to get there on time we left home, as Saber and Tara had done, at eight o'clock. As this meant more time out of the house at the beginning and end of the day, I was happy with the longer walk. However, as most of the pupils hadn't gone to my junior school, the respect I earned after the strap incident didn't come with me, and I went back to being the class joke, to be bullied by anyone who felt like it.

I'd learned how to handle this, though, from junior school. I knew that none of my family would step in to help me – Mena still tried to be as inconspicuous as possible, both at school and at home – so instead of arguing with the bullies I'd agree with them – 'Yes, my clothes are awful, aren't they' – and they'd stop, bored with me as their target.

I was in the top sets for most subjects, and I did well in class. I was good at sciences and maths and geography, and I still read anything I could get my hands on. I went to the library at lunchtime and I'd pore over every adventure story I could find, whether it was a Nancy Drew or Treasure Island. I also read all the My Naughty Little Sister books. They were my favourites, and I used to wish that the girl telling the story was me, because she was always being cuddled by her mother. I was always hopeful that this would be my reward, even though that never came. But because I was so pleased to read to the end of a book, and the sense of achievement this gave me, I never thought that Mother ought to be more like mothers in books – I hid that feeling under my pleasure at having finished the book.

The school never wondered why Mother never came to any evening events, or open days; why she never signed forms to excuse me from doing PE or why she never came to talk to my teachers. I avoided PE because Mother told me I had crooked legs and I didn't want to change into PE clothes because everyone would stare at me. I continued to avoid the lesson at school by forging Mother's signature on a note I wrote. If we had a supply teacher in, which happened a couple of times a term, they might ask me why it was in my handwriting, but I would tell them that Mother couldn't write English. Tara and Mena had both had to deal with this, and by the time I came along it didn't seem as if anyone cared enough to ask about my home. I was gradually losing confidence in myself. Trying to be invisible in the playground and in the classroom worked; I was never a bother to the teachers, so I was never really noticed. I slipped through these years, unseen and unregarded.

8

It was a normal afternoon; I had been hit by Mother for burning the *roti* I'd cooked for her dinner; she'd slapped me across the head and thumped me on the back, saying 'Do you expect me to eat this?' I brought her another one and went back to the kitchen and ate the burned one, to teach myself to cook properly next time.

I went to bed with a headache and backache that night. I felt drained, more than usual. I should have been excited, because it was my eleventh birthday in two days' time. I lay there in bed and thought about what I would wish for, and how I would keep my eyes shut as I wished it and not tell anyone, in case it might not come true.

I woke up the next morning late because it was Sunday, feeling very tired and my back was stiff. When I moved it hurt. Mena got out of bed before me which was very unusual.

'Are you all right?' she asked.

'I've got backache,' I replied, feeling stiff and sore in the bed.

Tara had awoken and was sitting in her bed rubbing her eyes; she had climbed into her bed downstairs as usual last night, only to discover that Salim had peed on it, and, after she'd roundly cursed Salim ('Don't you ever sit on my bed again, do you hear me, I'm going to leave the bogey-man in here, and if you go into my room he will take you away forever, do you understand?'), which left five-year-old Salim terrified, she had come up to sleep in our room. This meant I had to climb into bed with Mena and push her sleeping body over to make room for me. Having been woken up by Tara in her usual bossy way I didn't sleep that well; however, I managed to sit up and put my feet on the floor.

'You don't look too good,' Mena said.

I looked at her and shrugged my shoulders; I got out of bed and turned my back to her to make the bed. I moved the blanket and I saw a big red patch on the mattress and at that point Mena gasped with surprise and said, 'Sam, you're bleeding, your back's bleeding.'

I froze in horror, not knowing where all the blood had come from; I thought if I moved I might bleed more.

'Let me see,' said Tara as she carefully lifted my dress. 'Yuck.'

'What is it?' I asked, panicking at their reaction to something I couldn't see.

'You're in trouble, you've started your period. I'm going to tell Mum and Hanif,' said Tara, vindictive as ever.

'No, don't tell, please,' I whispered, but she was gone.

'Are you hurting a lot?' asked Mena.

'No,' I said, trying to hide the pain of my sore back. 'You've got to help Mena. I'll get some water and clean the mattress, but first I have to change my clothes.'

Too late, I could hear Tara coming upstairs. She bustled into the room, glowing with pleasure at my unhappiness – it gave her something to do.

'Hanif wants you, she says to come downstairs.'

'I'm okay, I'll clean the mattress and change my clothes.'

'She wants you *now*.'

I looked at Tara and she raised her eyebrows as if to say, Do you want me to go down and tell her you won't come?

'Are my clothes really bad?' I asked Mena.

'Yes.'

'You don't have time to change, just go,' said Tara.

It felt horrible walking in clothes covered in blood. I could smell it as I walked downstairs and it was disgusting. I was frightened, but I didn't know what I had done wrong.

Hanif and Mother were sitting on the sofa bed as I got downstairs. I looked at them in shame and then I looked at the floor.

'Turn around,' shouted Mother.

I did.

'Come here,' said Mother. I went over to the settee and she lifted my dress and pulled down my shalwar. I just stood there afraid that if I said anything, like Why am I bleeding? she would hit me.

'You bitch, you've started your period too early, you stupid bitch.' I didn't know what this word – *period* – meant. Period in Punjabi, *ganda kapra*, means 'dirty cloth time', so that all that stuck in my mind was the word 'dirty'.

'Go and wash yourself and I will come and sort you out afterwards,' said Hanif. Although her voice was no kinder in tone than usual, I nearly cried with relief at being allowed to go and clean myself. I quickly pulled up my shalwar and ran towards the kitchen.

'Don't you dare wash those clothes in the bathroom, wash them outside,' called Mother.

I walked into the bathroom and found some of my clothes hanging on the line near the back wall. I was relieved that I didn't have to go back upstairs to get dressed.

Hanif followed me into the kitchen, and handed me some knickers and a piece of cloth folded up into a rectangle shape.

'Wear these and if you need any more cloths let me know. Place it between your legs like this.' she demonstrated by putting the cloth in between her legs.

I went back into the bathroom wondering what was going on, why had Hanif given me these knickers? I filled the bath with warm water and had a wash. I felt ashamed of myself; if only I hadn't spilled that cup of tea this wouldn't have happened. I twisted my head as far as I could to try to see where my back was bleeding from but I couldn't see. This is when I saw where the blood was coming from. I quickly got out of the bath, dried myself, put the cloth between my legs and struggled into the knickers that Hanif had given me; they were an old pair of hers and were far too big on me. I had to tie them together at the front to stop them falling down. I'd forgotten what it was like to wear underwear. Once everything seemed safely in place, I pulled my shalwar up.

'Have you done it?' Hanif had stuck her head round to check up on me.

I nodded.

'This will happen every month. The cloths are in a bag in a cupboard under the stairs, and there are knickers beside them; use those when you need to keep the cloths in place.'

I nodded again, not really understanding what she had just said; all I wanted to do was go out and wash my clothes and be on my own.

I opened the back door and put my clothes on the ground, picked up the bowl and took it indoors, then filled it with water and took it out again and soaked my clothes. As I squatted down to wash my clothes Mena came out.

'Are you all right?'

'Yes. Hanif said this is going to happen to me every month.'

'Yes, I know. I'm lucky I haven't started mine yet. I'm going in, it's cold.'

She left me feeling confused; what did she mean, she hadn't started hers yet? Mena was in the class above me, which meant that she'd already had her sex education lessons.

Not long after my periods started, we had our classes on sex and I told some of the girls I had already started my periods and word quickly spread around the class. One of the popular girls in my class, who'd normally never be seen talking to me, came up to me at playtime and asked what it felt like. 'Horrible,' I said. 'It's like you've got stomach aches.'

As the months passed, I found out for myself that regardless of whether I got hit or not I bled every month. It was many years before I stopped feeling 'dirty', and stopped blaming myself for causing my period to start.

To keep out of everyone's way, Mena and I would sit up in our room as much as possible; no one would ask us to do things for them, up there. One evening I was upstairs when Mena came running in, saying excitedly, 'Tara's getting married!'

'What?' This was a big surprise; Tara, now aged sixteen, was too old to play games with us any more and so she had little to do with us, except when she wanted me to do something for her. 'Who to?'

'To Bashir.'

'That man who came from Pakistan a few months ago?'

Mena nodded. Bashir was a cousin, the son of one of Mother's sisters. He seemed all right, although he could only speak Punjabi; he was tall and, because of his moustache, we used to joke that he looked like Tom Selleck. He was living in rented accommodation a few doors away.

'When's the wedding?' I asked. A wedding meant a party, so I was as excited as Mena.

'Very soon by the sounds of things. Mother wants them to get married as soon as possible.'

'Does Tara like him?' I hadn't even seen the two of them together.

'Like him? That doesn't matter. She is going to marry him because Mother said so.'

'That doesn't seem fair,' I said, but I knew from the films we'd watched that in traditional families like mine they'd arrange marriages when the children were small, as young as babies sometimes; once both children were old enough, the marriage would take place. No one expected otherwise, and so Mena didn't even bother to comment.

'Amanda and I used to play marriage,' I said to Mena. 'We'd drape white towels over our heads for our dresses, and march through the dining room to meet our princes,' and I stood up to show her what I meant. The princes, I told her, were one of our teddy bears.

Mena started giggling.

' "Do you take this prince as your husband?" Amanda would say to me, and I'd say yes, and then she'd turn to the prince and say, "You may now kiss the bride." '

Mena pulled a pillow over her mouth to stop her laughter being heard downstairs; no sense in letting Mother know we were having fun.

We knew from the films that you couldn't fall in love with just anyone, but had to marry the person your parents had chosen for you. To refuse would be to dishonour the family, and Mena and I were well aware that this was the worst possible behaviour. When people didn't obey their family and ran off after a secret marriage, they'd have to live as far away as possible. But they'd always be tracked down, perhaps by people paid to hunt them, and killed to show that the family honour was saved.

It turned out that everything I expected from the wedding was different to the reality. Tara lost no time in explaining to me what she wanted: it was traditional for the daughters of each family to dance for the guests in a competition, and she expected me to take my turn. She decided to teach me to dance herself, and put a movie on the video and made me watch one song again and again so that I could have a go at it myself. I'd had no practice in dancing, so although I tried my best I kept getting it wrong.

This infuriated Tara. 'Can't you do any better? She's moving her arms to the left not to the right!'

'I'm trying,' I said, as I twisted all over the room in an effort to match what was on the screen, but I felt awkward and clumsy.

'You're useless! A monkey could dance better than you.'

Tara came to stand behind me, holding my wrists tightly in her hands, lifting my arms up and turning me round so as to force me to do the moves correctly. When I stepped on her foot for the third time, she let go and pushed me away. 'I'm not having you dancing at my wedding if you can't do it properly,' she exclaimed and flounced out of the room, which gave me an idea, as I didn't want to dance anyway.

When she reappeared I carried on making mistakes, tripping over her feet and flapping my hands out of time with the rhythm. Tara eventually howled with fury and shouted at me, as she flicked off the TV set, 'Forget it! You're just no good! There's no way I'm going to let you dance at my wedding. Get out of here now!'

I bit back a smile and went into the kitchen, where Mena silently raised her eyebrows at me, questioningly. I winked at her.

For the big day, when it came, Mother had bought us all new outfits. Saber came into our room wearing a smart white shalwar-kameez, which he complained about. 'Why can't we wear normal clothes?' he asked, curling his lip in disgust.

I thought he looked rather good. 'You can wear mine if you want,' I said, holding up my smart new blue outfit, which had gold embroidery down the sides of the dress and on the ends of the matching scarf. It was the first new outfit I had had since Mother had made me an orange shalwar-kameez to go visiting in when I was nine, which I still wore now, even though it was a bit small on me; it made me feel special, as it was the only present I'd received from Mother.

Saber smiled sarcastically at me. 'No, thanks,' he said and stomped out of the room.

'I hate pink,' said Mena, looking down at the suit laid out on the bed.

'I'll swap if you want to, I like it.'

'Yes, please.'

So we switched outfits. The pink shalwar-kameez had embroidery in the same places as the blue one; once we were both dressed, I thought Mena looked lovely. 'Wow, Mena, you look like a princess!' I said; I hoped that she'd be thinking the same about me. Mena teased her long black hair in front of the mirror, and then let me look at myself.

The mirror on the wardrobe door showed me a stranger. Dressing nicely had done nothing to disguise what I saw in my reflection; in fact, it had only made it worse. Instead of a princess, I saw a miserable little girl with a sad face and messy hair, looking lost and lonely. She wanted to tell someone how much she ached inside. She wanted to have friends. She wasn't greedy; one friend would do. A special friend whom she could tell how tired she was, tired from the housework, tired from the beatings, tired of no one appreciating her. She hated the way everyone made fun of her, and she wanted it all to stop. She wanted to run away from it, but had nowhere to go except deep inside herself. She wanted to know why her life was like this.

I turned away from my reflection. I couldn't take any more.

'You look great,' said Mena. I could tell she was just trying to encourage me. 'Well, okay,' she said, seeing the expression on my face.

I couldn't speak for the sadness welling up in me. I didn't need a mirror to tell me what I looked like, because I wasn't the little girl I'd been when I first came here. I was someone else, someone I didn't know.

Saber stuck his head round the door and said, 'Mother said to come downstairs when you're ready.'

Downstairs, everything looked different. All that was grey and unclean had gone; furniture had been moved, and white sheets covered the floor of each room. The walls and windows were covered with brightly coloured fabrics, and shiny, dangly decorations caught the light. It actually looked quite attractive.

Mena and I went into the kitchen; at least I hadn't had to cook for the wedding, as Mother had decided there was too much food to be prepared. She'd organised the food through someone she called 'Uncle'. Mother was making tea, while Hanif washed up. 'Sam, go and put the paper cups in the rooms, and then stand by the door and show people in.'

I took the stack of cups and placed them next to the bottles of juice and Coke on a table in the front room. Welcoming people at the door was fun; everyone had dressed up for the occasion, and all the women were dressed in sparkling shalwar-kameez. Our dingy house had never seen such light and colour, never heard such noise. How could anyone hear what anyone else was saying?

I was sent rushing from one room to another: 'Count the plates.' 'Go and get the serving bowls.' 'Fill the salt shakers.' 'Get the yogurt from the fridge.' 'Cut the cucumber.' All the time I tried to keep my nice new clothes clean, because of course Mother and Hanif had aprons but I didn't.

Mother issued her next orders. 'Go and see if Tara's ready. The *molvi* is going to be here any minute.'

'Where is she?' I'd forgotten about Tara, in fact I hadn't seen her all day.

'In Hanif's room,' Mother said, over her shoulder. 'She's been there all morning with her friends getting ready. The *molvi* will be here at one o'clock. Tell her not to come down on her own; I'll come and get her.'

I ran upstairs and knocked on Hanif's bedroom door.

'Come in,' a voice said.

Inside, Tara's friends seemed to fill the room, fluttering here and there, giggling together. Tara had her back towards me.

'Mum said hurry up,' I said, 'because the *molvi* is coming soon. But she also said she'll come and get you, so stay here till then.'

At that, Tara turned around to face me. She was wearing a long red skirt and matching kameez that was covered in golden embroidery, with golden shoes. A huge, gold, three-tier necklace matched her earrings. Her lips were deep red, and her eye make-up matched her blushing cheeks. She looked as if she'd just walked right out of a film, and I gaped.

'Wow, Tara,' I whispered. 'You look beautiful.'

And for the very first time in my life, my older sister smiled with pleasure at something I'd said to her.

'Tell Mum I'm nearly ready.' she said. 'Oh, do me a favour, won't you? Run downstairs and get me a glass of Coke.'

I ran down to the kitchen to fetch her drink.

'There you are. Cut these onions, Sam,' Hanif snapped as I walked in.

'But I have to go and give Tara some Coke. She's ready, by the way.'

'Then you'll have to hurry up and cut the onions first.'

So it wasn't until fifteen minutes later that I returned to Tara and handed her the cup of Coke.

'What took you so long?' She snatched the cup out of my hand, and the vision in my head shattered. 'I'm dying of thirst. And what's this paper cup? Couldn't you even get me a proper glass?'

A voice behind me gave me a start. 'Are you ready to come downstairs now?' Mother had come upstairs after me.

Her friends went quiet, while Tara replied softly, 'Yes,' and walked over to Mother.

Mother fitted the red scarf over Tara's face, and led her downstairs. The rest of us came down, and I noticed that as Tara got to the foot of the stairs everyone stopped chattering. Groups parted to make way for her. It all seemed so magical.

There was a chair set out near the window. Mother sat her down, carefully arranging her clothes, while all the women stared at her. I heard them whispering. 'She looks beautiful.' 'How much gold have her parents given her?' 'It's good she's marrying her cousin.' 'His parents are in Pakistan, so she won't get any hassle from them.'

Mother gestured to Mena to come and sit on the floor next to Tara. The women in the room came forward to give Tara money, which she handed to Mena to put in her handbag. The money was to persuade Tara to lift the scarf from her face. There were gasps around the room, then voices saying, 'Doesn't she look beautiful?' 'Wow, she's so lovely.' 'May Allah bless you with all the treasures in the world.'

Tara seemed to shine; everything about her seemed different today, although she was looking down all the time, keeping her eyes on the floor as if she didn't want their praise. I stood to one side and watched with the same excitement as everyone else in the room, but I knew that she was trying to do as Mother had told her.

I'd been in the kitchen cleaning up after the evening meal a few days ago when Hanif and Mother were coaching Tara.

'When we bring you downstairs, you're not to look up or smile,' Mother said.

'You don't want people to think you're happy to leave your parents' home,' said Hanif.

'When it is time for you to go, we want you to cry and hug us,' Mother added. 'You shouldn't look happy, because people might think we've treated you badly and that you're glad to leave.'

'The *molvi* is here,' shouted Manz from the front door, and Hanif turned to me. 'Fetch me a chair from the kitchen,' she demanded. 'Hurry!'

I handed over a kitchen chair which was put down next to Tara, and an old man, wearing a white shalwar-kameez and a black waistcoat, sat. He leaned over to her and started talking, too quietly for the rest of us to hear the words. Tara carefully repeated everything he said, and then he stood up and moved towards the front room; the chair was passed to me to hand to Manz, who was waiting by the door of the other room.

When the *molvi* went in after him, I peered round the door and saw Bashir, in a green suit and looking nervous, listening intently to the *molvi*'s muttered words. I wanted to see more but Mother shouted from the kitchen for me to come and help serve the food.

She handed me some paper plates. 'Go and give everyone a plate. And take the bag of forks and share them out, too.'

The women were sitting on the floor. I went around the circle, counting as I handed out the plates and forks. I could hardly believe that there were twenty-seven women and ten children in the room, when usually it seemed a squash with just Mother and us in there.

Back in the kitchen bowls of rice were standing steaming on the counter.

'What are you waiting for? Take the rice to everyone!'

That done, there were delicious-smelling bowls of meat curry and salad, which made my mouth water as I carried them through.

Once the women were serving themselves, I went back to the kitchen to find Mother and Hanif sitting eating. Good, I thought, as my stomach grumbled.

'Now take plates and all this food to the men in the other room,' said Hanif, indicating another stack of bowls and plates.

More walking to and from the kitchen, with no one offering to help. On my last trip back, Tara waved me over to her.

'Get me some food,' she demanded. 'I'm starving.' I filled a plate for her and went back to the kitchen, expecting to have something else to do, but was surprised instead when Hanif said, 'Hurry and have something to eat. Then you can clear the plates.'

I helped myself to some food and looked around for somewhere to sit. Hanif and Mother were sitting on the only chairs left in the kitchen, so I sat on the floor in the corner. I took a mouthful of curry, and stopped as I put it into my mouth; it tasted wonderful. Probably because I didn't cook it. I couldn't remember when I had last eaten someone else's cooking. I hungrily devoured my plateful, and then quickly took a second helping.

I'd just finished when Hanif handed me a bag and paper bowls. 'Clear the plates away now,' she said. 'Then share out these small bowls for the sweet rice.'

In the front room, I started collecting the plates. 'Is there any sweet rice?' a woman asked.

'It's coming,' I said. 'But can you please hand out the bowls while I clear the plates?'

With a friendly smile, she took the bowls from me. I cleared up, then went to fetch the spoons and sweet rice. When I returned the lady took the rice from me and placed it on the white cloth on the floor. Then she placed a gentle hand on my cheek. 'I wish my daughters worked as hard as you do.'

For once I felt appreciated, and I beamed at her.

Back in the kitchen, Mother and Hanif were standing over the pots discussing what to do with the leftovers.

'Do you want some sweet rice?' asked Mother. I nodded. 'Get a bowl and take some then.'

I ate quickly, hoping that I'd be able to go to bed soon. The excitement of the day and the constant helping out had exhausted me. But no. 'When you're done with that,' Mother said, 'go and clear the bowls away from both rooms.'

Just as I was finishing, Bashir came in and sat on the chair next to Tara. They looked at one another shyly. The men followed him into the room. 'May Allah bless both of you,' they all said as they took it in turn to pat her on the head, and then they said goodbye.

As soon as they'd left, the women started to sing a monotonous song. The only words I understood were, 'Our daughter's leaving us. Our daughter's leaving us now.' About halfway through the song, Tara and Bashir stood up. Hanif and Mother hugged them and started to cry. It seemed like the louder the women sang, the louder Mother and Hanif cried. They started sobbing very loudly when Tara moved towards the front door.

Hanif led Tara out, and we followed the women outside. Mena and I stood at the gate to watch everyone walk the fifty yards to Bashir's place. The women waited at his gate while Hanif took Tara and Bashir inside and shut the door. Mena and I ran back into the house.

'Is she going to live there now?' asked Mena as we headed upstairs to our bedroom.

'I don't know,' I said with a shrug. Honestly, I didn't care, I was so tired. Besides, it also meant one fewer person to tell me off all the time.

'I'm the eldest, so I get her bed,' Mena said with a laughing yawn. And she snuggled up in Tara's bed. I didn't mind. I would have the bed nearest the window, and could open the curtain whenever I liked to read by the light outside.

9

With Tara out of the house, Dad would sometimes stay over, crashing in Saber's room, although Saber hated that. Dad never mentioned the children's home, or coming to see me, or sweets in his pockets, or anything. It was as if that time had never existed, but he'd always place a gentle hand on my head, and give it a friendly rub, which meant so much as no one else in my family ever touched me except to hurt me. I knew he cared, I knew he would take me away if he could. I imagined him working far away somewhere, somewhere children weren't allowed. I imagined him working undercover as a private detectivee; solving mysteries, catching the bad guys, that's what my dad did. As no one told me anything anyway, and as I knew better than to ask questions, I had no reason to believe otherwise. Mother had told us we were never to go out with Father because of his mood changes; although I never saw him lose his temper, Mother had scared us so much that we wouldn't dare go. Father said to us Mother agreed we could go out with him, but that, as it turned out, was often a lie.

Late in the autumn of 1980, someone at our high school gave our class a talk on child abuse and the teacher said if anyone was being mistreated we should let one of the teachers know. I hesitated at first but then a week later – after I'd received a beating for not washing Manz's collars properly – I decided to tell our form tutor, Mr Pritchard.

It wasn't easy. Not just because I couldn't find the words to express what was being done to me at home, not really, I also couldn't say them – my stutter was so bad. Eventually I managed to stumble out, while my form tutor looked sympathetically at me, that 'I was hit at home the other day by my mother, and she's hit me before as well, and I want it to finish.' I cried when I said this, and he patted me gently on the arm as he gave me a tissue to wipe my tears.

'I'll talk to someone, Sameem, and we'll make sure this doesn't happen again.'

All the way home that day, I felt a mixture of elation – this was all going to change – and dread – what would happen when Mother found out? I had no idea how it would be stopped, of course, and so didn't expect what happened next.

A few days later there was a stranger in our house when we walked in from school. Mena and I looked at him and Mother, and, sensing something, Mena scuttled off upstairs; she didn't want to see what was going to come next.

'Hello, Sameem, don't worry, I'm a social worker' – and he introduced himself – 'and I've been sent to check up on what you told your teacher. I've been talking to your mother.'

I looked across at her, my stomach falling to the floor in anticipation of her anger. I could tell she was furious by the way she stared at me.

She started talking in Punjabi, saying, 'What have you told him?' and wheezing at the same time, pretending to have an asthma attack.

The social worker asked me, 'Are you okay?'

My mother immediately coughed out, 'You'd better say yes or I'll kill you.'

So I did.

'Why did you tell the teacher your mother is hurting you?' he asked.

I shrugged my shoulders.

'Your mother is very ill and very sorry she pushed you the other day.'

Mother added, 'Sorry, sorry,' in English and started crying. 'Go upstairs, *kutee*.' I didn't need encouragement to keep away from her so off I went.

Mena was waiting upstairs: 'What's going on? Who is that man? What's he saying to Mother? What did she say to you?'

'Shh,' I hissed at her, as I tried to hear what was being said downstairs. The door was shut so I couldn't make out their words, but the social worker left shortly afterwards.

'Sameem! Sameem!' Mother called me downstairs.

'Coming!' I shouted back. I didn't move but stood near the bedroom door trembling; I didn't want to go downstairs; I knew what would happen.

'You must go, please, or she'll get really angry, she'll hit you even more.' Mena pleaded with me. 'If you don't go down she'll probably kill you.'

I crept downstairs. Mother sat there. I waited at the foot of the stairs, across the room from her, my hands round the banisters, trying to keep myself safe from her grasp.

'Come here,' she said, her hands flat beside her on the sofa.

'No, Ami,' I replied, 'You're going to hit me.'

Suddenly she started shouting at me, cursing me, all sorts of terrible words, as she stood up and rushed across the room so fast that I didn't have time to back away. She grabbed me by my hair and pulled me away from the stairs. I started shrieking and crying as she yanked my hair in one hand and began slapping me with the other. She slapped my head and my arms as hard as she could, but I wriggled free and fell flat on the floor, hoping to stay out of her reach, all the time begging her to stop.

She stood back from me and I briefly thought, Maybe that's it, when she turned around with the *pika* in her hand; she started striking me across my back and sides with it as hard as she could, still shouting at me. The blows I usually received were nothing like this; the pain was fierce and sharp, a red-hot lashing of agony that made me yelp like a wounded animal. The pain was so intense that I couldn't draw breath quick enough to plead properly with her: *stop, stop.* I put my arms up to shield my head and she hit them a few times, but then returned to hitting me on the back and on my legs. She didn't stop, and I thought it would never end, as blow after blow whipped into me. I felt sure she wouldn't stop until I was dead.

Hanif, who all this time was sitting on the settee watching, decided to stop my mother. 'That's enough,' she said. 'The girl is bleeding.' I didn't know this until she spoke. Blood was oozing out of the wounds on my arms, my back, and on my legs. Mother told me to get out of her sight, so I crawled upstairs. As I did so Mother shouted that Manz would be home soon, and that she would pray for him to beat me too.

I lay on my bed and sobbed and sobbed. Mena didn't say anything but wiped the blood off me and helped me get changed, when I could sit up to help her. I didn't want to leave my room ever again. I didn't want to do anything again. I wanted everything to stop.

This wasn't a turning point or anything; I still felt that I was letting Mother down, that I was in the wrong. I didn't like getting hit but I believed that she hit me because she had to, that I made her do it. I know now that this was stupid, but somehow I was so battered that I fell in with whatever Mother said to me. It was all my fault.

Manz didn't hit me when he came in that evening, which was strange. I just didn't get any supper that night, as I didn't go downstairs. Despite what Mother said, Manz only lashed out at me in anger, like when I hadn't washed his clothes properly. Mother was rude – behind his back, of course, never to his face – about his temper, saying to us that he was *kad damak*, which meant 'rotten': in other words, mentally ill. Once, Manz beat me for answering Hanif back; he punched me, and pushed me to the ground, where I banged my head. But I had to show him I was better than him, so, that night, after I'd gone to bed, I pulled the curtain back a little so that the light came in enough to let me finish my homework. Achieving something that he couldn't do anything to stop made me feel a lot better.

My twelfth birthday passed like any other birthday, unnoticed. I was glad no one said anything at school, because I used to lie – 'Oh, I'm getting a doll's house,' I'd say, if asked – but I hated doing it and didn't see why I should. Of course the truth wouldn't have helped either, because I couldn't explain to anyone why my birthday was ignored.

When Dad made his occasional visits, which happened two, sometimes three times a month, he'd sit and talk calmly with Mother for hours. We got used to this, until one day when he showed up on a Saturday, during the day. After we'd had lunch, and when I was just finishing the washing-up in the kitchen, he came in and casually said, 'Do you and Mena want to go out?'

'Mother will say no,' I said, knowing what would happen if he asked.

'No, she won't,' he replied, grinning. 'She said it's okay.'

When Dad lied, he always said 'honest', as if trying to convince himself as well as you. I didn't hear it this time. I nearly shouted with excitement. 'Really? Shall we go now? Oh, I'll just go and get Mena.'

Dad chuckled.

I found Mena lying on the bed, her back to the door. 'Dad wants to take us out. Mum says it's okay.' I was a bit breathless from running up the stairs, but also from the adrenaline rushing through me.

'Liar,' she said, without even turning round.

'No, Mena, honestly. We can.'

She sat up, and looked questioningly at me.

I nodded. 'Yes, it's true.'

She jumped up and brushed her hands down her clothes. 'Then let's go!'

Dad said to Mother, as we came down the stairs, 'I'll bring them back in a couple of hours,' and we followed him out of the door, not daring to look at Mother's face as we went, in case she saw how much this day out was going to mean to us and immediately stop it. Only when the door was shut behind us did Mena and I feel sure that we really were going out.

'Where are we going? What are we going to do?' we both asked him as we walked away from the house.

'Where do you want to go?' said Dad, smiling at our joy.

Mena shrugged her shoulders. It had been so long since we'd been out with Dad that we'd forgotten all the things we could do.

'Let's go to the moon!' I said, and we all laughed.

'I haven't got a rocket. What about the zoo?' Dad wondered.

Mena and I looked at each other. We both felt a bit too old for that, so I said, 'No, we don't want to go to the zoo. But is there a library we could go to?'

'I think there's one near the town centre; shall we go and see?'

Dad only had to look at our faces to know that was what we wanted to do. Smiling again, he said, 'Okay, the library it is then,' and we set off together to the centre to find it.

It was such a contrast, being with Dad: he listened to us, he didn't tell us what we should be doing all the time, and, best of all, he smiled at us, rather than looking away or cursing us. With Mother, I was always trying to please her, trying to do better what I'd done before so that she'd be happier with me. With Dad, I didn't need to make an effort all the time; he seemed to be as happy just being with us as we were just being with him.

The library, when we got there, added to my sense of peace. As we walked in, an enormous sense of stillness, of safety, washed over me. This was a calm place where knowledge and adventure dwelled. I didn't realise how much I'd missed such surroundings.

Dad showed us the area of the library marked 'Children's books' and then went over to talk to the lady behind the counter. We drifted in different directions; Mena found a large picture book and headed to a chair to looking through it. I, on the other hand, looked at the markers on the tops of the shelves until I found what I wanted. At the end, in the older children's books area, was a whole bookcase marked 'Mysteries'. I ran my hands down the spines of the books, their names telling me of adventures in faraway places, in which brave children were rewarded.

I'd started to pull one off the shelf when Dad came up. 'I've just been speaking to the librarian, and filling in a form. You can take three books each, but you must return them by the date the lady will stamp inside the book.'

For a moment I couldn't breathe. To have something to read in bed – was it true? 'We can take books home?'

'Yes, of course,' said Dad. 'Don't take all day choosing, though, I must get you home before too long.'

In the end I chose a Famous Five mystery, a Nancy Drew, and a Hardy Boys mystery. Mena chose a big fairytale book.

'You can take two more books,' I reminded her.

'I only want this one.'

I quickly turned to Dad. 'If Mena only picks one book, can I choose two more?'

'Sure, if you're going to carry them.'

I pulled out another two Famous Fives, then Mena and I headed towards the exit.

'Sam! Mena!' Dad called after us, waving us back to the counter. 'You can't just leave like that. The lady has to stamp your books. And remember, you have to bring them back by that date.'

The lady stamped the form in the front of each book and then waved her hand over the page to help the ink dry. She looked at the books I had brought over, and said to me, 'Do you want me to put them in a bag for you?' and I nodded. When I took the bag she handed me, it was heavy, and I held the handle with one hand while I balanced the bag on my other arm.

Dad saw me struggling, and sighed. 'Pass me the bag, then,' he said. He carried the bag all the way home, only passing it to me when he went to buy some sweets and chocolates which Mena and I agreed we'd keep to eat that night while we were reading.

When we walked in, Mother immediately asked, 'Where did you go with them?'

'I took them to the library,' we heard Dad say as we slipped upstairs, going into our room to put the books under our beds. 'They have some books which they have to return in a month.'

'You got them books, English books?' Mother shouted at Dad, in Punjabi, loud enough for us to hear upstairs. 'They learn enough English at school! What do they want books for?'

Mother hated anything that was written in English. Letters were thrown, unopened, into the rubbish; she'd only pay a bill when someone came to the door, ready to cut off the gas or electricity.

I went to the top of the stairs to hear more; Mena waited in our room, cowering away from Mother's anger, as usual. Dad's voice was soft and gentle as he tried to calm Mother down. 'They have a couple of books with pictures and stories about animals. I'll show them to you if you want.'

Mother's reply was too muffled for me to hear properly what she said. After a while, Dad came to the stairs, and I rushed back into our room so he wouldn't know I'd been listening.

He called up. 'Mena, Sam, I'm going now.'

We went quickly downstairs to say goodbye.

'Thanks, Dad, for taking us to the library,' we both said as we hugged him on either side.

He gently rubbed our faces and said, 'See you soon,' before leaving.

Mother said nothing about the books. All that evening I was cheerful, although I couldn't wait till it was time for bed and I could go upstairs to read. Even the jobs I had to do didn't get me down, and I happily washed the dishes, swept the floor, cleaned the cooker, and massaged Mother's head because it was hurting. This was a task that usually fell to me. I'd be expected to rub and knead her scalp for about twenty minutes, pushing down hard so that my fingers ached. Sometimes Mena would do it; then Mother would lie down and I would be expected to walk up and down on her legs – all the time avoiding her knees – and up on to her back and stretch out her arms for her. Kneading her head was the hardest, though, as with Mother lying down my back would ache as much as my fingers from the awkward position I'd have to stand in.

Eventually, everything was done, and Mena and I could go upstairs, to read our books. Just then, Manz came in from work, and the first thing he said to me was that I hadn't washed his clothes.

I'd started answering back to them recently; someone would tell me to do something and I'd mumble a retort. Then if whoever I'd spoken to said, 'What?' I'd just say, 'You heard me,' and walk away. Hitting me had got to the point where it didn't seem to make an awful lot of difference; the self-harming I was doing made their violence seem ordinary. So although I didn't answer back very much, my obstinacy in refusing to do their bidding even got Mother's attention. Which was the point, of course.

Tonight, I'd been working hard all evening, and the house was spotless, the dishes cleaned and put away, Manz's supper cooked and ready to be heated up. He didn't value any of the work I'd done, he just saw what I hadn't done. All I wanted to do was to go and read, and all that came into my mind was the image of Hanif sitting on the settee while I slaved away. I snapped, blurting out the words before I thought about what I was saying. 'Ask your wife to wash your stupid clothes.' And I started up the stairs.

'What did you say?' Manz had reached up and yanked me back downstairs by my hair.

I knew what was going to happen; it was as if I were outside my body, watching. I noticed Mena, higher up the stairs, and although I started to feel his blows, I continued to observe what was going on, Mena, cowering against the wall, and I wondered why; Manz was beating me, not her. It must be true: it's harder to watch someone you love go through something awful than actually to go through it yourself.

He slapped me, pulling my hair, punching me in the side of the head so that I fell down on to the floor, where he kicked me, and stamped on my feet. He used my hair to pull me up to my feet so that he could more easily punch me in the stomach; I collapsed to my knees as the air rushed out of my body.

He wouldn't hit my face. He didn't want to leave marks that anyone might see, and I hated him all the more for that – the calculated way in which it was done. So I wouldn't cry, I wouldn't let him have the satisfaction of hearing my yelps of pain. I bit my lip till it bled, and the tears ran down my face.

He shoved me back down on to the floor, and gave me one last dismissive kick. He hadn't spoken at all, unlike Mother who cursed and yelled at me when she beat me. Now he broke the silence, and said, 'That should make sure you don't forget to wash my clothes next time. Now get up and get me some food. I'm starving.' Then he walked away as if he'd pushed some leaves away from the front door with the side of his shoe; I meant that little to him.

I dragged myself into the kitchen, and pulled myself up with the help of a chair so that I could stand by the sink and wash the tears off my face before I looked to see what damage he'd done. I blew my nose loudly, and cursed him under my breath, saying all the horrible things I could think of, trying to feel better.

As I stood there, Mena came in quietly. 'What did you say that for?'

'What?' I said. 'It's the truth, isn't it? She should be here giving him his dinner but instead she's just sitting down.' I coughed; my sides hurt when I did so, but, touching them gingerly with my left hand, I could feel nothing was broken. 'Will you dish up the food, Mena? I'll take it in but can you help?'

I took Manz his meal.

'Do we need any bread tomorrow?' he asked me; even though he'd just dished out the worst beating he'd ever given me he didn't acknowledge it at all.

'No, we have lots of bread. Do you need anything else?' I wanted to get away from him, and the refuge my books had promised all evening seemed even more important now.

He shook his head as he started to shovel food into his mouth, so I went upstairs quickly and found Mena already waiting there.

'Shall I get the books out?' she asked.

'No, not yet; let's wait a while. When Manz comes up to bed, he'll make us turn out the light.'

He followed us not long afterwards; we heard him walking up the stairs, and, on the way to his room, he opened our door, and, without coming in, stuck in a hand to turn off the light. 'Go to sleep now,' he said. 'And don't turn the light back on, okay?'

I almost gasped in surprise. He'd never said that before. Had Mother told him about the books we'd got that day?

When everything was quiet, Mena said in a whisper, 'What shall we do? We can't read now.'

I had thought about this before, although I'd never yet had a reason to do it. 'Look,' I said. And I stretched up a hand to pull back the curtain, and the light from the street lamp outside flooded the room. It was an orange glow, but it was bright enough to read by. 'See? We can read and we're not doing anything Manz told us not to do.'

I leaned over the edge of the bed and slid the books out of their bag. I handed Mena her large picture book of fairy tales, and chose one of the books for myself. The cover showed a young girl shining a torch into the trunk of a tree, and I lay there, savouring the pleasure of the moment, making up my own story from the picture before I had to follow the one inside. Leaning by the side of the bed gave me more light, so I stayed there.

After we'd been reading for about ten minutes, Mena whispered again, 'What's your book about?'

'It's about a girl in the country; she's following some clues.'

'I'm reading 'Hansel and Gretel'. It's about two children who find a house made out of all the yummy food you could imagine, but they don't know it's owned by a wicked old woman.'

I'd read the story dozens of times when I was younger, in the children's home, but I didn't say so because I knew Mena had never had the chance to do so before. Some time later Mena fell asleep, the book lying on the bed beside her, and I took it away from her, and, keeping note of the page numbers, closed both books and put them down the side of the bed, ready to pick up in the morning, if there was time. I went to sleep, the aches and pains in my body fading as I dreamed of having my own torch, and solving my own mysteries.

10

Dad was still coming round to take Mena and me out, but he tried to time his visits for when Mother wasn't in so that she couldn't forbid us to go. If she was out for the afternoon, she'd often ask Tara to come and stay in the house. Tara tried to tell Dad he couldn't take us out, saying, 'Mother's not here.'

He would reply, 'She's not here to ask, so come on then, I'll take all the blame when we get back. Hurry up.' As we got up to leave, Dad would say, 'Would you like to come?' Tara always shook her head but she never stopped us from going. Dad would take us to the park where we could run in circles round him and have ice creams or some other treat, or we'd go to the Arboretum where we would walk under the trees holding his hands, or take a ride sitting beside him on the miniature train. We never wanted to go home; but we had to eventually.

I was a different person when I was with Dad, and could be the child I was. At home I had no playthings, and I was never allowed to make any noise, as this would set off one of Mother's headaches, so in the park I could scream and shout for joy, I could be free. Because no one at home seemed to care about Dad, I felt I was more like him than anyone else in my family; no one cared about me either. I loved his gentle side, when all I got at home was anger; I loved the way he just walked away when Mother said the terrible things she did, as if they didn't hurt him. I too put on a brave face; I tried to ignore everything they said and did to me, but all the while, deep inside, it hurt. When Dad went home at the end of the evening, I longed, more than anything, for him to take me away with him.

I did know, however, that he was ill. I don't know exactly what Father's diagnosis was but I knew he needed an injection once a month to calm him down. He'd come to the house and, after a while, a nurse would arrive at the door. She would talk to him about his needing an injection and Father would protest for a few minutes, saying it made his hands shake. Mother would say 'If you don't, you'll get angry and I won't have you coming to the house at all,' so he'd let the nurse inject him. I watched through the door as he pulled his pants down a little so the nurse could inject him in the buttock. I shuddered when she jabbed him with the needle. It was horrible watching my dad being forced into having this done.

We lived in Walsall until I was twelve. My only respite from the drudgery and fear at home came when I had to go into hospital. I had terrible trouble with my feet, which required attendance at hospital outpatient clinics and, sometimes, operations. My toes used to curl under themselves and become rigid, so that I couldn't straighten them.

Hospital was heaven for the peace and rest it gave me. Here I did not need to work; here I could eat food that reminded me of the meals in the home I'd grown up in, and here no one beat me.

When I first came to live with my family, Mother would call me something and point to my feet; it took me about six months to learn that she was saying, 'crooked feet' or 'cripple'. Mother would often try to straighten them by tapping them with a hammer, threatening me with a hard blow if I didn't do something about them. She thought I was doing it on purpose. I was always careful not to get too chatty with anyone in hospital, in case they asked questions, so I would try to sleep as much as possible, except when the food came round. I'd lie there, while smiling nurses brought me delicious things: chips and fish fingers, or pies and, best of all, pudding. It was not having puddings that I minded most at home: cake and custard, treacle pie, cornflake tart. I had become used to the savoury foods but I really missed the sweet stuff I'd been brought up on. Mena's feet were also operated on. The only visits we had were when Mother came to take us home.

I always wanted to stay in hospital, but I knew I had to go home, just like I had been taken away from the children's home. After two blissful weeks I'd be sent home with my leg in a cast, which would remain on for another five weeks. While I was in the cast I would hobble around to do the housework, which would have built up in my absence because no one else would do my chores for me. Never mind that I had a leg in plaster, with instructions from the doctor to rest my leg. I wanted to shout, 'Mother, look, I can do all the housework in a cast, tell me I'm clever, tell me how great I am,' but I didn't, and she never praised me.

When it came to having the cast removed, Mother would take me back to hospital. We would go in a taxi, and Mother would demand a refund for the fare from the hospital, but, instead of using the money to return home by taxi, she'd pocket it and we'd walk back. The doctor would look at the cracked and frayed end of the plaster cast and tell me off for having walked on it too much, but Mother wouldn't pay any attention to that, so of course I wasn't allowed to either.

With Hanif's baby, Frazand, around, my chores increased. As she seemed to be so busy with him, I had even less help than usual; only Mena came into the kitchen to help wash up and clean a little. But all the wiping, dusting and brushing, as well as all the clothes washing and cooking, remained my jobs.

I was constantly tired, trying to do all the domestic chores, and yet still find time to do all my homework. Being tired meant that I snapped at Hanif a lot more than I'd ever done before, especially if she made demands when I was in the middle of something else. Also, Hanif had started getting fat again, and Mena and I had decided, when we were in the kitchen cleaning up one evening, that this meant she was getting ready to get another baby soon. I could hardly bear thinking about this; I was already swamped by the chores I had to do, so another baby would make it impossible for me to manage.

So when one day Mother called me in to see her I just assumed I was going to get a slap, or worse, for answering back to Hanif, or for not doing something properly or fast enough. It was 1982, and I was nearly thirteen now; I'd been growing a bit taller but I was still small for my age compared to the well-fed girls at school.

Mother beckoned me over to her, as, by instinct, I'd stayed as far from her as possible. When I got close, she suddenly reached out and pulled me towards her, wrapped her arms around me, hugged me, and speaking into my ear as she did so, said, 'Sam, you are a good child, a good daughter, you work hard for your family, you work hard for me, well done.'

I couldn't believe it! All my hard work, all the effort I'd put into doing a good job, and I'd finally done it well enough!

'Because you work so hard, because you do what you are told, I'm going to take you back to Pakistan to see where I come from, to meet your family there.' She sat back from me, held my face in her hands and looked into my eyes as she said this. 'Just you, Sam. Just you and me.'

Mother never, ever touched me, except to hurt me. She never spoke nicely to me. At long last she'd noticed, and – I couldn't help it – tears of gratitude poured down my face. I smiled through my tears, I babbled something back but I don't remember what, I was so overwhelmed by this unexpected feeling, this glow that came from somewhere deep inside and filled every part of me. All that I'd done, all that I'd ever put up with, had been for only one reason: to please Mother. To have her recognition of all that I'd done – I'd never expected the day to come. And now it had arrived, and, for my reward, I was going to go on holiday, with her – just the two of us on our own!

I knew nothing about Pakistan; the others, who'd been there, never mentioned it, and of course Mother had never said anything to me before about the country. But we'd had a holiday at the seaside when I was at the children's home, and I was sure there would be shops and a beach and other children to play with in Pakistan. Or maybe not – but it wouldn't matter, because a holiday meant no chores, no cooking, no cleaning, and Mother happy with me the whole day long.

When I came home from school the next day, there was a visitor in the house, who was introduced to us as 'Auntie', although Mother called her 'Fatima'. She was an aunt to an in-law, not a blood relative, and she was about Mother's age; but she was kind where Mother was harsh. I immediately liked her, more so when, the following evening after dinner, I was carrying the plates through to wash up, and I heard her say to Mother, 'My daughters don't do half of what Sam does. Why do you make her do all the housework on her own? Why doesn't anyone help her?'

That night, and the following one, Tara, who had come for dinner, and Hanif came into the kitchen to cook and serve dinner, and when it came to clearing away even Mother brought her dirty plate to the sink, instead of yelling at me to do it for her as she always did. Despite my newly intensified adoration of Mother because of her plan to take me on holiday with her, I couldn't help noticing how much nicer it was when Auntie was about and everyone did their little bit to help me as a result.

It wasn't just at home that Auntie's presence made a difference. She took Mena and me to the park just around the corner, the same one that Dad took us to, but, unlike him, she expected us to run over and play with other children, to explore the park freely and wander through at our own pace.

The park was full of trees and flowers as well as lawns and a playground, but, best of all, in the centre was a boating lake. All sorts of birds drifted past on the water as we sat and watched; most beautiful of all were the swans. Dad, perhaps nervous of what Mother might say, never let us get too close to the water; but close up I was able to see how big the birds were, and how white their feathers were. They seemed to glow in the sunlight, and they glided by so gracefully that I didn't want to go home, I wanted to stay here and watch them for ever.

As I sat there I remembered Cannock Chase, and the open land around the house, and the stories that Auntie Peggy read to me. I remembered one about an ugly little bird that no one liked, and which went away and changed into a swan, the most beautiful bird of them all. Perhaps, I thought, that's me; I'm going to go to Pakistan, where the horrible Sam who gets it wrong and has to be told off will change, and the girl hidden inside will shine out. When I come home, Tara and Hanif and all the others will not recognise me, everything will be different, and I'll never be unhappy again.

'Sam. *Sam.* C'mon, Auntie says we have to go.' Mena interrupted my thoughts, tugging on my sleeve.

'What, now?' I asked.

Mena nodded.

I got up and walked as slowly as I could, reluctant to leave this little piece of paradise behind.

Auntie was walking in front of us as we came out of the small patch of woods near the gate, where the playground was. I was still lost in my daydream and hadn't spoken to Mena. 'Look over there,' she suddenly said. 'There're swings,' and she smiled at me, and I realised I wasn't the only one who found it hard to go home.

For the three days Auntie was with us, I was so happy. She was gentle and nice to me, so when the time came for her to leave, and she gave me a hug, I held on very tightly; she was tall and I felt as if I were being encircled and cared for when she held me. I didn't want her to go but I couldn't say so in front of Mother or I'd have been hit for saying something so silly. I knew that when Auntie had gone, I would be on my own again with the saucepans and the mop and the brush.

Auntie eventually disentangled herself from me, chuckling a little as she did so. She lifted my head up with her hand and looked thoughtfully at me before turning to Mother. 'She looks like you, you know.'

Mother said, 'Yes, I think so too,' which surprised and pleased me.

Even Tara agreed. She said, 'You're the prettiest of all of us,' but the way she said it was mean.

Soon after Auntie's visit I had to go into hospital to have my foot worked on again, and, as usual, I came out with my leg in plaster. On the Saturday morning, Mena went downstairs before me to use the toilet. I heard her feet running back up the stairs and she burst into the room and said, 'Sam, we're moving. Come on and see!'

Moving? I had no idea we were moving. Where to? I hopped out of bed and followed her down, wondering what was going on. Sure enough there were Mother and Hanif in the kitchen, packing everything into cardboard boxes. 'You're up at last, good,' said Mother. 'You can help now.'

'Here, take this and put all the pots and pans in,' said Hanif, as she handed us a box. I started to lift the stuff off the shelves, and put the smaller pots in the bigger ones before placing them in the box; but I was confused about what was going on. I decided not to ask Mother what was happening as she was ranting away to Hanif about something, pointing at the front room.

'Are we all going to Pakistan? Are we moving there?' I whispered to Mena.

'I don't know, no one's said anything to me either.'

At that point Hanif came back into the kitchen so we shut up; it was safest not to ask, I'd discovered. Mother, though, had told me we wouldn't be going to Pakistan for another three months. So what was all this commotion for? Was everyone else coming to Pakistan after all? Was all this stuff going to sit in boxes till then? How would I be able to cook with everything packed away?

Finally we finished in the kitchen; it took me a while to help everyone, as with my leg in plaster I couldn't move very fast or climb up to reach the higher shelves. When we had filled our boxes, though, Hanif said, 'Right, go and pack your room now – your stuff into these boxes,' and she gave the two of us some boxes to put our clothes and few possessions in.

As we had so little anyway, it didn't take long to pack them away. Clothes, pillows, quilts, blankets; at the very bottom of the blankets box I hid the books from the library that we'd never returned. I'd never wanted to take them back because I never believed I'd ever have another book of my own in my hands again.

I still wanted to know what was going on, even though Mena kept telling me not to bother, we'd find out soon enough. But I was more curious than she was so I stuck my head round Saber's door to see if he, or even Salim, knew any more than us.

Saber was just finishing his own packing, and he looked up at me. 'Are we taking the beds, d'you know?' he asked.

'Dunno.' I shrugged my shoulders. 'No one's told me to do anything with them, so I guess they're staying here. Do you know where we're going to?'

'No idea, no one's told me anything. Take my boxes down for me, will you, Sid, I'm going out for a bit.' And he ran off downstairs before I had a chance to protest.

Mother started calling that she needed help with her things, so I stomped down to the front room ready to be given my orders.

Shortly afterwards a van drew up at the front door and Manz hopped out from the driver's seat. Hanif went to sit in the front seats, and Manz came into the house and looked about at the boxes piled everywhere.

'Okay, everyone, let's get this van loaded,' he said. 'I want to get to Glasgow tonight.'

Glasgow? Where's Glasgow? I looked at Mena and she looked back at me; neither of us had any idea what was going on. Also, we'd had nothing to eat all day, and I was hoping there'd be time to eat something before we got in the van, but with Manz there ordering us about it didn't look as if we'd get the chance.

Eventually the van was loaded, and Mother went to sit in the front with Hanif, the baby, and Salim. Saber mysteriously reappeared just as the last box went on, and Manz put a rug in the back with the boxes and told Mena, Saber and me to get in.

Once we were in, Manz pulled the back of the van shut, and it was suddenly airless and very dark. Although I knew the other two were in there with me it was a bit spooky; just then Saber started making scary noises. '*Woohoo wooohoooooo!*'

'Shut up, Saber, or I'll kick you,' I said. 'And with this cast on my leg, that'll hurt.'

'You're going to have to find me first.'

As suddenly as it went dark, a shaft of light came into the back of the van. Manz had got into the front and opened up a small window that closed the back of the van off; now we could hear them, see each other, and even get a little bit of air. I looked across at Saber, leaning against the boxes at the back of the van, and smiled meanly at him. 'Now I can see you,' I said. The van started up, and we moved off.

With the light and air coming in I relaxed – I had tensed up instantly the van went dark – and so the three of us talked for a while. We realised that none of us knew where Glasgow was, so we played a game instead. At least we tried to; Saber kept spoiling it. 'I spy with my little eye something beginning with F,' he'd say, then, before we had a chance to say anything, he'd say, 'Oh, furniture again, I win, like all the other times.' And he stopped talking and went to sleep.

'Oh, he can be so irritating sometimes, Mena,' I said to her quietly. 'Sometimes he can be so nice and sometimes such a pain.'

'I know. Look, let's do the same as him, it's been a long day so far.' And she too started to try to doze.

I sat awake for a bit longer, every bump and rattle of the van stopping me from resting, or so I thought, until I jerked awake – the van had pulled up, and the engine was turned off.

'Are we here?' said Mena. Saber stretched and yawned, and then Manz yanked open the back.

'Everyone out,' he said. Saber was first, then I slid over to jump down, and couldn't believe what I saw: there, outside the house we'd stopped by, was Auntie's happy round face, beaming at me!

'Auntie Fatima!'

'Hello, Sam! Welcome to Glasgow!' she said. 'I got the keys to the house this morning.' She passed them to Manz, then came to me, holding her hands out so as to help me down from the back of the van. Grinning, I stepped into her embrace and hugged her, even though my leg went mad with pins and needles after so long slumped on the floor.

She hugged Mena, too, and then turned to the house. 'Isn't it great? It's bigger than your old one so there's more room for all of you. Come, let me show you.' And she took the two of us with her, leaving Saber, this time, to help Manz unload the van.

The house turned out to be a large ground-floor flat, with three bedrooms, a kitchen, a front room, a bathroom, and a spacious cellar. All the rooms were huge and the ceilings very high.

We walked into the first room. 'This is for you two to share with your Mother,' said Auntie, smiling at us as she said so.

I felt Mena go still beside me, and I knew she was thinking the same as me – there goes any peaceful evenings reading, we'd be at Mother's constant beck and call – but we said nothing. We looked around; the walls were dirty yellow in colour, and the carpet tatty, but it wasn't bad. It smelled damp, like the house in Walsall, but I guessed that if we could open a window every now and again that would go.

It didn't occur to me to question what was decided by everyone else, as to who was sleeping where. I knew I always came last in any arrangements.

The next room was bigger than the first, and there were huge windows which filled the room with light. Again, the place was dirty and tatty, but Auntie said we'd have the TV in here, which meant that it would no longer be in the room with Mother, and therefore we could watch what we wanted.

(Over the years Mena and I developed tricks to get our way with the TV. On the rare occasions when Mother came in here we'd find excuses to get her out: 'Mother, you look tired, would you like your head massaged?' And one of us would sacrifice a bit of time to rub her head, to make her sleepy so that we could all watch TV in peace.)

'Now here's the cellar,' said Auntie. Mena and I looked through the door at the darkness at the bottom of the rickety-looking steps, and decided not to go down. It was several weeks before I felt brave enough to do so.

Manz and Hanif got the second bedroom; Saber took the third for himself. I was pleased to see an indoor toilet and a proper bathroom. There was another, smaller, room near the back of the house, the boiler room, that Salim took over. Mother protested that Salim would be too hot in there, but he wanted it and, as he was the youngest and spoiled, it didn't take a lot of persuasion for Mother to come around to the idea.

'And finally the kitchen. Come and look at the garden,' said Auntie, and we duly did, though on the way I couldn't help but notice how bare the kitchen was, and how dirty the tops of the counters were. But it had room for a table, and somewhere to sit, once we'd got chairs or a settee, so it was another place to go. And the garden, as we saw through the window, was huge. Overgrown, of course, but at least there was something there.

'Now I brought a little food as I knew you'd all be hungry after your long journey,' said Auntie, and she laid out plates with curried eggs and *rotis*. Wisely she'd brought masses and I ate hungrily, as I'd had nothing all day.

Auntie lived next door in Glasgow. Her eldest son was married and her eldest daughter, who was nearly twenty, was really kind. We went to her house sometimes and she would always ask us if we were hungry, and put out food. If Mother nodded her head at us, this meant we could eat.

I loved the spacious new house, but I was puzzled at first. Had we fled Walsall? It felt like that to me; we were running away from the life I knew, from school and from the outside world. It may have been because Manz was about to go into business in Glasgow, but how could I know, when no one told me anything? Even so, I loved it in Glasgow; we could be more normal, or so I thought. We could watch *Starsky and Hutch* on the TV, and even walk into town – there were more Asian people around, and Mother believed this meant Mena and I couldn't get up to any mischief, as she'd get to hear about it.

Saber took over the cellar, making it his den and spending hours down there, away from everyone else. He'd tell us ghost stories about what lived in the dark corners, and Mena would listen with large, worried, eyes. The stories reminded me of the ones that Amanda and I used to tell back in the home, so I didn't believe a word of what he said, and laughed at the endings.

'You don't believe me, Sid, do you?'

'No, of course not. There's no such thing as ghosts.'

'I'm not so sure,' he said. Then he looked me in the eyes. 'If you're certain about that, why don't you find out? Come down to the cellar tonight, I dare you!'

I hardly paused. 'Of course I'll come down. Just not tonight; I've got all that washing-up to do first.'

'You're scared,' he said delightedly. 'See, Mena, she's frightened.' And he sat back, smugly convinced he'd got me.

'No, I'm not. I just don't have time. I've got to get those pots scrubbed or I'll get it.'

His smile faded. 'Okay, well what about later, when everyone's asleep? I'll take you and Mena down. I promise I won't tell any ghost stories, we could just sit and talk.'

I thought for a moment. It would be fun to do something like that for a change; I was becoming a bit restless in the house, anyway. 'Okay, let's go down.' But I didn't want to wake up Mother or Manz; they wouldn't see it as 'fun', just as something else I shouldn't be doing. 'We'll have to be very quiet, okay?'

Once I was in bed I thought he wouldn't come. It got later, and the house seemed quieter and quieter – I thought any noise we might make would be bound to wake Mother. Suddenly the door creaked open and Saber's head was visible in the gloom by the door. When he saw that I was awake and looking his way, he gestured to me to join him. I looked at Mena. She was awake, I could tell from her breathing, but she was pulling the blankets tight round her, as if to say I'm not coming, leave me alone. So I crept out of bed and whispered to Saber, 'Mena's not coming. You promise not to scare me?'

He nodded, and together we moved down the hall to the cellar door. Saber went ahead, switching on the light and going carefully down the stairs. Halfway down he stopped and looked round. 'Come on,' he hissed.

I was still at the top. The silence in the house, and the darkness ahead of me, made me feel a lot less brave than I had been earlier. It was the same as when I'd had to use the toilet in Walsall when everyone else was in bed; I started to spook myself by imagining things.

'Come on,' he said again. Gingerly I took my first step on the stairs, and then the second. Nothing creaked or groaned, so I felt okay. Saber gestured that I should shut the door behind me, to keep the chance of being heard to a minimum. I did so, though the thought that I was shutting off my escape, should there be something scary down there after all, did run through my mind.

At the foot of the stairs, it seemed darker still. The small sliver of light that came under the door barely went beyond the passage we were now in; all I could see was the gleam of Saber's eyes. 'Turn the light on,' I whispered.

'There aren't any,' he replied. 'I've got candles, though, let me light them.' And he went off into the darkness, leaving me standing there.

I heard him strike a match and then the room in front of us started to glow. Saber reappeared, carrying a candle, which sputtered and waved but gave out enough light for me to see around. The walls were brick, covered with cobwebs and dust, with graffiti scratched into them.

'Come on in here, Sam. This is where I hang out when I'm down here,' said Saber. I followed him in and saw that he'd made it quite nice, really; he'd found a mattress and put a sheet on it. There were other candles stuck to the floor, which he was busy lighting, and a pile of comics next to them.

I sat down and picked up one of the comics, and started to flick through it. 'I come down here and read those, sometimes. When I want to get away from everything upstairs.' Saber was squatting by the wall opposite me, watching me. I put the comic down. 'When it gets horrible up there.' There was a silence between us, and I felt a lump in my throat. 'When they hit you, and swear at you,' he continued. 'I really hate them when they do that.'

I couldn't speak.

Saber shifted and looked round at the wall. 'There's a hole in the wall here, where I've put some biscuits. If you like, you can come down here when you want and eat some, and read the comics. When you want to get away.'

Tears came to my eyes, and the lump in my throat dissolved. 'Thanks, Saber,' I managed to croak. The silence felt a bit awkward, so I picked up my comic again. 'Where did you get money for all these?' I asked.

'Dad,' he said. 'He gave me pocket money every week. And I'd read them at his house after school. I hate it now because I don't think he's going to visit us any more. It's too far for him to come.'

'You went to *Dad's*?'

'Shh, Sam, not so loud. Yes, sure.' He shrugged.

'So that's where you went to,' I said.

'Huh?'

'Nothing.'

We sat there for a while, not saying anything more, until I started to get cold. 'I think I'd better go back to bed, now, Saber,' I said, and he nodded.

'Come on then,' and he started to blow out the candles.

I waited until he was done and then we went to the bottom of the stairs together. When I was back in bed, my toes cold, I smiled into the darkness.

I was growing now, and Hanif looked at me oddly one day in the kitchen and said something that made Mother look round at me. Oh, no, I thought; what now? Mother went out of the room and came back clutching a white object, and said to me, 'It's time you started wearing one of these. Hanif will show you what to do.' I looked in bewilderment at the material scrunched up in my hand, till I unravelled it and realised I was holding one of Tara's old bras. Hanif showed me how to put it on, and then sent me into the bathroom to take off my clothes and dress myself. Like the underwear we used once a month, it didn't fit properly, but I was too used to that to let it bother me.

Tara didn't live with us. After we'd moved to Glasgow, Tara and her husband, who worked as a waiter, had come up to stay for a few days and then they moved into a flat about a mile or so away. Soon afterwards, Mena, Saber and I went over to see the flat. On a side table, Tara had a photo of Mother in a silver frame, and Saber picked it up, looked at it for a moment, then said to the photo, 'I've come here to get away from you, and now you're watching me here as well,' and he put it back on to the table, face down. We all laughed, and I couldn't help but notice that Tara laughed as much as the rest of us.

We had a certain amount of freedom in Glasgow and I loved the clean air and the light that stayed late into the summer evenings. But when autumn came round, and I started noticing other girls in the street in their uniforms, I grew a little anxious. Nothing had been said about school, yet, and there didn't seem to be any sign that anyone was going to mention it.

I talked to Mena one night about this, while we were washing-up. I had my hands in the sink and she was drying the dishes. No one had said anything to her, either. 'Why don't you get Mother relaxed and ask her then, when she won't shout at you?' she suggested.

After we'd finished, I went and gave Mother a head massage. She often complained of headaches, so she was always happy to receive a massage. I knew that I could make Mother sleepy very quickly because I knew which parts of her head to stroke and rub to make her relax. I worked on her head for about ten minutes, till she was almost asleep. 'Mum,' I said quietly, 'aren't we going to school here? I've already missed a few weeks, and it's going to be hard to catch up.'

'Why?' she murmured. 'You and I are going to Pakistan in October, you won't need school.'

I finished her massage and she went to sleep. I stared down at her head, boiling with rage at her, but had no idea what to do with my anger. I marched back to the kitchen and told Mena.

Mena didn't look bothered. 'I don't like school anyway, I don't really mind.'

'Well, I do!' I almost shouted. 'I'm in the top sets for everything! What am I going to do at home all day?'

Mena pulled a face, and turned away. I was doing well at school; maybe she wasn't, and maybe she didn't care about it as much as I did. But I had no one to tell, no one to complain to.

The days seemed to pass very slowly here. Perhaps it was because of the endless daylight; perhaps it was because I was stuck at home. I started my own routines, like waiting till the man upstairs threw his newspapers out, every Monday, because then I'd rush out and grab them and have something to read for the rest of the week. In Walsall, we'd guessed the time by what other people did: the man over the road had left for work at the same time, eight thirty, every morning, for instance. Here in Glasgow there was a church down the road which struck the hour and caused everyone else in the house to complain at the noise, but I loved it. At least with the clock I could tell the time. Hanif had the only clock in the house, which meant that she knew when to give me my chores.

A month passed and one day Mother came home with some new clothes she'd bought especially for me. 'See, Sam,' she said. 'Not long now.'

And she sat down and told me all about Pakistan, which made me even more excited about the trip. She told me that her family had lots of land there, the weather was nice and warm, and I wouldn't have to cook or clean because they had servant girls to do that. Every story made me more keyed up; I imagined a place where everyone was ready to burst into song, or explode into a happy dance, just like in the films we watched. There would be plenty of everything, and every-one would be friendly, and, best of all, Mother would be kind to me. She was kind to me now but I still had to work to please her; in Pakistan, she told me I wouldn't have to work and yet Mother would still be there with me. In some confused sort of way Pakistan came to seem like my prize, my gift for having endured all that had happened to me; I had suffered, and now I would be happy. I listened more eagerly to everything Mother told me about the country; I would be so happy there with her.

There was only one problem; Mena wouldn't be with me. Mena, who shared almost every thought and knew all that I dreamed of. 'I wish you were coming, too,' I said to her one evening.

'Me, too.' After a pause, Mena added, 'I won't be able to do all the work you do.'

'I'm sure Hanif will help,' I said, and we both giggled. 'If there's no one else doing the work, she'll have to do it herself, won't she?'

The day came for us to leave. Mother packed our cases, which Manz put in the car. I hugged Mena, and she hugged me tighter.

'I'm going to miss you,' she said. 'When are you coming back?'

'I don't know,' I answered, suddenly aware that I hadn't thought of that. But there was no time to ask Mother.

'Come on, hurry up. I've got to go back to work,' Manz urged. I kissed Mena on both cheeks, said goodbye, got into the car, and then we were on our way.

It was quiet in the car on the way to the bus station; no one spoke. At the stop, Manz hurriedly took the suitcases from the boot and set them on the pavement, kissed Mother farewell, and drove off without saying anything to me. Our luggage was placed on the bus and we boarded it and sat down, and not having anything to do on the long journey south, I went to sleep. I awoke blearily to find we'd arrived at the airport, and our bags were being taken off.

Mother started giving me orders once more. 'Go, get one of those,' she said, pointing to the trolleys. 'Stay with me. Push this,' and she walked ahead while I struggled with the trolley.

The airport terminal was very busy, and I kept as close to Mother as possible. We stood in queue after queue, where women with make-up smiled at me, and our luggage disappeared down a conveyor belt, so that at last I didn't have to push anything. Then a man looked at Mother's passport and we sat about in a large waiting room, ready to board the plane. Mother never spoke to me, and of course I didn't ask her anything, or get up to look in all the brightly lit shops. I wished I had something to read.

Eventually, we were allowed on to the plane. I had a seat next to the window, and I looked out the whole time we were on the ground and as we took off. The vibration of the plane scared me and I held on tight to the armrest, casting a furtive glance at Mother for reassurance, but she had closed her eyes.

The engines roared, the plane accelerated so quickly that I was pushed back into my seat, and suddenly I felt very heavy as the plane lifted off the ground. My ears started ringing, and I swallowed hard to make them pop – Mena had taught me to do this before I'd left – and then the plane straightened out, and everything was quieter.

Outside, the cities and towns became little playthings, and I watched as we flew higher above them, the cars moving to and fro like lines on paper. Then we flew through the clouds – it was a bit bumpy for a while – and emerged into bright sunshine. A *bing* sounded, and a few people started moving about.

I read the magazine in front of me, every word, but did as Mother did, and slept most of the way. When I woke up, it was because Mother was shaking me, telling me we had arrived in Pakistan.

I I

I walked down the stairs from the plane, the intense heat taking my breath away. I felt faint and sick, and my stomach churned. Once in the terminal a coolie approached us and Mother started haggling with him; she seemed to be an expert. Tired and horrible as I felt, I thought it was odd to see that Mother was good at something in the outside world. After they agreed on a price, he helped us with our luggage and led us out of the terminal.

Outside again, the heat overwhelmed me, and I was sick near the door. Relieved but embarrassed, I looked around for Mother but she'd gone ahead. I started to panic. Some children about half my age approached me, holding out their hands and begging, 'Please give us some money.' 'I'm so hungry; I haven't eaten for days.'

I felt sorry for them; they were, so thin and bedraggled, their hair tangled and faces filthy. But I didn't have any money. They pushed closer, and I could smell as well as see how dirty their clothes were.

Then I saw Mother waiting near the taxi stand; she beckoned me impatiently, shouting, 'Come on! What are you doing? Hurry up!'

Everything looked strange after the grey sky and dark colours of Glasgow buildings; it was strange to think that only twelve hours ago I had been in a different world.

Along the road we travelled everyone wore the same style of clothes as we did back home, but that's where the similarity ended. Children walked around with trays of tea calling out, 'Cup of tea for two rupees, who wants to buy some tea?' They pushed and shoved at the car windows and made me laugh, but they didn't spill a drop. Women sold things from baskets, shouting the price as they walked along. Men cooked at the roadside on open fires and strong spicy smells filled the car even though the window was closed. The buses and lorries were painted and decorated in all the colours of the rainbow, and there were bicycles weaving in and out of the traffic.

Then we left the busy town and drove along a country road, slowing down now and again as we passed through small towns, each just as busy as the last. Everything looked dirty, and it was so hot.

When we finally stopped it was dark, and we seemed to be in the middle of nowhere. There were no streets lights; it was pitch black all around, with only a faint light in the distance.

Suddenly the clip-clop of a horse's hooves came closer and closer, and to my amazement, out of the darkness, a horse and cart pulled up beside us. The passenger jumped out and greeted Mother with a big hug and helped the taxi driver put the suitcases into the cart. He then picked me up and kissed me and helped me into the cart. He told me that he was my Uncle Ghani. I thought he said 'Gandhi' and, as it was so dark that I couldn't see him clearly, pictured him as an old man with round glasses. He even sounded old.

I sat on the hard wooden seat next to Mother. The cart jerked forward when Uncle clucked at the horse, and I almost fell off. The seat was uncomfortable, and it was a very bumpy ride, but this was my first time riding in a cart pulled by a horse and I couldn't stop smiling.

The air was filled with strange sounds and smells: dogs barking in the distance and rushing water close by, as if we were riding beside a river. Mother and Uncle chattered away. The faint light I had seen in the distance slowly grew brighter as we drew near, and finally Uncle stopped the horse and said we'd arrived. I felt very tired as I jumped down, and all I wanted to do was get into a nice warm bed and go to sleep. Mother led the way without saying anything to me, but I followed, ever the dutiful daughter, so pleased to be here with her, alone.

We walked through a big archway into what could only be described as a medieval village. Shadows huddled around open fires that filled the air with wood smoke. I could just about make out the outline of small hut-like houses in the background. The shadows rose to their feet and turned into people who ran towards us shouting, 'Auntie is here! Auntie is here!' They hugged and kissed Mother, then turned to me and hug and kiss me, too. It was lovely to be welcomed so warmly, but it was also a bit bewildering. Who were these people, anyway? No one had ever told me anything at home, and it looked as if I was expected to cope in the same way here – picking it up as I went along.

We made our way across the open area, while the people returned to sit around their fires, and we walked under another archway that led into a gloomy lamplit courtyard. Mother walked through a doorway to the right, into a room that was lit by a single bulb plugged into the wall. So they did have electricity after all; I'd started to wonder about that. The room was furnished with two beds along the walls and a huge standing fan in a corner. Finally running out of energy, I sat on one of the beds.

A tall, thin woman walked in and hugged Mother, then hugged me, too, and introduced herself as my Aunt Kara.

'Are you hungry?' she asked.

I shook my head. 'But I'm thirsty,' I said quietly, feeling very unsure of myself.

She left the room and returned a few minutes later with two glasses of water. I took one and gulped it down. I didn't realise just how thirsty I was until the refreshing water touched my tongue.

Kara took the glass from me and said, 'You must be very tired.' She removed my shoes, and as I settled down, put a thin blanket over me. The bed felt hard, but I was so tired I fell asleep in no time.

It took me about a week to adjust to the time and get used to the food and change of environment. Mother and Kara started to go out to visit friends, leaving me on my own. Mother always told me not to go outside the gates until she returned, which was often not until the end of the day. Sometimes Kara left a few *rotis* for me to eat for lunch. Other times, when she didn't, my cousins Amina, Nena and Sonia, who lived next door and were about the same age as me, came around to play and brought some food.

When Mother and Kara returned in the evenings, Nena, Amina and I went for long walks on the farm. We stopped and picked sugar cane, chewing on the delicious sweet flesh inside, or climbed trees to eat the small green *bir* fruit that I loved, and sat up there and talked for hours.

I liked sitting in the trees and watching the birds flying home to their nests, which were only an arm's length away. I liked the long walks through the farm and the fresh taste of the fruit we picked straight from the trees. I liked the way everyone helped each other with the chores. I didn't do half as much work as I did at home. And if there wasn't anything to eat, someone else was always cooking food, which they gladly shared. Best of all, no one hit me.

About a month later, however, things changed, and although no one told me anything, as usual, I could sense a different mood about the place. Mother stopped going out, and guests started coming to visit instead. There was one family who came every day, bringing baskets of fruit and clothes for me. Kara made tea for all the guests, but she made an obvious extra effort when this particular family came around, serving them food as well. I decided that they must be important. One day, Mother finally introduced me to them.

'This is Uncle Akbar and his two sons, Afzal and Hatif, and his daughter, Fozia.' Akbar was thin and small, no taller than me, but I was thirteen and he looked about sixty. Afzal and Hatif both seemed to be in their late twenties and looked very much alike. Only their noses and hair differed: Afzal had a more pointy nose than his brother, and his hair was longer, coming down over his ears. Their sister, Fozia, looked a lot older and had features similar to her brothers, but she smiled as she greeted me.

'Come and sit down next to us,' she said, as she took my hand.

I felt awkward and shy, the way these people all watched me closely, and I didn't know what to say as I sat down on a chair beside her near the tree outside. I knew from experience that they'd sit there chatting with Mother for hours, so I sat for a while, trying not to show how bored I was, when Nena dashed through the front gates and asked if I wanted to play. I waited for Mother to nod her head, then quickly got up and left.

Later that afternoon, Mother asked me which boy I liked the look of, Afzal or Hatif.

I frowned. Boys? They were grown men, and I'd hardly paid any attention to them at all. Why would I have had any thoughts about what they looked like? I shrugged and said, 'I don't know. Why?'

'Nothing,' she said quickly. 'I'm just asking.' And she left it at that.

I went out for an evening walk with Nena and the rest of the children. Nena and I had become good friends, and, as we walked to the river bank and sat down, we talked about life in Pakistan and how different it was from life in Britain.

'I like it here,' I said. 'I don't have to cook and clean as much.'

'But there is nothing to do here!'

I laughed a little. 'I like that. I used to get hit a lot, but I haven't been hit at all since I've been here.' I lay back on the river bank. The sound of the water running by was soothing and I stared up at the clouds in the sky. 'Mother asked me something strange today.' I told her what Mother had said.

Nena laughed and said, 'It sounds like you're getting married soon! They're a nice family.'

I lay still in horror, but Nena didn't seem to notice. She told me how Uncle Akbar's wife died some years ago and how he had brought up the boys with the help of his family and his daughter, Fozia, who was married and had two children of her own. Nena chattered on about all this as if it were normal to get married at my age.

I couldn't be getting married! I thought as we walked back to the house. I'm only thirteen years old.

But it turned out to be true.

Mother told me that Afzal liked me and wanted to marry me. At first, I thought she had to be joking – I was too young. But she went on to explain that since she didn't know when we could make another trip to Pakistan, I might as well marry him now. These words chilled me to the bone: marry him *now*?

The next day I went out alone in the morning and walked to my favourite tree. I climbed to the middle and sat down on a branch with my back against the trunk. I stayed like that, in a daze, for hours. All kinds of thoughts rushed through my head. I wanted to run away, but I didn't know where I was. I'd never been out of the village and had no idea what was beyond the trees and farmland. Where could I run to? I just sat there wishing I was back in Scotland, wanting to scream at the top of my voice, why, why? What had I done to deserve this? I looked down from where I sat. It was a long way down.

Suddenly I heard Nena calling me. 'Sam! You're in big trouble!' She stood right below me, shouting up at me. 'Where have you been? We've been trying to find you all morning!'

'I've been thinking, that's all.'

'Well, you better come home. Everyone's worried about you.'

I climbed down the tree and followed Nena home quietly. When I got there, Mother took one look at me, started swearing, and beat me. It was the first time I had been beaten since we'd arrived in Pakistan, and – perhaps because I'd lived without being hit here, and it had felt like a sanctuary – it hurt.

'If I ever find you out of the courtyard again, I will kill you! Do you understand?'

'Yes,' I whispered, nodding meekly.

'You're going to be married next week,' she said.

I sat for hours under the drooping tree in the yard, crying. The bruises on my body hurt, but that's not why I wept.

'Stop crying and come to bed,' Kara called from the doorway. 'You'll upset your mother and she'll hit you again.'

I hardly slept that night. I'd actually begun to think that life was getting better. How stupid of me to expect that. I should have known that someone somewhere was laughing at me, saying, 'Let's see you escape from this nightmare.'

When I managed to fall asleep, I had a dream about a wedding. There was a huge party, and in the middle a girl sat and smiled. She was every bit as beautiful as Tara had looked on her wedding day, and, as I stared at her, she looked over at me and gave me a conspiratorial grin, which I returned. The dancers whirled past her and I woke up.

No one talked about the wedding over the next few days. Neither did I. I began to hope that everyone had forgotten or that maybe it really was a stupid joke of Mother's. Everyone was getting on with day-to-day life just as they had since we arrived.

Several days later, we had just finished breakfast when Akbar walked through the gate with his family and some other people. They were all dressed up in fancy clothes as if they were going to a party and I assumed they were here to take Mother with them, because we hadn't made any preparations for a party. Mother came out of the house smartly dressed and told Kara to take me inside and get me dressed.

Get me dressed? I wondered. 'Dressed for what?' I said to Kara as we went inside.

'Your wedding, silly,' she said, smiling at me as if this were a game.

Married? Today? When Tara got married, the preparations took ages: clothes were piled up beforehand, the house decorated, friends and family came around and sang songs, played music, and danced. It was exciting. The night before her wedding, all the women and girls sat around in a circle and drew patterns on their hands with henna. Yet here, six days had passed and no one came around to sing, decorate my hands, fix my hair, play music, or sew any clothes.

Kara said she had a red suit that I would wear. I pictured Tara's wedding clothes – the beautiful red shalwar-kameez with matching scarf, all covered with gold embroidery – and her beautifully made-up face with gold dots around her eyes and red lipstick that matched her outfit. And gold necklaces and bangles sparkling in the light. Well, all that might not be so bad.

But Kara dragged a big suitcase out from under one of the beds, pulled out a plain red suit, and ironed it. It looked old, nothing like the sparkling clothes Tara had worn. Kara told me that this suit belonged to her daughter.

'It is expensive,' Kara said. 'She brought it a couple of years ago and only wore it a few times, but then she got pregnant and it wouldn't fit her any more.' Kara handed it to me and told me to change because the *molvi* would be here soon.

I reluctantly took the suit and put it on. It was a bit loose and the sleeves hung well past my wrists, but Kara said I looked fine.

Just then Nena came in. 'Let me comb your hair,' she said as she picked up the brush. I sat on the bed, numb and speechless, while she sat behind me brushing my hair and tying it back. Then she stood in front of me and looked me over carefully. 'You look nice,' she said with a smile and a nod. 'Auntie, have we got any jewellery?'

'No, she looks fine the way she is.'

I told myself this must be a rehearsal, I couldn't be getting married, not today. I wasn't wearing any make-up or jewellery, and all I had on were old clothes that didn't fit properly. I didn't need a mirror to know that I didn't look anything like as grand as Tara had. I felt sick with fear. My throat seized up as Kara handed me a red scarf. I put it around my head and she pulled it down over my face. She left the room and I started to cry.

Nena patted my shoulder. 'Oh, Sam, don't cry. It's always upsetting when you leave your parents' home, but it'll be all right.'

But that wasn't why I was crying, and I couldn't explain to Nena.

Then Kara came back, leading the *molvi*.

'Hello, daughter,' he said in a soft, mumbly voice. 'Just repeat everything I say.' And then he started speaking in Arabic, in such a low voice I had trouble hearing him.

I repeated the few words I understood and just mumbled the rest. A few minutes later he and Kara left the room.

Nena gave me a hug. 'You'll be leaving soon. But after a few days, I'm sure you can come back for a visit.'

Mother came into the room and said, 'It's time for you to leave, now. You're to go with your husband's family to your new home.'

My husband? My knees started to shake when I tried to stand, and I had to sit back down quickly, before I fell. I looked up at Mother and started to cry again.

She just grabbed my arm and pulled me to the doorway. She pointed to Uncle Akbar. 'That is your father now, and that is your husband,' she said as she gestured to one of his sons, who stood there with a smile on his face.

No, no! I thought. This can't be true! I'm in a nightmare.

'Go on, now,' said Mother, and she gave me a push in the direction of these men who were little more than strangers to me.

I tried to say I didn't want to go, but not a word came out. I shrank back from the doorway.

Mother stepped closer to me, towering over me as she looked down. 'Don't you dare make a scene, Sameem. Just get up and go with your husband.'

I looked at her, hoping she'd seen the tears in my eyes and understood how frightened I was, but she looked away.

I had no choice but to go through that door. I felt sick and was trembling. I was being taken away by someone I didn't even know. As they led me towards the car I looked back, but the gateway stood empty. No one had lingered even to wave goodbye.

We drove out of the village, past the river, and on to the main road. Afzal sat next to me. He was speaking, but I was too numb to make out the words. Everything was a blur. After about twenty minutes we entered another village. My so-called husband leaned towards me and said, 'This is your home now.'

They took me through a huge wooden gate that opened up into a yard. It was very similar to Mother's house: with the same kind of open-fire cooking area and a water pump in the corner. Akbar led me through the house and into a bedroom, where he told me to sit on the bed. He went out, leaving me alone with Afzal. I heard the sound of the bolt being pulled across the door and locking with a loud clang.

I wanted to get up, unbolt the door and run, run as far as I could in any direction. I knew something bad was about to happen because the hairs on my neck stood up. My heart raced with fear. I looked down and saw an ant walking towards me. I kept my focus on it. As it went under the bed, I wished I was that ant. I wanted to disappear under the bed too.

Afzal came and sat next to me and stroked my face. I couldn't help it – I flinched at his touch. He said something to me, then leaned forward to kiss me. I had never been kissed by anyone like this – Auntie Peggy used to kiss me on the forehead sometimes, especially if I'd been hurt in some way, but no one in the family had ever kissed me. His face was hairy, and he smelled. His stubble rubbed on my skin, scratching me, and I wanted to push him away, when suddenly to my horror he put his tongue into my mouth and pushed it around. I reared backwards, away from him; I wanted to be sick, I couldn't breathe, what on earth was he doing? I knew I should do what I was supposed to do or I'd get hit, just like at home, but I'd no idea what I was supposed to do. And this was revolting.

He tried to kiss me again. This time I said no; I didn't want him to do that to me a second time. Something flickered across his face and I turned my head away from his gaze. I could feel him staring at me and I could hear him breathing. I turned my attention back to the ant on the ground, moving about purposefully. I so wanted to be that ant, to be able to go and hide right now. I wanted to scream, Take me away from here, take me home, but there was no one to hear me. We were shut in a room away from people, and there was nobody here who knew me who would come to help me anyway.

Afzal put his hand on my chin and lifted my head up. He leaned his head towards me and I pulled backwards again but he anticipated my motion and pushed me on down, so that I was lying flat on the bed. He brought his face towards me again but I turned to one side; in my head I was shouting loudly, No, no! stop! But the air around us was still, apart from his heavy breathing. At last he pulled away, but not to let me go; as I gulped down air, panicking, he leaned back on to me and started to pull at my clothes. I was incapable of reacting; it were as if I was paralysed by all that had happened. He started to undress me, and though I wanted to scream and tell him to stop, not a word came out. When he appeared satisfied with what he'd been doing to me, he rummaged down the front of his shalwar-kameez and moved himself on top of me. I had no idea what was about to happen and this final invasion of my body, a part of me I was barely conscious of at all except to know that it was mine and mine alone, finally forced me to scream in agony. As he crawled about on top of me and hurt me, he seemed to expect me to be in pain, for he'd begun making shushing noises immediately, but didn't stop. All I could do was hide my face with my hands and pretend it wasn't happening. I closed my eyes so tight that my tears struggled to come out. Why are you doing this to me? I was crying out inside. Please stop, please stop hurting me.

And then suddenly he did. He juddered to a halt, rolled off me, adjusted his clothes, and stood up. I took my hands away from my face and curled into a ball, all my middle parts aching with pain. Afzal disappeared through a door on the opposite side of the room. Once the door was closed, I snatched up my dress from where it lay on the floor near the bed and quickly pulled it over my head. I looked around for my trousers and saw them dangling from the foot of the bed. As I got up and placed my feet on the floor I shivered again; the floor felt cold and so did I. I stood near the bed with my legs trembling so much I could hardly stay upright. I didn't know what I was supposed to do now. I didn't know what to feel. I didn't understand what had just happened.

Then the door opened and Afzal walked out of the other room. I looked down, focusing on the floor again where three ants were making their way to the door, and I could only see his feet as he stood near me.

'Are you all right?' he asked.

I nodded. I didn't know what else to say; if I said no, he might hurt me like that again.

'The bathroom is through there,' he said.

I lifted my gaze enough to see that he was pointing to the door he had just come through. He unbolted the door that led out, and light flooded into the room. I hadn't noticed how dark it was until then.

Somehow, without knowing how I got there, I found myself in the bathroom. I stood under the shower and the water jolted my senses. I was sore between my legs, and there was blood on my thighs, which I washed away. The pain didn't go as easily. I slid to the floor, crying under the spray.

After a while, someone knocked on the door and a woman's voice asked me if I was all right. I didn't answer, and she knocked again.

'Are you all right?' And this time, her voice sounded a little concerned.

The last thing I wanted was for her to come in while I was still in the shower, so I told her I'd be out in a minute.

I dressed quickly, opened the door, and went into the bedroom. I took a deep breath and said, 'I want to go home.'

She gave me a puzzled look. 'This is your home now,' she said.

'But I don't want to stay here. I want to go and see Mother.'

Just then Afzal walked in.

'She says she wants to go home,' the woman told him.

'You can't go until your mother comes for you,' said Afzal.

'Please,' I whispered. I took a breath to try to make my voice stronger. 'Take me home. I want to go home; I just want to go home!' I broke down in tears.

'Take her home,' said the woman.

'Not now,' Afzal said. 'I'll take her in the morning. If I take her home today, her mother will wonder why she's back.'

Placing a hand on my shoulder, he said he'd take me back in the morning. But that meant I'd have to stay the night, in that bed, where he might touch me again – something I dreaded.

'Are you hungry?' the woman asked. Without waiting for an answer, she stood up. 'I'll get you something to eat.' She left the room.

Where was she going? I didn't want her to leave me alone with him again. I stood up to follow her, but Afzal held his arm across the doorway. 'I love you,' he said.

I heard the clanging of pots just outside, so I sat back down on the bed, hoping that he wouldn't do anything to me while someone else was nearby.

As I waited for the woman to return, tense and unable to relax, I wondered why it was that everyone who was supposed to love me hurt me and bruised my body. First there was Mother's 'love', shown by beating me throughout the years; and Manz's clouts around the head, injuries that left me with permanent bumps on my skull. Now this. Well, there was no part left on the outside of me that hadn't been battered or bruised, so maybe it made sense that someone started on the inside. Now I knew that there was no part of me that I could keep just for myself, untouched by people's 'love'. I felt numb, broken, worthless, defeated.

When the woman came in with the food she'd prepared, I looked at her this time; it was Afzal's sister, Fozia. She wore a pretty pink shalwar-kameez, and her hair was tied loosely and hung down around her shoulders. She smiled at me and set the tray on a table in front of a two-seater settee in the corner of the room. I didn't want any food to eat; I just wanted to go home.

'Have something to eat,' Afzal said.

I didn't want him to shout at me, or hurt me, so I followed him to the settee. I looked down at the food, which smelled good. There was a bowl of rice and two different curries, one lamb and the other chicken. There were also *rotis*, salad, and yogurt chutney.

'What do you want?' Afzal said as he handed me a plate on which he put a *roti*. He was trying to be gentle now but I didn't trust him after what he'd just done to me. 'There's always plenty of food. I buy it in bulk to sell to the street traders. I can look after you well, you know.'

I pointed to the lamb curry, and he handed me the spoon. I poured a little on to my plate and tore the *roti* in half, then I sat on the settee and started to eat. He sat next to me and served himself from the dishes. I wanted to move away from him, but instead I just nibbled on the *roti*.

'Do you need anything else?' Fozia asked.

'No, we're fine, Fozia,' Afzal said. 'Join us. You've made more than enough food.'

'I've already eaten,' she replied. But she didn't leave, and I was grateful for that.

While I ate, I looked through the open bedroom door and straight into a kitchen. It was a lot like the one we had in England; it had wall units and a sink, unlike at Mother's house here, where all the cooking was done on an open flame, and the washing-up at the pump. Past the kitchen, there were some stairs leading up to the roof.

We finished eating and Fozia cleared away the dishes, but, instead of taking them to the kitchen, she took them outside and piled them near the water pump. I wondered why she didn't use the kitchen sink.

The thought of the pump outside made me want some fresh air. 'I need to wash my hands,' I managed to say.

'Use the bathroom sink,' Afzal said, pointing.

I felt more lost than ever. Despite using a sink all my life up until just a couple of months ago, I had expected to go outside and wash them under the water pump; I wasn't accustomed to using a sink anymore.

With a sigh, I walked into the bathroom and closed the door behind me. I hadn't really paid much attention when I'd gone in to shower. Now I saw that all four walls were tiled from top to bottom, and there was what looked like a toilet in the corner: it was built into the ground, so you still had to squat, but at least it could flush. I quickly washed my hands and dried them on the hand towel that hung from a peg near the sink.

No one was in the bedroom when I returned, so I made my way outside, where I found Afzal talking to Fozia.

Afzal turned around and looked at me. 'Do you want to sit out here for a bit?'

I nodded.

He walked to the other side of the yard and brought back a chair. I sat down while he got another chair and sat next to me. It was getting dark. I couldn't bring myself to look around, so I focused on Fozia washing the dishes. From the corner of my eye I could see Afzal watching me, which made me uncomfortable. Then the sound of voices came from the other side of the wall, and the gate slowly opened.

'Ami, Abu asks when you're coming home,' said a little girl. She stopped when she saw me and stared. I just stared back. She was about six years old and wore a red shalwar-kameez, but smarter than mine, even though it was my wedding day.

'Yes,' Fozia said quickly. 'I'm coming in just a few minutes.' She carried the dishes back into the house.

The girl was still staring at me.

'Say *salaam* to your auntie,' Afzal said to the girl.

She put her hand out and almost in a whisper said, '*Salaam*, Auntie.' I smiled and shook her hand. 'What's your name?' I asked.

'Shabnam.'

Fozia came out of the house. 'Come on, Shabnam, let's go,' she said. Then to Afzal, 'Do you need anything else before I go?'

'No,' Afzal quickly replied, so she took the little girl's hand and they left. Leaving me alone with Afzal again.

I had to stay with him that night, and it terrified me. I prayed for strength. The thought that I'd be back safe with Mother tomorrow helped me get through.

★   ★   ★

I woke up the next morning to the now familiar sound of cocks crowing. What a nightmare, I thought. Then I heard water from a shower and, gasping, sat up. It wasn't a nightmare. It was worse: it was real.

After I showered and ate the breakfast that Fozia brought around, Afzal asked me if I still wanted to go home and I quickly nodded. Of course I wanted to go home. I didn't want to stay here.

'I'll go and get the car,' he said.

I breathed a sigh of relief.

He returned a few minutes later and I got into the car. He drove out of the village and along a main road for what seemed an eternity. My heart raced as we finally turned on to the dirt track alongside the river: I was going home.

I opened the door and jumped out of the car as soon as it came to a stop. As I walked towards the house, Nena ran up to me. Instead of giving me the hug I expected, she grabbed my shoulders and asked, 'What are you doing here?' She looked at me as if I had done something wrong.

Thinking Mother would be pleased to see me, I smiled as I saw her come out of the house.

'Why are you back?' she demanded. 'Why didn't you wait until I came to get you?'

My smile melted away. She didn't ask me how I was. She just walked off, saying she was going to town with Kara and would be back soon. It was as if she didn't know what I'd been through. Or maybe didn't care.

I just stood there looking down at my feet, which had somehow stuck to the ground. I couldn't move.

'I told you,' said Afzal as he sat on the chair under the tree. 'You should've waited for her to fetch you.'

His complacency decided me. I took a deep breath and managed to walk into the house, closed the door, and stood with my back against it. No one cared about what had happened to me. No one asked if I was all right.

Thoughts whirled around in my head. I had done everything that had ever been asked of me since I'd come from the children's home. I cleaned and cooked, I always watched what I said and wasn't cheeky, but still they beat me. They called me names and mocked my stutter. They hurt me so much. And now this.

I didn't belong here. I didn't belong anywhere. No one loved me. No one cared about me. The people who said they cared about me couldn't, because look what they'd done now: given me to a complete stranger, as if I were property, and let him hurt me even more. I couldn't trust anyone. Nothing could be worse than this.

I'd had enough of being hurt. I could put up with being beaten and sworn at. I didn't mind the housework and being tired all the time, I coped with it. But this, what had happened to me in the past twenty-four hours, this was something far beyond anything that had gone before. I thought that Mother had brought me on holiday because she loved me. Now I saw it was all a lie. She'd betrayed me. She'd given me away to someone who hurt me more than she did, and didn't care when I came back to her. Would I be passed on to someone else who would hurt me even more?

This thought hit me like a blow, and I sank to the ground, shaking. What if this wasn't the worst to come? How could I be sure this was the end of all my torment? What was it about me that no one wanted to love? I must a horrible person, that was it. If only someone would tell me what was wrong with me. If I knew what it was, I could change it. Was it too much just to want someone to care about me?

I felt deadened by these thoughts. Looking up from the floor I saw a shelf, on which sat a small brown bottle. The world wouldn't care what happened to me if I wasn't there. No one would miss me. I didn't have the strength to fight any more. Death was surely the only way out. I no longer had any hope for myself. I reached out and took down the bottle. It contained white tablets of some kind. I opened it and emptied out the contents into my palm. My hand scarcely trembling, I swallowed about fifteen tablets. I waited a while, but nothing happened, so I shoved some more down my throat and waited to faint or something.

Why was it taking so long? Why didn't I feel anything happening? Then the door opened and Afzal walked in. I quickly stashed the empty bottle back on the shelf, hoping his eyes hadn't adjusted to the dim room enough to see.

He stepped over to where I sat and held out his hand. 'Come on, let's go home.'

Feeling beaten and tired, rejected even by the death I'd sought, I burst into tears and, refusing his help, stood up. We approached the door and my legs started to wobble. I felt faint and managed to stagger a few paces to fall down onto one of the beds. As everything swirled around me, I closed my eyes and prayed for the end to come now.

12

I woke up. A man whom I had never seen before was sitting on the edge of the bed. He had a stethoscope around his neck, so I assumed he must be a doctor. He looked at me with a smile and said, 'You gave us quite a scare.'

'I want to die,' I muttered, feeling a little dazed. 'Why didn't you let me die?'

'Don't be stupid.' Afzal's voice, nearby. 'You don't want to die.' His face appeared from behind the doctor.

Sunshine poured in through the door. It was warm, but I shivered. I wanted to run away. I tried to lift my head but I couldn't; someone had put a ton of bricks inside it. My mouth felt so dry it was as if they'd poured sawdust down my throat, too. I heard some rustling sounds and was able to move my head enough to see Kara, Mother, and several of the children dressed in their school uniforms.

The doctor stood up and left, saying that I should have plenty of water to drink. Mother followed him out. Afzal came and sat in his place.

'I'm very thirsty,' I managed to say despite nails clawing the inside of my throat. 'Could you get me some water?'

Nena went and got me a glass of water. When she returned, I struggled to raise my head to drink it.

Afzal moved to a kneeling position next to the bed. With one hand he raised my head and with the other he took the glass from Nena and put it to my lips. I sipped the water, and it felt refreshing. I drank it all.

'Do you want some more?' Afzal asked softly.

'No,' I said.

'I'm glad you're awake,' said Nena, patting my shoulder. 'I'll come back to see you this afternoon when I get back from school.'

'School?' I asked, confused. 'You don't go to school on Friday.'

She gave me a strange smile and said, 'It's Monday today, silly. You've been asleep for more than two days.' And she left with the other children following her, all of them saying goodbye.

'I'm going to look after you,' Afzal said. 'Just tell me what you want or need and I'll get it for you.' He stood up slowly and set the empty glass on the floor. 'When you're better, I'll take you home.'

That thought terrified me. Death might have defeated and rejected me this time, but I wasn't going to give up so easily. I wasn't planning to get better; I'd take some more tablets as soon as I could get up. There was no way I was going back with him.

'The doctor says you might be *hamila*,' Afzal went on. 'That could be why you fainted. He couldn't understand why you didn't wake up for two days, but he said the body can go into shock if someone as young as you is expecting.' He smiled. 'When you are, you'll be going back to Scotland soon.'

What? Going back to Scotland? That changed everything. Just the thought of going home made me feel better. I didn't know what 'expecting' was – though I did know it wasn't the reason why I hadn't woken up for two days – but I was determined to get that way.

I finally stopped hoping that my mother would love me. I had tried to kill myself and it hadn't worked; self-harming wasn't going to do anything for me any more. There was no release in it for me any longer, and that's why I stopped. I was no longer Sam who made mistakes and got things wrong and had to be punished; I was no longer the girl who'd done nothing wrong, and yet still got beaten for it. The biggest shock of all was when I realised that my aspiration, the target that had kept me going through all the years of cruel words, slaps, punches and worse – of wanting Mother to love me – had gone. I just didn't care any more; nothing mattered.

The next day I still felt dizzy, but I could sit up with my head resting on a pillow.

Kara asked me at lunchtime if I wanted to sit outside in the sun. I nodded, and she helped me off the bed. The room spun and I squinted my eyes as we walked outside. I tried to focus on the tree in the yard but it kept moving; first to the right, then to the left, then back to the right again. I clutched Kara's arm to keep my balance.

'Lean on the wall while I get a chair to put under the tree,' Kara said.

I pressed myself against the wall and rested my head on it, but it, too, kept shifting. There was nothing to grip hold of, and I felt myself falling to the ground, but then Kara was there and somehow I was still standing. She took my arm and helped me to the chair. I laid my head back on the pillow as the mid-morning sun filtered down through the tree. My head was pounding, so I closed my eyes, wishing everything would just stop moving.

'What would you like to eat?' Kara asked.

I opened my eyes in surprise. I hadn't been asked that question before; I always just ate what I was given. What instantly came to mind was a plate of chips topped with tomato sauce. I hadn't had chips for ages. 'I'd love some chips.'

'Chips? What's that?'

I explained how they were made and Kara said, 'Okay, I'll try to make them.'

Not long after, the delicious smell of the chips frying floated past, and my mouth began to water. I couldn't wait for that first taste.

'I hope this is what you mean,' Kara said as she handed me what looked like chips and smelled like chips. They didn't taste quite as I'd expected, but I put that down to not having tomato sauce to smother them with. They were so good I asked for more, but Kara said that was all for now because doctor's orders were not to give me too much to eat on the first day. She gave me a glass of water and told me to rest. I slept most of the day and was awakened by Afzal in the evening.

'It's getting cold,' he said. 'Let's take you inside.'

My head didn't spin as much as before. I felt cold, but I walked into the house unaided.

Afzal went home that evening, but said he'd return the next day. And he did.

★   ★   ★

'I'm taking you home today.'

That didn't scare me now. Mother had told me that we were going back to Scotland in a few weeks. As long as I kept that thought alive, I knew I could get through anything.

I went home with him that evening. As we approached the house, it looked different: cleaner and brighter. I could smell chips as I walked, and a girl about ten handed me a plate as soon as I sat down. The room didn't look as dark and gloomy as before; it had a red carpet on the floor and smelled of incense.

There were people sitting on the chairs and the bed staring at me. I recognised some of them, like Hatif and his sister. The rest were mostly women. Everyone nodded at me as I looked around at them, but it was strange because I didn't know who they were.

Akbar came in, handed me a glass of water, and said, 'If there's anything you need, let Afzal know.'

A plate of chips, cooked by someone else? Someone else cleaning up after me? Someone else offering me drinks or anything else I wanted? I could put up with this for the next few weeks. I'd soon be on my way back to Scotland; only Afzal, and what he did in the bedroom at night, daunted me.

Over the next few days I settled into a routine. I got up in the morning, took a shower, then waited for Fozia, who lived next door, to bring breakfast round. Afzal told me he loved me every day and caused me pain every night.

I hated the nights. At dusk I prayed that the sun would stay out a bit longer, that the crickets wouldn't start to chirp, signalling that night-time had arrived. Because that was when Afzal was alone with me. He touched me in places I didn't want him to, and then crawled on top of me and hurt me. I thought he was punishing me for something I'd done wrong, for I'd got used to people punishing me for no reason. When he was done, he rolled over and slept, while I turned the other way and cried.

Thinking about going back to Scotland helped me keep positive and accept my surroundings. Four days after I went back, Mother came to see me. She had news from home; Hanif had had a baby girl.

Mother had also told Manz about my marraige. She stayed for ten minutes and then told me to get ready because she was taking me home. And we'd be leaving for Glasgow in a week or so.

On the way back to her house, I could hardly sit still. Mother was going to book the return flights that week, and we talked about not letting anyone know we were on our way home. Mother even told me which clothes I should pack.

When we got back to Mother's, I went to the toilet and found out my period had started. I asked her for a sanitary towel.

To my surprise, Mother started cursing. Then she said, 'You're not expecting yet! You're not going back to Glasgow until you're expecting, even if it means leaving you here for a while!'

Tears started to my eyes. 'Wh . . . what do you mean?'

Mother stormed out, leaving me terrified. I couldn't stay here – I had to get home. I ran crying outside into the fields and climbed up my favourite tree.

'I prayed to you,' I said to God. 'I asked you to help me. I don't know how to cope and I asked for your help. I'm begging you to help me.' I couldn't stop crying as I looked up into the sky.

Nena had followed me, and she now stood at the bottom of the tree. 'What's the matter?' she shouted up to me. 'Why are you crying? Sam, please talk to me.'

'Go away! Leave me alone!'

'I'm coming up.' And she climbed up and sat on a branch near me. 'Well? Why are you crying?'

'Because I'm not expecting and that means I'm not going back to Scotland.'

'I thought you said you liked it here.'

'I did until I got married. But now I just want to home. I hate it here.'

'Oh, Sam, I'm sure you'll be expecting soon. Let's get down and go back to the house. There's no need for you to sit up here crying. It's not going to help.'

We climbed down and slowly walked back to the house in silence.

I stayed with Mother for a week and then went back to Afzal's. I thought about trying to commit suicide again. But as long as there was a chance of getting back to Scotland, I decided to keep my focus on that, even if it meant feeling like a zombie for the next few months. I did as I was told, I sat where I was told, and I went where I was told.

Other than at night when he hurt me, Afzal treated me far better than Mother ever had. He wouldn't let me do any housework, made sure there was enough for me to eat, and asked me every day if I needed anything. He gave me a lot of beautiful new clothes, in all the colours of the rainbow. But none of it stopped making me feel like a prisoner.

I couldn't leave the village and instead spent most of my time next door at Fozia's house. Afzal, Hatif, Akbar and Fozia's husband left for work together, then Fozia made breakfast for us and the children after they left.

Her house was similar to the one I lived in with Afzal: it had a small kitchen and bathroom at the back and stairs leading up to two rooms that, like the kitchen, were hardly used.

'Why don't you use the kitchen?' I asked once, curious to know why she sat outside and cooked on the open fire when there was a kitchen inside.

'It's too hot to use it in the summer,' she replied. 'I only cook inside in the winter or if it's raining.'

Her voice was kind and patient, so I asked about something else that had been on my mind. 'When is it going to rain?' I'd been here for a few months now and it hadn't rained once.

'I don't think it'll rain for another few weeks.'

'A few weeks?' I exclaimed in surprise. 'How can you tell?'

'It's the same every year. It won't rain until the weather is going to change.'

We talked on and off all day while I watched her going through her usual routine. The children disappeared to a cousin's house after breakfast and didn't return until dinner-time.

Fozia earned some money sewing clothes for people in the village, and we'd have at least one visitor each day. We'd chat to the visitors for a while over a cup of tea, and before leaving they'd give Fozia a large piece of cloth. Then I'd watch her turn it into a shalwar-kameez within a few hours. Afterwards it was time to cook the dinner before everyone got home from work. Every other day a girl came around to clean the bathroom and sweep inside and out. She looked ragged and stared at me while sweeping, although she always kept her face expressionless.

'You're here to sweep, not stare,' Fozia chided her once when she caught the girl looking at me. She quickly turned her head and swept the floor harder.

I felt sorry for her. After all, I knew what it was like to work and not be praised. So I went to the bathroom, and when I came out, I said, 'You've done a great job cleaning the bathroom. It's sparkling.' And I gave her a friendly smile.

She stopped her sweeping and looked up at me. 'Huh?'

'The bathroom, you've done a great job.'

A grin blossomed on her face, and she bowed her head. I could tell no one had complimented her before. From then on she smiled as she swept the floor, and I praised her as often as I could.

'You know, I pay her to sweep up,' Fozia said one day.

'I know, but what I say to her is priceless.'

They took me back to see Mother a month later, and the first question she asked was, 'Have you started your period this month?'

I nodded miserably, knowing that it wasn't the answer she wanted to hear, and knowing that I wouldn't be going back to Scotland yet. Instead I was taken back to Afzal's house.

A couple of weeks later, someone told me that Mother was returning to Scotland in three weeks' time. My heart sank. I made up my mind that night that if she left me here, I really would kill myself. I couldn't cope here on my own. Mother might not care for me much, but she was the only link I had to Scotland. If she weren't here, I had nothing; if she left me here, I might never get back home.

Two weeks later, I visited Mother yet again, and as before she asked me if I'd started my period this month. I shook my head, wondering why she kept asking me that question. I knew it was connected to whether I was expecting or not, and whether I could go back to Galsgow, but I didn't know how.

'Are you sure?'

'Yes.'

Kara came in and hugged me. 'Don't move around too much,' she said. 'We don't want you falling ill again.'

This time I stayed at Mother's, and for the next few days Afzal fussed over me. He bought me fresh fruit and vegetables each day and wanted to know if there was anything else he could do for me, all because I was expecting. I didn't know why this was such a big deal. I didn't even know what this word, *hamila*, meant. All I knew was that it was going to get me back to Scotland, and that was good enough for me. I also noticed that Mother was nicer to me and Afzal stopped what he'd been doing at night. Somehow, I'd finally made them happy.

Mother booked the tickets and I stayed at Afzal's house for the last week, where Fozia treated me like a queen. She had always been kind to me, but now she served me breakfast in bed and told me to rest. I didn't understand what all the fuss was about. I wasn't ill or anything, so why were they treating me like this?

I returned to Mother's the night before we were due to leave. At one point during the evening, Afzal took me aside.

'Don't forget me when you go back,' he said. 'I'll see you again as soon as you apply for me to come to Britain.'

Wondering what he meant but not really caring, I just nodded. 'Take care of yourself when you get back and if you need anything, just let me know.'

I nodded again, but the truth was that I wasn't paying much attention to what he was saying. My mind was back in Scotland. I was excited to be going home, but I didn't want to show it. Deep inside, I was afraid that I'd start my period and that Mother would then leave me behind.

Later, when Mother and I packed our suitcases, carefully packed most of the new clothes I'd been given, looking forward to having a whole new wardrobe to show Mena when I got home.

The house was full that night. Most of the villagers came to say goodbye, and we didn't go to bed until after two in the morning.

Afzal and his father spent the night in the next room, while I spent the night with Nena squashed in my bed talking away.

'I'm going to miss you,' she said. 'It's been nice having you here. I hope you come and visit us again.'

Yeah, right, I thought. If I have my way, I'm never coming back. But I didn't say it aloud, knowing it would probably hurt her feelings. I just nodded and fell off to sleep.

We awoke early the next morning. The sun was shining and there was a cooling breeze. I washed quickly, then sat under the drooping tree and had some breakfast. Nena joined me.

'What time are you leaving?'

'I don't know.'

'What time is Sam leaving?' she shouted to Kara, who was collecting the eggs from the chicken pens in the corner of the yard.

'After lunch,' Kara replied.

Nena smiled at me and said, 'You have time to take a walk. So you want to go after we finish breakfast?'

'Yeah, okay.'

We left as soon as we'd finished eating, passing through the village and heading towards the farmland.

'Let's go and climb your tree one last time and then we can walk to the river,' Nena eventually suggested.

'Okay,' I said again.

We sat in the tree looking out on to the farmland. It was a hot, May day. I'd got used to the weather and food, and the people in the village were nice. Part of me liked it here; it was so quiet just sitting in the sun, so peaceful. If only the serenity hadn't been spoiled by my marriage. If not for that, I might even have liked to stay; if not for that, I wouldn't be yearning to go back to Scotland.

But I did miss my life in Glasgow. Had someone told me a year ago that I'd be thinking this, I would've thought they were mad. Yet here I was missing the housework, missing looking after Hanif's children, and, most of all, missing Mena. At least there I'd had control over my body. Sure, I got hit, battered and bruised but those wounds healed in time. But what Afzal had done to me, invading my privacy, hurting me inside – I didn't think that would ever heal. And what Mother had done – showing how little she cared – had meant that I would never do as she wanted, ever again.

We got back to the house as Afzal and Uncle Ghani were putting the luggage on to the horse cart for the journey to the town centre, where we'd get a taxi to the airport. I sat in the middle, while Kara and Mother sat on either side of me. Afzal sat in the front with Ghani. We rode through the village with Nena, Amina and some of the other children following us on foot. They stopped at the gates to the village as we passed through them and waved us goodbye.

'Bye, Auntie. Bye, Sam. We are going to miss you! Bye!'

I waved back, smiling at the children, relieved that I was leaving, and a bit guilty, too, that I wouldn't miss them at all.

The morning sun was hot, but the breeze cooled us as we rode by the river. It became hot and dusty, though, when we reached the main road for the ten-minute ride to town.

This was when I looked at Afzal properly for the first time. I'd scarcely done more than glance at him up till now, probably because I didn't want to put a face to the person who was hurting me. I could tell what his thin-framed body looked like but not his face. Now I saw that he had a narrow face that matched his tiny eyes. He didn't have a beard or moustache. His wide mouth smiled when he saw me looking at him, and this made his eyes smile, too. I realised with a start that though I'd lived with him for months, I didn't really know him at all. It didn't matter that people said he was my husband; I didn't think of him that way. He was just a man, and that was all. I said goodbye and turned away.

This time, on our journey back to the airport, nothing seemed the same as it had on our first time on these roads. Every town we passed was the same, with unwashed people selling on the street corner, spicy smells covering less appetising human odours, and single-storey houses sitting far back from the road and blending into the dusty landscape. I certainly wouldn't miss this, I thought.

An hour later we reached Lahore. The houses along the route to the airport were huge with big gardens and guards outside the front gates. The roads weren't as dusty, nor did it smell of sewage, as in the towns we had passed through. Trees lined the roads. We passed a university that looked very grand. I wasn't sure if we were even still in Pakistan; this wasn't like the Pakistan I had lived in for the past eight months.

The driver pulled up in front of the airport. The heat wasn't as intense now as it had been out on the road, but it was still hot enough for me to sweat. Once we had checked in, Kara hugged us and wished us a safe journey. As we walked towards the departure lounge, I looked back. Kara was still watching us, and I gave her one last wave.

There were plenty of seats in the lounge. We sat down, and the cool air from the air conditioning felt great. I was so tired that I'd almost drifted off to sleep when Mother said, 'Come on, it's time to board.'

I slept all the way to London, the relief at finally getting away helping me to relax. At last I could rest without Afzal bothering me. I woke up as we were touching down in London, where we had to change planes to Glasgow. I stayed awake for the hour-and-a-half journey, as they served tea and snacks; I had had nothing to eat since breakfast in Pakistan.

Glasgow city centre looked amazing, clean, and fresh-smelling. It felt wonderful! Everything was wonderful now I was back. I felt like shouting at the top of my voice, 'Look, everyone, I'm home!'

No one seemed to be up yet when we knocked on the door of our house. After a minute or so, Mena opened the door, half-asleep and yawning. Her eyes grew wide as she saw who it was, and she shouted as she hugged me, 'You're back, you're back!'

I grinned and hugged her back.

Mena helped bring the bags inside, and then Mother went straight to her bed complaining of a headache, saying she was going to sleep and that no one should disturb her.

I followed Mena to the kitchen, where we had some toast. She said while we'd been away they'd eaten what she called 'English' food every day – chips, just like me. I envied them their freedom, living without Mother's rules and restrictions. Mena asked me a lot of questions about Pakistan all at once.

'What was it like? Was it hot? What's your husband like?'

I answered her in kind. 'Horrible. Yes, very hot. And horrible.'

'Manz has been filling me in. Did you know that Hanif had had a baby girl?

'Yes, I know; mother told me.'

I looked around and saw that the kitchen was clean; the dishes were washed and stacked on the draining board. And not a sound came from the other rooms. I asked Mena the time.

'It's about eight o'clock. No one has woken up yet.'

'We had to get up at six o'clock in Pakistan,' I told her, 'and help do the chores even on a Sunday. I didn't mind that until I got married.' I sighed, then smiled at her. 'But I'm so glad to be home. I don't want to go back to Pakistan ever again. Are any of Hanif's children up yet?'

'Oh, don't you know? They all moved out just after Mother left. They live in a council house over in Govanhill. And did you know Saber got married just after you left?'

A vague memory tickled the back of my mind. Mother had mentioned it, but with everything else that had happened I'd forgotten. 'What's she like? I asked. 'Tell me all about it.'

'Her name is Tanvir, and she arrived from Pakistan just a few days after you left. She's a distant cousin. Paji arranged the marriage, but the wedding wasn't as big as Tara's. Tanvir stays in her room most of the time and only comes out when Saber wants something to eat or she has to wash his clothes. She's okay, I guess.' Mena shrugged. 'She looks after Saber pretty well and he adores her. Oh, look! He's even bought her a washing machine. And a microwave!' She pointed to the new appliances.

'Is Saber working now?' I asked, wondering how he could afford these things.

'Yeah, he works as a waiter in a restaurant in town. And there will soon be children running around the house again: Saber told me Tanvir's expecting.'

'So am I,' I quickly replied.

Mena stared at me for a second and then said, 'You can't be! You're only fourteen! You're not allowed to have a baby until you're at least sixteen.'

Having a baby? Was that what *hamila* meant? I was going to have a baby? My stomach felt like it dropped into my feet as all the pieces of the puzzle suddenly fitted into place. I burst into tears.

Mena took me in her arms. 'Don't cry, Sam.'

'But they only told me I was expecting. I didn't know that meant I was having a baby.'

Mena held me tightly. 'It's going to be all right. Don't worry.' Then she held me away from her and wiped a tear from my eye. 'Just think, you'll have someone of your very own to love and to play with.'

But no matter what she said, I only felt scared and confused. It was May 1983, I was fourteen years and two months old, and I was going to have a baby.

13

As the weeks went by, I got back into my old routines of cooking and cleaning, though the new machines Saber had bought made my job easier. I didn't get sick from being pregnant, whereas Tanvir, on the other hand, suffered from morning sickness, and afternoon sickness, and any-other-time-of-the-day sickness.

'Don't eat that,' everyone would say to her. 'Don't eat this. Drink lots of water. Get her some juice. Are you comfortable? Put your feet up and rest.' Everyone fussed around her. I was glad I wasn't sick, but I could have done with a bit of the attention she was getting. Since I was having a baby, too, why did I have to keep doing all my old chores? Why couldn't I get some rest?

With Hanif and her children gone, at least some things were easier. However, I found that Hanif had been through my things while I was in Pakistan and thrown lots of stuff away, including the orange shalwar-kameez that Mother had made for me. Although I could no longer wear it, that suit had meant something to me – some small token from my mother – and I was, for a brief moment, devastated that it had been chucked out. Mother, of course, didn't care how I felt.

I think Mother thought that marrying me off would get rid of my stubbornness. But everything was different for me after my experiences in Pakistan – both the day I found myself married, and then when I came back and Mother sent me away again. That was when I realised she was never going to look after me, I was going to have to do that myself. So when we came home to Glasgow, Mother was the same, but I had changed. She didn't know that her plans hadn't worked, though; she still thought she could tell me what to do, just as she did with everyone else. She was always on the phone to Pakistan, giving Afzal's family orders, saying that if they didn't do as she wanted she'd break off the marriage. She was trying to control everything, all the time. Of course Afzal couldn't legally come over until I was of age, and she would use this as a lever to get her way.

Afzal wrote one letter, telling me how he loved me and that he couldn't wait to come to Scotland, but he didn't mention my pregnancy or how I felt, or anything like that. I thought about him sometimes: I thought about what he had done to me and I forgave him for it; I thought about him coming here and looking after me and the baby, and thought that he would come over in a few months, before the birth of my baby, but he didn't. Mother said, 'He could have sent you something over in that note,' and I'd wondered, what she meant. What could he have sent me? Mother tore up the letter afterwards, probably because of my being under age, but mostly because she wanted to control me; I was just a tool for her plans: she'd use me if it fitted in, and not if it didn't. She never thought, Is this the right thing to do by Sam? She always thought that because it was right for her, it was right for me too.

Glasgow, though, seemed to suit Mother. She went out a lot – to Auntie Fatima's and others – and had more of a social life here than in Walsall. She started attending prayer meetings and made about four or five friends that way, and she'd go their houses and they'd come to hers. She'd never shown any interest in anything like that before, even in Pakistan. Mena and I weren't involved; we'd be expected to go with her to the big prayer meetings, but these only happened about twice a year so that wasn't too much for us to put up with. Mother became very strict about religion, but she wasn't very religious in her home life. It seemed to us she only went because Auntie Fatima did, and because that's where her circle of friends came from. But, as she hadn't had nearly so many friends in Walsall and because she seemed so much happier here in Glasgow, we never complained.

Tara's house was about ten minutes down the road, but it was as if she had never left because she was at Mother's house most of the time. Mother, Hanif and Tara would sit and chat about what was happening in Pakistan, and then Tara would complain about her husband, and ask how to stop him coming home drunk all the time. Mother would say, 'Kick him out, teach him a lesson.' Like my father, my brother-in-law was kicked out of the house a lot.

Three months after we returned from Pakistan, Mother said I had to go to the doctor that day. As always I couldn't ask why – I never questioned anything Mother said, but now I no longer trusted her – but I did wonder if it was to find out if I was pregnant or not. And, if I wasn't, would Mother send me back to Pakistan?

When we were at the surgery, Mother said, 'When we're with the doctor and he asks about the baby, leave all the talking to me.'

Dr Walters, who had been our GP since we'd moved to Glasgow, was an old doctor but he had a kind voice as he looked at me after he'd finished the examination. 'What are you going to do? How are you going to look after a baby? You're just a baby yourself.'

Mother put a hand on my leg – *don't say anything*, the gesture said – and spoke to the doctor. 'I took her to Pakistan, and she went out and slept with a boy one night. That's how she got pregnant, doctor.'

I caught my breath and bit my lower lip. But I didn't dare call her a liar. I wanted to, but I couldn't, not in front of him. A knot of anger at her cheap dismissal of me formed in my stomach, and now, for the first time since getting pregnant, I felt sick, but it was because I was sick with rage and disgust. I looked at her, but as usual, she wouldn't catch my eye.

'I'll be with her to help her all the way,' Mother said quickly, as if she knew I wanted to tell the Dr Walters the truth.

Shrugging his shoulders, he gave me a prescription for iron tablets and told me to take one every day and said that he'd make an appointment at the maternity hospital for me.

On the way home Mother asked for the prescription and tore it up, saying, 'You're not to take those tablets. They will make the baby big, and you'll have difficulties when it wants to come out.'

Tears stung my eyes as I walked home at her side.

A few weeks later, it was time for my appointment at the hospital. I attended the antenatal clinic. Tara came with me, and I was certain it was to make sure that I didn't say anything I shouldn't. As we were waiting to be seen, she said, 'If they ask you anything about the pregnancy, tell them you slept with someone and you don't know where he is now.'

These words made me feel as if I had done something I shouldn't have. When I walked into the room, even the nurse seemed to look at me with a disapproving frown. Perhaps the doctor had made notes on my forms, and she'd read them. I wanted to shout to everyone that I hadn't done anything wrong.

The nurse examined me and took a scan. She rubbed some jelly on my bulging stomach and ran a little machine over it, all the while looking not at me but at the small screen the machine was attached to. Blurry grey shapes swam in and out of focus. She started talking, telling me in a brisk voice was she was seeing. 'Ah, here we go now,' she said. 'Here's the baby. There's baby's head and arm, see?' And I stared where her finger was pointing. That's when I saw my baby for the first time. The head wasn't very clear, but I could see the tiny heart, beating, when the nurse pointed it out. Seeing that almost took my breath away. A baby was growing inside me, and there was its heart beating; I could see it right there on the screen. I was really going to have a baby!

The nurse took some blood, and then the midwife came and explained that I was sixteen weeks pregnant and I had twenty-four more weeks until the baby was born. Her voice was kind and made me feel a little better.

'Have you felt the baby move?' she asked.

'I didn't know it should,' I said, shaking my head.

'Oh, yes.' She smiled at me and gave my shoulder a squeeze. 'Maybe you weren't expecting it, but now that you know, I bet you'll feel it move.'

On the way home, I told Tara, 'The midwife said I should feel the baby move.'

'I wouldn't know, so be quiet.'

Her sharp tone kept me silent for the rest of the journey. The elation I'd just experienced seeped away.

And as if by magic, that night as I lay in bed I felt the baby move. An overwhelming sense of wonder flooded me. I put both hands on my stomach, willing the baby to move again, and it did. This time when tears came to my eyes, they were of joy. I told no one; no one wanted to know about my baby. Mena, as always, kept quiet so as not to antagonise Mother who, of course, never asked me anything.

I, however, did antagonise Mother. I'd started answering her back when we were in Pakistan, and at first she'd ignored me, so I carried on once we were back home. At first she'd simply swear at me, but it didn't take long before I felt the first slap from her. She was careful to avoid hitting my tummy, and really the slaps weren't enough to bruise, but I carried on standing up for myself, because the smacks were the only contact I had with her. She would never touch me otherwise, and so – stupid as it sounds – I didn't mind being hit by her.

Manz wasn't around much, and so I wasn't bothered by him as I had been in the past. In many ways I was like a child, with the freedom of being at home, with no school, no Manz; it were as if I was having the childhood I'd missed out on before, even though I was pregnant. In Pakistan I'd felt grown up, but back in Glasgow I started jumping on the beds with Mena. I was becoming more distant from Mother; her hold on me was loosening. What she said, what she did, mattered less to me than ever before; I didn't care.

Over the next few months I got bigger and bigger, making it difficult for me to keep up with my daily chores. I couldn't stand up for long, as I was very tired, and my feet swelled up, but I was still expected to cook and clean. Mena helped as much as she could, but, unlike Tanvir, there was no staying in bed all day for me. I didn't suffer from any of the more unpleasant side effects of being pregnant, and I was excited that I was going to have a baby soon.

Mother made me cover my bump with a shawl when any of her friends came round and I had to stay in the kitchen; I wasn't allowed out to the shops because Mother said people would stare at me. In her version of what had happened, I was supposed to be ashamed of being pregnant, but I wasn't; I would take my time outside even when I emptied the bin, walking back slowly, enjoying the fresh air and sunshine.

When I was nearly nine months pregnant, Mother told me to tell her if I started to get cramps, especially if they came and went with regular intervals in between.

'That's when the baby is ready to come out,' she explained.

I lay in bed that night, feeling the baby kick and move. I'd never thought about how it was going to come out until Mother brought it up. I'd just assumed that the baby appeared, all clean and wrapped in a blanket, while I lay on the bed looking drained but happy. That's because the only time I'd seen a newborn was on the telly, and those were the pictures they always showed.

Once at school I'd listened in with some other girls while one told her friend about her baby brother, who'd been born the day before. She said that the baby had had to be cut out of her mother's tummy and that they'd then stitched her mother's tummy back together again, and we had all squealed in revulsion.

Lying there in bed, I couldn't get the picture out of my mind, of being in a room in hospital and being cut open – it seemed horrific to me. But then I remembered Hanif; she'd not seemed to suffer after her babies were born, so maybe it wouldn't happen in our family. I clung to that belief all through the next few days, as I didn't know who to ask about what was going to happen next.

Early one morning, several days later, I woke suddenly to feel a pulling at the base of my stomach. It quickly became clear this was the cramping Mother had mentioned, and as I lay there for a few minutes it didn't stop. Finally I thought it was time to wake Mother, who had now moved into a different room.

I was afraid Mother would shout at me at me for waking her up, but to my surprise, when I called out, 'Mum? Mum?' she came into our room right away.

'How long between them? How long have they been going on for?'

'About half an hour. I don't know.'

She turned to go back to her room. 'Tell me when the next one starts.'

'Now,' I said, trying not to let my voice shake. 'I'm having one right now.'

'All right. Lie down and tell me when you get another one.'

The cramp lasted about fifteen seconds. It wasn't all that strong, more uncomfortable than painful. The noise had woken up Mena and she asked, 'What's the time?'

'Go back to sleep,' Mother called out from her room. 'It's only twenty past seven.'

Mena snuggled back into the covers, but she didn't go back to sleep; instead she lay there and looked at me, and I concentrated on looking back at her so that I wouldn't feel too frightened. Eventually another cramp started.

'I'm getting another one now,' I called to Mother.

'Okay. Twenty minutes apart. I'm going to call an ambulance.'

Mena held my hand when the pain of the cramps ran through me, and I started to become really frightened. Up till now I had been happy to feel my baby move inside me but this was different, this was pain. I wanted someone to comfort me, to tell me it was going to be all right, to let me know what was going to happen next. Mother stayed outside, waiting for the ambulance.

Ten minutes later, it arrived; the two attendants asked me to walk out to the street with them, so they could help me on board. Mena followed as far as the front door. Just before I stepped into the ambulance, I looked back at her, and smiled and waved goodbye.

We drove away. No one from my family came with me or to hold my hand in hospital; it were as if I was offensive to them in the state I was in and had to be taken away. Even Manz had gone in the ambulance with Hanif when she had had her babies.

At the hospital, nurses busied themselves around me, and then I was left alone. The cramps started to worsen. A doctor came to see me and told me, 'You still have a long time to go. I'm going to give you an epidural.'

I thought that must be the medical term for taking the baby out. The idea of him cutting me open scared me, and I looked over in panic at the nurse who'd come in with him.

She placed a hand on my head. 'Don't worry. It's just a prick in the back. It'll stop the pain.'

I breathed a sigh of relief. 'Oh, okay.' Everything was so confusing and unfamiliar, but stopping the pain was something I could understand.

As the nurse had said, the doctor gave me an injection in the back and moments later the cramps disappeared.

'Okay,' the nurse said. 'You'll be fine now. We'll leave you here for a bit, but if you need anything, just press this and someone will come right away.' She pointed to the button on the wall just above my bed. 'Is anyone from your family here? It would be okay for them to come in now.'

I shook my head. 'Just me,' I said, smiling. 'But could I maybe have something to read?'

She went out and returned a moment later with some magazines; I read, while every so often the nurse checked on me. I dozed off a little bit later.

At five thirty that evening the epidural must have worn off, as once again I was jerked out of my sleep. This was much worse, though, as a shooting pain ran through me, starting in my groin and racing up to the top of my stomach, and back down again. It forced the air out of me in a surprised shout and I felt an urgent need to push. My sides and back went rigid and I thought I was going to pop. Even before I could press the button to call for the nurse, several people must have heard my shout and came rushing in and wheeled my bed into the labour room.

Nurses bustled all around me while I felt these awful spasms. One put blankets at the end of the bed while another removed the one I had over me. At one point, I had a fleeting thought about how strange it was to be the centre of attention, but that quickly gave way to the cramps that kept flashing through me in waves. I wanted to ask them to give me something for the pain, but instead all I could do was pant and try not to scream. Why I didn't bellow I don't know – maybe it was all those years of being told to keep quiet that took over.

A nurse examined me, then announced to the room that the baby was nearly ready to come out.

'I – need – to – go – to – the – toilet,' I managed to puff out, as the pain gripped me.

'No, dear, that's the sensation of the baby coming out,' said a nurse who was standing near my head and wiping away sweat from my face. 'Don't worry; it's okay.'

'But – I – really – want – to – go – to – the – toi— *aaaargh!*' I screamed as something far worse than any of the cramps so far seemed to tear through my belly, and threatened to rip me in two.

The nurse slid an arm under my shoulders and raised me up, then put two more pillows behind my head. 'Sit up,' she said. 'It's easier to push.'

I didn't understand what she meant. Besides, the pain was making it hard to think straight. Everything was a muddle. I could hear voices all around me but, through my fog of agony, I didn't register what they were saying. Before long, I didn't care what was happening around me; I just wanted the pain to go away.

I felt my back split right down the middle as two nurses held my legs open. Another nurse came into the room and stood at the foot of the bed.

'Keep it up,' she said, her voice strong and encouraging, 'keep it up. You're doing great.'

What was I doing great? I wondered. The nurse wiping my face gently brushed my hair out of they way, and I had a sudden moment of clarity while my body stopped seeming to come apart; no one had touched me so tenderly for years.

Then this enormous pressure in my groin slipped in an alarming way, and I felt as if the world itself was shifting. 'Make this one a long one,' someone – I didn't know who – said. 'Come on, push as hard as you can. Push! *Push!*'

'I can't,' I cried, tears pouring down my face. 'I can't do it any more! Please help me. Please!' I pleaded with them.

The nurse beside me held my hand in one of hers, and I squeezed it hard. She said in a soft voice, 'It's going to be all over soon. Just a couple more pushes. You can do it.'

Now my hips seemed to heave apart. I screamed, and then I felt something lodge between my legs.

'Take it out! Take it out!' I screamed in a panic.

'One more push. Come on, one more big push.'

'*Aaarrggghh!*' I cried and pushed at the same time.

Then all the pain disappeared.

The room was silent for a moment.

And a baby began to cry.

The nurses placed it on my stomach. One of them said, 'It's a boy.'

Laughing and crying at the same time, I placed my hands on him. 'Shh, baby, shh,' I murmured, all the pain and agony forgotten in the immense love that filled me.

A pair of arms reached underneath mine and started to lift the baby up. 'I'll take him now; we have to weigh him and get a tag on him,' and she tried to take him away.

'No!' I said, holding tighter to him. I wanted to keep him with me. I didn't understand what they were saying about weighing him and tagging him. If they took him away, it would be for good, I thought in terror. They would make me go home and would keep my baby. I started to cry as the nurse cleaned me up and stitched me.

'I'm sorry,' said the nurse, misunderstanding my tears. 'I'm trying not to hurt you. But I do have to do this. We can't have you getting an infection, now can we?'

'Where have they taken my baby?' I managed to say as my throat seized up. 'Can I see him again, please?'

'Not right now, dear, because I'm— '

Another nurse came in and interrupted her. 'How long are you going to be?'

'Not long. I've nearly finished.'

'Can you take her back to the ward when she is ready?'

'Yes. As soon as I've finished, I'll take her straight away.'

Soon the nurse put me in a wheelchair and pushed me back to the ward. Without my baby. I wanted to shout for them to give him back to me, but I had a huge knot in my throat and it was all I could do to breathe.

In the room, the nurse pulled the covers back on a bed. 'Can you manage?' she asked. I nodded wearily and pushed myself out of the wheelchair. In the next bed, a woman held a tiny baby to her chest, and I wondered why she got to keep her baby but I didn't get to keep mine. Perhaps it was because I was too young. I lay down thinking about the little life I had touched for only a moment, and I began to cry again as the nurse helped me get comfortable.

Yet another nurse came into the room, pushing something in front of her. She stopped at the foot of the bed. 'Do you want him here or shall I put him next to you?'

My boy! In a glass cot on wheels.

I smiled at the nurse through my tears, and I'd never had such a big smile on my face, felt so happy, or been so proud. 'Could you put him next to me, please?'

With a grin at me, she wheeled him to the side of my bed. 'Press the button on the wall if you need anything or if he wakes,' and she left.

I looked at my son's tiny face and the way his even tinier hand rested on his chest as he slept. I stroked his hand with the lightest of touches, just to make sure he was real. A sense of joy overwhelmed me as I struggled to keep myself from falling asleep.

My very own flesh and blood! My baby. My son.

I had been tricked to go to Pakistan; I had been forced into a sham of a marriage; I had been forced into conceiving this child in the first place. But now he was here I loved him immediately, and fiercely, and I knew in the instant I laid eyes on him, the moment I touched him, that I would love him like nothing else in my short life so far. I lay on the bed, my head turned towards him, my body aching and sore, but a glow radiated through me as I gazed at him. The agony of the last few hours faded from my mind as I stared at him, feeling that I had done something special: I had made life, and this life wasn't just anyone, it was *him*, and he was with me now. I felt a peace I'd not known in years as I slipped asleep.

I was awakened by a nurse. I sat up blearily as she took my son out of his cot and placed him in my arms. I smiled down at his beautiful face.

'Have you thought about a name for him?' she asked.

'Azmier,' I said. 'He'll be called Azmier.' Mother had always told us what the first son to one of her daughters would be called; she'd promised her own mother to name him Azmier, after a holy site in India that my grandmother had visited, but Mother always thought that Tara would bear the first son. Hanif had wanted to use this name for her son but Mother refused; she wanted the name kept for her daughter.

'That's a nice name,' the nurse said. 'I think Azmier's hungry,' she said. 'Shall we try and feed him?'

I had seen Hanif breast-feeding her baby and I wanted to do that too, but I thought there'd be more to it than there was. The nurse opened my gown and put Azmier's mouth to my nipple. He latched on hungrily. 'Wow!' she exclaimed. 'I've never seen that before! We usually have to try a few times before the baby will feed.'

I smiled at her and then looked back down at Azmier. None of this seemed real. I stroked Azmier's hair to make sure it wasn't a dream. As he nursed, I began to feel tired again, even though I'd just wakened from a nap, and nearly fell asleep. The nurse must have expected this, because she kept popping in to check on us every few minutes.

After a while, Azmier fell asleep himself. I didn't want to put him back in the cot, partly because I didn't have the strength, but also because it was such a joy to hold my son. So I just held him and gazed at him, smiling at how perfect he was. I'd just begun to drift off to sleep with him in my arms when the nurse returned.

'Could you put him in the cot?' I asked.

She carefully lifted him out of my arms and set him in the cot. He settled right down, as if he hadn't noticed he'd been moved. The nurse gently stroked his black hair and smiled, then turned her attention back to me. 'Would you like me to bring you a cup of tea and some toast?'

Until that moment, I hadn't thought of food. 'Yes, please.'

'Do you take sugar?'

'No.'

'Okay. I'll be right back.'

As I sat waiting, it occurred to me that I'd never been asked if I wanted a cup of tea before. It made me feel very grown up. But then, of course I was grown up: I had a baby now.

The nurse returned a few minutes later. 'Here you go,' she said as she set a tray on a table and wheeled it into place next to my bed.

I ate the toast first and then sipped the tea. It was absolutely delicious; for the first time in months, it seemed, I could enjoy the taste of food again. Being pregnant had made my taste buds disappear.

The next morning I woke up at six o'clock. Azmier was just lying there quietly in his cot with his lovely brown-black eyes wide open.

'Hello. How are you this morning?' I said, reaching over to stroke his soft skin. I could still hardly believe that this was my baby.

A nurse came in. 'Breakfast will be around before long,' she said. 'Would you like to take a shower first?'

'Oh, yes. That would be lovely.' I started to get out of bed carefully.

'Are your things in here?' the nurse asked, bending over a little to open my bedside cabinet.

'What things?'

'Your personal items.' She stood up and gave me an odd look.

'No, I didn't bring anything with me.'

'Not even a nightie? Or slippers?'

'I've got my shoes,' I said quietly, and my face burned.

She sighed and said, 'I'll go and see what I can find for you.'

I felt silly. I couldn't have known that I needed to pack a case to bring with me, but I felt embarrassed that I hadn't thought of it. In the hospitals I'd been to as a child, we never had to take anything because there were always pyjamas and towels and toothbrushes there. I waited hoping she would manage to find something, because I really wanted a shower. She came back a few minutes later with a bundle of items.

'Here you are,' she said, handing me a towel, a bar of soap, a pair of pyjamas and some slippers. 'The shower is around the corner. I just checked, and it's empty. Put those slippers on first. Don't want you catching cold. And here.' She opened a packet of sanitary towels. 'You'll need one of these right away. I'll put the rest in your cabinet.' She also handed me a pair of paper undies.

I walked round to the shower wearing the green slippers she had given me and holding the towel and pyjamas in one hand while using the other to hold the back of my gown shut.

Although I felt cleaner after a hot shower, I was a bit wobbly on my feet as I walked back. I got to my bed just as Azmier started to cry.

'He sounds hungry,' said the woman from the next bed, who was awake now and feeding her baby. 'Is it a boy or girl?'

'A boy.' I picked him up and sat on the bed and started to feed him. 'Is yours a boy or girl?'

'A girl,' she said, and a tender smile crossed her face as she glanced down at her daughter. 'I had a very long labour. I came in two days ago, and I had her just before you came into the ward.'

'Really?' I thought about my own labour, which hadn't even been a full day and felt suddenly lucky. 'That long?'

'Yeah, but it was all worth it.'

'Yeah.' I smiled at her, and somehow I knew that we were sharing something special. 'I know.'

'I'm Julie, by the way.'

'I'm Sam.'

'You look very young,' Julie said.

I just smiled and didn't answer her obvious question. I definitely didn't want to talk about my age and why I had had a baby so young.

A nurse came in. 'Is he sleeping?' she asked.

'No, he's wide awake looking at me.' I glanced down at Azmier yet again and smiled at him.

'Shall I show you how to change him then?' I nodded. 'Bring him through to the changing room.'

She led the way to a room that had six changing tables lined up against the wall. Some plastic baths were stacked near the sink in the corner of the room.

'Set him on his back on one of the tables.' I chose the one closest to me. She stood next to me. 'Good. Now open up his clothes.'

I undressed him just as I had undressed Hanif's children countless times, and I changed his nappy automatically, without waiting for the nurse's instructions.

She chuckled. 'You've done this before, haven't you?'

I caught her eye and returned her smile. 'Yes, I have. Lots.'

'I can tell because new mothers usually have to be told everything step by step. So who have you practised on?'

'I have two nephews and a niece. I look after them a lot.'

'Fair enough. I bet you know how to give him a bath, too, don't you?'

I just grinned at her.

She gave a dramatic sigh. 'I wish all the mothers here were like you!'

We chatted about babies and Azmier while I gave him a quick bath. He let out an indignant yowl when the water touched his skin, and I spoke soothingly to him. Although I knew what I was doing, I found that there was a huge difference between bathing Hanif's babies and bathing my own. When I was done, the nurse handed me a blue Babygro and a vest.

'Come on,' she said. 'Let's get you back to the ward.'

First I put the clothes on Azmier, then I wrapped him up in his blanket, leaving his little arms free. Back on the ward, the air was filled with the appetising scent of toast. As I placed Azmier in his cot, I heard a voice behind me say, 'What would you like for breakfast, dear?'

'Can I have some toast and tea, please?'

The lady gave me a nod and a smile. 'Certainly. Would you like some cereal, too? You must be starving.'

I climbed back into bed. 'Yes, I am. Could I please have some cornflakes?'

I pulled the high-rise tray in front of me and she placed my breakfast on it. With a sharp pang of nostalgia, I realised that I hadn't been served breakfast since I'd left the children's home. It was such a simple gesture, but it meant so much to me.

The breakfast lady placed a small card and a pen on the tray. 'Tick what you want for lunch, and I'll come back for it in a bit.'

I looked at the menu while I ate. I ticked jacket potatoes and salad, and for dessert I ticked apple crumble and custard. My mouth practically watered at the thought; I hadn't had that in ages!

'I can't stand hospital food.' Julie interrupted my thoughts.

'Umm,' I said non-committally. But inside, I felt sure I'd like it very much. It would be a wonderful change from what I'd grown used to.

Once I finished eating, I pushed the table away and adjusted the bed to lie flat. Azmier was fast asleep, and I felt tired, too, so I pulled up the covers and lay there thinking of how I'd been looked after when I was younger, how the kindest, loveliest woman I had ever known was Auntie Peggy, and how she had treated me with care and consideration all the time I was with her in the home. I vowed that I would be like her; that Azmier would grow up knowing love and feeling protected. That, in other words, I wouldn't be like my mother. I felt a power I hadn't had before; it came from Azmier, and my love for him, and my need to protect him. Smiling at my son as he lay in his cot, I quickly fell asleep.

The next two days were wonderful. I spent them doing the same things I'd done my first morning: waking up, taking a shower, feeding Azmier, eating and sleeping. Sometimes Julie and I talked, sometimes I read magazines, and sometimes I just watched my beautiful son.

It was after lunch on the third day, just after I'd changed Azmier's nappy and was placing him back in the cot, when I heard Tara's voice behind me.

'What are you doing?'

I spun around and saw her standing at the foot of the bed. Julie was giving her daughter a bath, so Tara and I were alone in the room. I smiled at her, glad that someone had finally come to see me. 'I've just changed his nappy. He's awake; would you like to see him?'

I expected her to say yes, and started to turn around to pick him up, but all she said was, 'Has anyone been asking questions about the baby?'

I straightened up, and my smile fell. 'What do you mean?' I thought she'd be happy and excited to see my baby.

'You know what I mean,' she snapped. 'Has anyone been asking where the father is?'

I frowned. 'No. Why would they?'

At that, she turned her back on me and walked away. I stared after her. She hadn't asked me how I was or how the baby was, how much he weighed or if she could hold him, or even if I needed anything. Before I could make a move, though, she retraced her steps back to my room.

'The nurses told me you're coming home in two days,' she said, and now I heard a hard edge in her voice. 'I'll come and pick you up about lunchtime.' And then she strode out. This time, she didn't come back.

When the day came when I was to leave the hospital, I had to ask the nurse if I could keep the clothes Azmier had on, as I didn't have anything of my own for him to wear. I also asked if I could keep one of the blankets.

The nurse gave me a sympathetic look. 'Well, we're not supposed to, but we'll make an exception in your case.'

'Thanks,' I said, relieved but wondering what was so special about 'my case'.

I changed into the clothes I'd worn when I arrived; they were now very loose. In my cardigan pocket I found some coins, and, after counting them, I jingled them in my hand. I bagged a few cotton nappies to take home with me, then sat and waited. Time crawled by. One o'clock. Two o'clock. Where was Tara? Three o'clock. It was way past lunchtime now. Four o'clock. I got tired of waiting. I decided I would just take the bus home – I had enough change – so I picked up Azmier and went to the nurses' station and told them I was leaving.

'Has someone come to pick you up?' one asked me in surprise, looking around.

'No,' I said, trying to keep my voice steady and firm. 'I'm taking the bus home.'

Both nurses gasped and looked at me with shocked expressions.

The first one cleared her throat. 'I can't stop you taking the bus, Sam, but you'll have to wait a bit longer so I can take you to the entrance.'

'Okay, that's fine,' I said. 'Where shall I wait?'

'Why don't you go back to your room. I'll come and get you in a few minutes.'

So I went back and sat on my bed. By now it was four fifteen and I was getting more impatient than ever. I was just about to go back to the nurses' station when Tara walked in.

'Are you ready?' she asked.

'What kept you?' I demanded. 'I've been waiting for ages.'

'I told you I would come and get you, didn't I?'

I looked at her and shook my head. 'Let's just go,' I said.

As I followed her past the nurses station, one said, 'Oh, good! Someone has come for you. We were getting a bit worried at the thought of you taking the bus home.'

Tara looked back at me. 'What, you were going to take the bus home? Are you mad?'

'I didn't think anyone was coming to get me.'

'She's mad,' Tara said to the nurse and kept walking.

'No, I'm not!' I snapped at her.

She stopped at that and gave me a cold stare. I stared right back. I'd never stood up to her before, but now I felt different. I had my baby, and I had to be strong for him.

Tara looked away first. And she didn't speak a word to me as she drove me home.

As we walked into the living room where Mother sat waiting, the first thing Tara said to Mother was, 'She's been really cheeky.'

The car journey had tired me out, and I sat down without arguing. Mother came over and took Azmier from me, telling me to go and rest and not to worry about the baby. But there was something I didn't like; I didn't trust them with my baby. I saw Azmier in my mother's arms, and I could see me there too, and it was also what she said – 'Let me look after him' – and I thought, What, like you looked after me? I recoiled in horror at the thought. So I reached out and took Azmier from her. 'It's all right,' I said. 'I'm not tired.'

Mena came in just then, her hands and half of her face covered in flour. I started to laugh as she stared at the baby. She looked at me and asked with a puzzled look on her face, 'What are you laughing at? I'm not going to pick him up, if that's what you're thinking. I was making the *rotis* but couldn't wait to see the baby.'

'I know,' I said, still chuckling. 'There's as much flour on your face as there is on your hands.' Mena wasn't very good at cooking. She tried, but the food would always be undercooked or burned. 'Who's that, Azmier?' I asked, lifting him. 'Is that your silly auntie trying to be a clown?'

'He's lovely!' Mena said, coming a few steps nearer. 'Look at those tiny fingers! The *rotis* can wait; I'm going to wash my hands so I can hold him.'

I looked up thankfully at her departing figure. Hers was the first positive reaction to my baby from the family, and it meant a lot to me.

At that point Azmier started to cry because he was hungry. I took him to my room to feed him. Mena came in after a few minutes and sat down next to me. She watched with an amazed expression on her face as he suckled hungrily.

'Doesn't that hurt?' she asked.

'A bit. Have you finished cooking? I'm starving.'

'Oh! Of course you would be. I'll go and get you some food.' She returned a few minutes later with some hot chicken curry and rice, which, although it wasn't what I'd craved in the hospital, tasted lovely. I ate it in no time.

That night, Azmier slept in my bed as there was no cot for him. He didn't even have any clothes other than the ones they'd given me at the hospital.

The next morning, a nurse came to check on Azmier and me, to make sure everything was all right and that we had everything we needed. I was embarrassed to admit that I didn't have any clothes for my baby. She glanced around my bedroom, then asked where the baby slept, so I told her.

'I'll try to get you a cot and some baby clothes,' she said.

And that evening she came back with a cot and four big bags of clothes.

Mena and I managed to put up the cot in the corner of the room while Mother went through the clothes. It suddenly struck me that she'd known that if she didn't buy anything for Azmier, the nurse would bring what he needed. That made me angry, that my own family wouldn't even buy new clothes for my baby, when Hanif had everything she needed, and more. Mother sorted the clothes into piles and put away the ones that were too big for him right now. I looked at the remaining clothes, which were second-hand but fairly new and clean. There was also a bag full of blankets. I took out a few, put them into the cot, and laid Azmier on top of them.

Over the next few days, I discovered how nice it was to have someone else to fuss over. Giving attention to and taking care of my son was more fun than anything I had done in such a long time. It reminded me of playing dolls with Amanda all those years ago, except that it was more important and more satisfying. And it helped me focus on something positive, which was a big change.

One night when I got up to feed Azmier, I looked closely at him as he nursed. His eyes were open and gazed into mine as he fed, then, when he'd had enough, his lids drowsily came down and his beautiful lashes fluttered as he slowly settled into sleep. I looked down at him and felt his chest rising and falling as he breathed in and out. His life was so precious to me that I made him a promise, whispering so as not to be overheard: 'You won't go through what I went through. I won't let them do that; you won't be sworn at, cursed, slapped or hit in any way. I promise. I won't do that to you, and I won't let any of them, either. I'll protect you from all of that. You won't have to do what they want, you will be whatever you want to be, and blossom like a flower.' And I bent my head and sealed my promise with a kiss on his forehead.

14

Manz bought a hardware store when Azmier was eight months old, and Mena went to work there. Once again, after months of sharing all the chores with Mena, I had to do everything myself, which exhausted me. As the weeks and months went by, however, I found that my motherhood counted for nothing with Mother around. She always knew better. If I wanted to do something for Azmier, Mother knew a different way. I couldn't take him out. I couldn't feed him the things I wanted to. I couldn't pick him up when he cried. Mother said if I picked him up every time he cried, he'd get into the habit of being fussed over.

The same rules didn't seem to apply to Tanvir and Saber's child. Sham was born less than a month after Azmier; they took Sham out all the time, dressed him the way they wanted, fed him whatever they wanted, and Mother herself picked him up when he cried. Why couldn't I do the same for my son?

Although I was busy, I always made time to feed, change and play with Azmier. He was a happy baby and didn't cry much, certainly not as much as I remembered Hanif's babies doing. He was potty-trained at fourteen months and started to walk at about the same time. When Sham took his first steps, Tanvir and Saber were over the moon, and so was everyone else. When Azmier started walking a week or two later, other than me no one noticed except Mena, who gave him a sweet and kissed him.

There was no word from Afzal after my mother sent him news of Azmier's birth, no birthday cards, nothing. I wanted Afzal to come over and look after us but because he didn't make any effort even to ask about his son, I felt let down at first. But then – as always – I knew I had to pull not only myself through but Azmier too. I had to focus on how I was going to protect him. It was hard at times; I would cry while Azmier was sleeping in my arms.

I told him stories that I'd learned as a girl from the books we had in the children's home, and sang him songs that Auntie Peggy had taught me as she cuddled me on the settee. I made up loads of stories about children living in the woods on Cannock Chase, and told him those night after night, when no one else was listening.

But I was changing. I'd started to stand up for myself more. I'd go into town with Azmier when I wanted; I'd say no if I felt I didn't want to do something. As the months went by, I grew in my independence. Dad was my example for this. When Azmier was nearly two, Dad, who had been staying with us for a few days, went out for something. He came back holding a bag and walked into the kitchen where I was standing. 'Move!' he shouted. This made me jump, I hadn't been shouted at by Dad before. He looked around and saw a pot he wanted to use but it needed a wash so he flung it in the sink. 'Wash it!'

I did as I was told, scared and trembling. Mother, Tara and Mena, hearing all the commotion came into the kitchen.

'What are you doing now? What are you in here for? Get out!' Mother shouted.

Dad turned around and shouted back, 'Fuck off, you bitch!'

That's when Mother told us all to run into the bedroom while she called the police.

The others ran out of the room. I walked slowly, turning my head to look at him. It was really refreshing to see that side of Dad; it was the awakening I needed, a sign for me to do the same. I mean if Dad could do it, then I could do it too; that's what helped me to start to develop the courage to stand up to them.

The police came and called for an ambulance. Mother told them he was acting in this way because he hadn't taken his medication and that he needed an injection to calm him down. Dad went away with them quietly. But I felt different; he had given me something, though he didn't even know it.

Mother used the visit from the police to scare Azmier: 'If you are bad, then the police come and take you away,' she told him. 'They put you in a room on your own and leave you there without any food or water and beat you if you try to escape. So always be a good little boy and do what I tell you.' I was very angry that she'd said this to him, as he was scared by what she'd said, but it was too late for her to take back the words.

I was even more angry the day she told him to call me Baji, or big sister, which is what Mena and I called Tara. I said to her, 'No, that's not right, I'm his mother and he should call me that.' She shouted that I was too young to be a mother, that I looked like a girl and she didn't want her new friends asking awkward questions. Suppose someone said I shouldn't have a baby at that age and took him away from me? I reluctantly agreed, because I was ashamed of the fact that I was a mother at fourteen, but when she was out of the room I taught him to call me Mum. If we were in front of her in her room, and he called me Mum, Mother would say, sternly, 'What did you call her?' Azmier would quickly say Baji, fearing her anger. I got a smack for standing up to her, but that seemed a small price to pay for hearing my son call me Mum.

I started having a dream, one that came night after night. I would feel very lonely, and realised I was in a room, an attic room, high above people I knew and could hear. There were boxes heaped up, all round the room, and glass cabinets with jewellery on the shelves, sparkling in the dim light. Someone – I'm not sure who – would say to me, go on, take a piece, it'll be fine, and I'd look through the cabinets until I found one that I liked best. It was a pendant, heavily tarnished but with a brilliant red rose shining beautifully out at me. I'd reach out to touch it, but always wake up before I could, and I'd lie awake, staring at the ceiling, wondering what it meant. In the morning, I'd be dissatisfied and irritable with everyone for a while.

However, my new independence soon brought the same old troubles down on my head. After a few months of owning the hardware shop, Manz bought another shop, a fruit shop, on the same street as the first. He told Mother to send me with Mena in the morning. I refused; who would look after Azmier? There was no way I wanted to leave him with Mother. 'I don't want to work for you for free,' I said. 'I'm already a slave around the house, and now you expect me to be a slave in your shop, too.'

And so Manz's beatings, for so long something left behind in the days before Pakistan, began again. When I was left bruised on the floor, with Manz towering over me, yelling, 'You're coming to help in the shop. Mum can look after your stupid boy and anyway, Tanvir's here. She can look after him,' I realised I had no choice.

Mornings up till now had been a joy, waking up to hug my son, to see his eyes open, and to begin the day with him. We'd eat breakfast, I'd start my chores, and he'd play by my feet as I did so. The following morning I was up and ready to go before he'd even stirred, and when Manz beeped the horn, expecting Mena and I to come running, I gave Azmier a quick kiss on the forehead and rushed out before I sobbed over him.

Manz parked on a side road by the busy high street. Shops lined either side of the road and Manz led the way to the hardware shop. Mena took the keys from him without speaking and let herself in. 'This way,' he said to me, without looking round, so I trailed after him along the road to a shop called Green Pastures, where he unlocked the shutters.

I looked at the shelves, lined with tins and jars on one side, and a counter on the other. Manz interrupted my thoughts. 'First, you get the potatoes ready. The sacks are in the corner.' He pointed towards the back of the shop. 'Weigh five pounds of potatoes in the scales next to them, put them in a bag, and tie it. Then stack the full bags neatly over here. When you've done that I'll tell you what to do next.'

I started work in the corner but of course it wasn't good enough for him. 'You're not going to get very far like that. Move, I'll show you how it's done.' He picked up an empty bag. 'You fill the bag first,' and he put a bunch of potatoes into it. 'Then you weigh them. See? Nearly five; that will do.' I didn't bother to say that his bag was way under five pounds, and that anyone could see that, as I didn't want another thump. He took the bag off the scale, tied it closed, and placed it on the floor nearby. Just then a customer walked in. 'Carry on, and don't be slow.'

I started to weigh and bag the potatoes, but all I could think about was Azmier. Had he woken up yet? Would someone give him breakfast? Or would he have to cry for them to notice him?

After a while, when I'd finished the potatoes, I went over to Manz and said, 'I'm hungry, can I get something to eat?'

He replied, 'Yes. And get Mena something, too, while you're about it. But hurry up.'

I didn't know what to eat so I decided to go and ask Mena what she wanted and have whatever she did. I walked down to the hardware shop, passing a bakery on the way. It was quiet in Mena's shop, and she was pleased to see me. 'How's it going?' she asked, smiling. I told her, and asked her what she wanted to eat. 'Go down the road to the bakery and get me some sandwiches, will you? Egg mayo, please.' And she reached into the till and passed me a five-pound note. I got myself a pasty and a cream cake, and Mena her sandwiches, and took them back to her shop where we sat behind the counter and talked while we ate breakfast.

'Don't you get bored, coming here every day?' I asked.

'No, not really. It's better than sitting at home and getting slapped and sworn at by Mother.'

That was true, but I had my son to worry about. 'Yes. I hope Azmier is all right. I wish I could have brought him with me.'

'I'm sure he is going to be fine, Sam. He's a tough kid,' said Mena as she finished off her sandwich. 'You'd better get back, now, you don't want Manz mad with you again.'

Manz had orders for me the moment I walked in. 'I want to teach you how to work the till so I can go to the cash and carry tomorrow. Are you watching? You punch in the numbers and hit this key. That's all you need to know. Go and pick a few items, and pretend to be the customer while I show you how to use it.'

I went and put a few items in a basket and brought them to the till where Manz showed me again and again how to use the till. Once I'd mastered it, I served customers for the rest of the day.

When we arrived home that evening, I was weary as we walked in but as soon as Azmier rushed up and hugged me I felt better. Nobody had ever greeted me as warmly as he did and I loved it. I held him tight, kissing him all over his beautiful face and making him laugh. 'Did you have a good day without me? Did you miss me?' I said. He giggled, then said he wanted his dinner. Mother appeared; I must cook dinner tonight and make sure I cooked enough for everyone's lunch tomorrow at the same time, so that Azmier could be fed during the day.

I set Azmier on his feet and headed to the kitchen, cursing them all under my breath. I'd spent a day standing at the till in the shop, and now all I wanted to do was sit and rest – just like Hanif and Tanvir. Instead, I had to cook for everyone else, and make their lunch too. I made curry and rice, enough for today and tomorrow. After Azmier and I had eaten, I put him in his cot, and went to bed myself. By eight o'clock, we were both asleep.

It seemed only moments later when Mena shook me awake. 'Sam, Sam!'

'What?' I said blearily.

'Hurry up, Manz is going to be here soon.'

It was the same as yesterday; Azmier was still asleep, so I kissed him and off we went, and when we got to the shops Mena headed for the hardware shop and I went with Manz. I helped him stack the shelves, then got breakfast for me and Mena. Before I left Manz said, 'Come back in fifteen minutes. I have to go to the cash and carry.'

Eating some sandwiches with Mena, I told her that I was nervous about being left on my own in the shop. 'What if something goes wrong? What if I charge the wrong amount? I don't want to be left alone in the shop.'

'That's how I felt when I was left on my own for the first time,' she said. 'But it doesn't matter if you make a mistake; just apologise. Look, if you really get stuck, ask someone to come and get me. I'll shut this shop and come down and help you for a while.'

Surprisingly, Manz too tried to sound reassuring. 'You'll be okay,' he said before leaving. 'Look, it's not that busy at this time of the day. I'll be back in about two hours.'

I hoped no one would come in to the shop but of course there were dozens of customers as soon as Manz left. I was so busy serving them that I didn't notice the time go by until Manz returned with a vanload of stock.

'Come and help me unload the van,' he said.

A 'How have you coped?' or a 'Well done for handling things on your own,' would have been nice but of course Manz said nothing of the sort. I helped him unload the van, and for the rest of the afternoon re-stocked the shelves and served customers. By mid-afternoon, I was tired and hungry. I wanted a drink but Manz said, 'No. We're going home soon. You can have something when you get back.'

I drifted off to sleep on the way home. In the kitchen I searched through the fridge and the cupboards, only to find there was nothing ready to eat. Azmier had complained he was hungry when I'd walked in, so I made some toast for both of us, but we had to eat it dry because there was no butter. With this inside us, I started making curry.

Smelling the cooking, Mother shouted from the bedroom, 'Don't make rice today, Sam. Make *rotis*.'

Azmier was in there with me, so I counted to ten, slowly. I still stuck my tongue out at her, which made Mena smile. 'Look, Sam, I'll help you with the *rotis*. You give Azmier the first one I make. He seems really hungry.'

Azmier gobbled it down greedily.

'He's not normally this hungry, Mena,' I said. 'I don't think anyone's feeding him.'

That night I hid a plate of food under my bed. Mena saw and asked, 'What are you doing?'

'What do you think? We'll have something to eat, now, when we get home tomorrow!'

At the end of the next day, just before we were ready to go home, I said to Manz, 'Mother said we're running low on some things at home. She wants me to bring some bread, eggs, butter and milk.'

'Well, hurry up and get it,' he snapped. 'I need to lock up.'

I put all the items Mother had asked for into a bag and slyly sneaked in a couple of chocolate bars, too. When we got home, I slipped the chocolates under my pillow, and then went into the kitchen.

'Once again, nothing to eat,' said Mena. 'And I'm starving.'

I put my finger to my lips, miming shh at her, then went to retrieve the plate of food I'd hidden yesterday. I pulled it out, heated it up in the microwave, and split it between Mena, Azmier and myself. We ate it along with some bread while I made dinner for everyone else. From then on, I got into the routine of hiding food each night so that Azmier could eat as soon as I got home.

Being away from my son all day was horrible, because it was obvious that he wasn't being looked after properly. Mena and I would come in and he'd always be hungry, and no one had thought to give him a bath or even clean his face or hands. I had no idea what he'd done all day and if I asked he always seemed to be happy, but I knew that he wasn't being played with or paid much attention.

I'd feed him, bathe him, read stories and sing to him, play games with his fingers or toes, and then settle him into bed, and it would tear into me that he needed more from me than I could give. He needed me with him all the time, and I'd lie on the bed watching him sleeping in his cot, and pray for a miracle to happen. What I wanted I couldn't describe, I just knew that I wanted him to have a better life than I had had.

While I was in the shop, I'd think about him, and what our life would be like if we ran away together. We'd find a little house somewhere, with a garden, and we could play in the sunshine together all day. I'd smile to myself, but then Manz would say, 'What are you doing? Daydreaming, huh?' And if there was no one in the shop, he'd cuff me, and my dream would be over once more.

15

Azmier's third birthday was quiet, as no one remembered except Mena and me. I'd hidden some chocolates in my pockets while working in the shop, and when we were alone, just the three of us, we gave him the chocolates and said, 'Happy birthday.' Sham's birthday, three weeks later, was different: Tara gave him a toy, Mother some new clothes, and Tanvir and Saber got him more of everything.

That night, Azmier (who was sleeping in bed with me now that he'd outgrown his cot) tossed and turned in his sleep, and I thought he must be a bit hyper from the day. I put my hands out to comfort him, gently so as not to waken him, and touched him on the back. He flinched. I didn't know what to do. He was sleeping, and I didn't want to wake him up and see what was wrong; I couldn't put on a light to look as I'd wake Mena. I waited till morning, and, when it was light enough, lifted up the back of his shirt.

My heart stopped. There, in the middle of his back, was a huge bruise, a fresh one, one that couldn't have happened because he'd fallen down the stairs to the cellar or banged against something in the garden. Silent tears slid down my face. My own little boy was being beaten, as I had been; I'd sworn to protect him and I'd failed. Just then I noticed that he'd also wet the bed – something he'd never done before.

Azmier turned round, ready to smile at me, until he saw the tears in my eyes, and he put his arms round me and said, 'Don't cry, Mama.' 'It'll be all right. Shh.'

I smiled at him, as I recognised the words as those I said to him when he was crying. I wiped my cheeks and hugged Azmier back. 'You're right, sweetie. It'll be all right.'

Then I got him up and dressed, and quickly stripped the bed. I put his pyjamas and the sheets in the washing machine, so that no one would know what he'd done, and that no one would hit him for wetting the bed. We ate some toast and then it was time for me to leave to go to work; I could hardly bear to leave him behind, I was so worried about what was going to happen to him without me there to take care of him.

On the way to the shop, in Manz's van, I came to a decision; we would run away, they'd left me with no choice now. I'd pack a suitcase and we'd go, anywhere, just away from here.

I waited till I could go on a break and told Mena while we ate. 'Where will you go?' she asked.

'I don't know,' I answered. 'Anywhere must be better than here.'

'But where will you live? What will you do? Don't go, Sam. They'll find you and kill you or take you back to Pakistan and leave you there.'

I looked at her; she was right. They would come looking for us, for sure. And what would they do if they found me? Would they send me to Pakistan? They'd hurt me; maybe they'd even kill me. Such things weren't unknown in our community. And because nobody knew me here, no one except the family, nothing would happen. Even Mena wouldn't speak to the police, considering how frightened she was of everyone. And what would happen to Azmier then?

All right, then, it wouldn't be easy. But I'd find a way, somehow; I had to get Azmier out of there. I had nowhere to go, no money to travel with, and no one to protect me from them. I was stuck here, for now, and I would have to find my own way out, but I had to come up with something.

For the next few days, I thought and thought about what I could do, but nothing came to me. Then one evening I came in and went to the kitchen to cook dinner, only to stare in surprise: there was Mother, surrounded, as always when she cooked, by dozens of open packets and bowls and dirty saucepans in the sink. All that cleaning up, I thought – why? Mother explained, 'We're expecting a guest tomorrow. Get more butter out. Pass me the onions.'

More mouths to feed, on top of all that cleaning. Mother bossed me about as if I didn't know my way around the kitchen, as if it wasn't me who cooked for her every night. 'Take down that large saucepan for me. Wash that bowl.' I understood why when, as she chopped the onions, she told me, 'Hajji Osghar is coming tomorrow, from Pakistan. His family are very rich and well-known. Now, don't make the curry too spicy. I'll prepare what I can tonight, and I'll cook the rice tomorrow.'

Of course: Mother wouldn't want Hajji Osghar going back home to tell his family and friends that she didn't look after him or feed him properly. That's why she was in here tonight; I bit my lip as I tried not to laugh at her.

You were called Hajji if you had been on the Hajj, that is, been on a pilgrimage to Mecca. It was a mark of honour, to be called Hajji, and so the following evening when we came home. I was expecting to see a pious-looking man with a beard wearing a white hat on his head, just like the man who taught us the Quran, in the sitting room. But I was told, instead, to wash up; not only had they eaten already, they'd even fed Azmier – a first – and then left the rest for Mena and myself. We sat down in the kitchen and ate before washing-up. We'd just finished when there was a knock on the kitchen door and a young man, clean-shaven and wearing jeans and a T-shirt, walked in.

'Hi, I'm Osghar. Can I wash my hands?' he said. He smiled nicely at us, and he spoke so politely and quietly that I paused; no one ever spoke like that in this house.

'Yes, of course,' I said. His manners were refreshing compared with what we usually got on our return from work. I handed him a towel, and he smiled again.

Just then Manz walked in and said, 'Are you done? Let's go, and I'll show you around town.'

After they left, Mena and I looked at each other and smothered our laughter behind our hands.

'Oh, my God! He certainly doesn't look like a *Hajji*,' I said, blushing. 'He looks *nice*.'

Mena let out a tiny gasp. 'You're married, Sam!' she said teasingly.

'Oh, yes.' I'd forgotten that, I really had. 'Well, there's no harm in looking!' And we burst out laughing again.

I was the first one up the next morning. I woke Mena, and then headed to the kitchen. Osghar, already there, smiled when I walked in; we said 'Good morning' politely to each other, but I couldn't ask him anything else as Manz came in and said it was nearly time to go. I made toast for everyone, and we left.

Osghar came with Manz and me, and later in the morning went with Manz to the cash and carry. When they got back, I went out to help unload as always, but Osghar looked round at me as he pulled boxes from the back, and smiled as he said, 'No, it's okay, thanks. We can manage.'

I nodded my thanks and went back into the shop, a warm glow inside me. Seldom did anyone from my family look at me when they spoke to me, usually, and nor did they speak so nicely to me. And I was smiled at all the time – it made me feel different, I wasn't used to it. Having Osghar around was great; he was kind and helpful, but he'd leave soon and then I'd be back to the same routine.

That evening I was finishing the washing-up, and told Azmier it was bedtime. He rushed out of the room and I heard him say to Osghar and Mother, 'Shh, don't tell her I'm in here, I'm hiding.'

When I followed him in, I could see him behind the curtain. I said loudly, 'Has Azmier come in here? It's his bedtime.'

Osghar joined in, smiling with me. 'I haven't seen him anywhere.'

'Hmm. I wonder where he's got to?'

'Maybe he's in the garden?' Osghar said, as I quietly stepped to the window.

I yanked back the curtain and said, 'Boo!'

Azmier screamed and laughed as I picked him up. 'No, not bedtime yet!' But he was gleeful and happy.

The next morning Manz was out and so Osghar stayed in the shop with me. After a few minutes of fiddling with the items on sale by the till, he said hesitantly, 'Your mother told me a story last night.'

'What?' I asked.

'I was surprised to find out that you have a three-year-old son. You don't look old enough. So I asked your mother how this could be.'

'And?' I pulled my arms around me, waiting to be judged.

'She said you slept with a man in Pakistan so they had to get you married to him.'

I felt a cold wave of anger sweep through me.

'But I don't believe her,' he hurried on, seeing my face.

Tears sprang to my eyes. I couldn't believe Mother would lie like that to a family friend. I should've known she'd twist things her way, of course, but it hurt all the same to hear it from Osghar.

'Hey, hey. I'm sorry,' he said gently. 'I didn't mean to upset you.'

'Oh, it's okay. I should have got used to the lies by now,' I said, wiping my eyes and blowing my nose. 'Do you want to hear the truth?'

He nodded his head.

'My mother tricked me into going to Pakistan when I was thirteen and forced me to marry someone I didn't know.' I told him the whole story. All the feelings I'd kept pent up so long – anger, frustration, misery, loneliness – I let out, and doing so made me feel better immediately. I hadn't realised how little I'd been able to speak about what happened; I couldn't tell Mena everything because she didn't want to know what might be facing her, too.

'So I'm seventeen now,' I carried on, 'and have a three-year-old son who I love but can't be with because I'm stuck in this stupid shop while he is at home. You know, yesterday was the first day I got home and found that Azmier wasn't hungry and that he was clean. Just the other day, I found out that they're hitting him when I'm not around. Now he's wetting the bed.'

I was suddenly embarrassed that I'd told a virtual stranger so much. 'I don't know why I'm telling you this. But you asked for the truth, and I swear this is all true.' Of course I knew why I'd told him; his kind eyes and gentle manner were something I'd not experieced for so long. I was just responding to his kindness.

Osghar paused, and then said, 'I don't know what to say. But what kind of mother would do such a thing?'

But at that moment Manz walked in and we had to stop talking.

Manz came over to me. 'You have an appointment with the immigration solicitor tomorrow. He wants you to sign some papers.'

SAMEEM ALI

'What papers?' I asked. What was he talking about?

'Just sign them when I take you tomorrow and don't ask any questions!' Manz shouted. Osghar looked at the floor.

I remained quiet all that evening. After dinner, Osghar again came into the kitchen and asked if he could wash his hands.

'I'm sorry about today,' he said. 'I didn't mean to upset you.'

'It's okay. I needed to get it out,' I said. 'I feel better after talking to you.'

He turned from the sink with his hands dripping, and I reached forward with the towel for him, and our fingers touched, briefly. We both looked into each other's eyes.

Tanvir walked in and broke the spell. 'Do you need anything, Osghar?'

'No, I'm fine.'

He put the towel down and followed her back to the sitting room.

I couldn't sleep that night, lying awake for hours thinking about Osghar. Something different was going on, and I couldn't tell what, not yet. I knew I should still be angry and frightened, but all I could think of was Osghar's smile, and the touch of his hands as I held out the towel for him.

In the morning, Manz asked Osghar if he'd stay with Mena while he took me to the solicitor's for my appointment.

I'd completely forgotten about this appointment. What could it be about? Why did I have to go? What could I possibly need a solicitor for? Was I getting divorced? Was there some problem with Azmier's birth certificate? Though I wanted to, I knew I couldn't ask Manz, as he'd just shout at me. Mena gave me a questioning look, and I returned a tiny shrug.

At the solicitor's, after Manz and I had sat in the waiting room for a while in silence, a tall man took us into his office and asked me to take a seat. It all made me feel very small, though I'm sure he didn't mean me to; his smart suit and accent, his large office with a huge mahogany desk, and papers stacked up on it, all seemed designed to intimidate me.

'I just need you to sign a few papers in relation to your application for your husband to come to Britain,' the man said.

The floor beneath me suddenly rolled sideways, and I had to grip the arms of the chair tightly. My husband? What? I never thought about that man in Pakistan that way. My throat filled with fire and rage but I couldn't say anything, not in front of this man. So that's why Manz wouldn't tell me – he'd tricked me, like Mother did, to get me here. I felt his eyes on me, making sure I did nothing to upset his plans. I realised, through the buzz in my head, that the solicitor had put some papers down in front of me.

'Please sign here,' he said as he marked a cross at the bottom of the first page, 'and here.'

Manz leaned forward, and put one arm on the desk next to the papers while he turned to me and gestured with his other arm for me to do as the solicitor asked. To an outsider, it might have looked like a brotherly gesture of affection, a 'look, let's do this together' gesture. I knew differently: the menace was clear. My hand shook as, with no choice, I signed the documents.

'And lastly here, please.' When I had finished, the solicitor signed them to – 'I'm just witnessing your signature here,' he explained – and slipped the papers back into an envelope which he placed in a tray in front of him. 'Thank you. I'll submit your application to the immigration office. As soon as I hear from them, I'll be back in touch.' And he stood up to lead us to the door.

I didn't say anything to Manz all the way back to the shop.

Inside, though, I was seething. That – that *man* – he didn't have an identity for me, he was just a man who had hurt me and then made no effort to contact his son – coming here! I would be expected to cook for him, I supposed, and to wash his clothes. I almost gasped with horror in the car – we would have to share a bed again.

Not that. Not that. I couldn't allow that. The thought of him touching me was disgusting.

And Mother and Manz, filling out those forms, as if I'd done it! How dare they? I suddenly realised that if they hadn't had to be witnessed by the solicitor, Manz would probably have forged my signature and not told me anything about it. I'd have come back from work one evening and there *he* would be, Azmier on his lap as if all that had passed was nothing.

My fury was so great that I had to turn to look out of the window, so Manz wouldn't see, and start breathing slowly and deeply to try to calm down as Auntie Peggy had shown me to help me control my stutter all those years ago. It didn't work now.

When we got to the shop I paid no attention to anything Manz said until it was time for me to go over to eat lunch with Mena. 'Send Osghar over here when you get there,' said Manz.

Mena started to question me straightaway. 'What was the appointment about?'

'Hang on, I'll tell you in a minute.' I said to Osghar, 'Manz wants you back at the other shop.'

'Okay. See you later,' he said, and as he left he gave me an encouraging smile, one I couldn't return.

'Come on! Tell me what happened,' said Mena.

As soon as the door shut behind Osghar, I let it all out. 'They're bastards! They've gone behind my back and filled in the forms to invite *him* over here. He has never written to ask how his son is. It's been more than three years! There's never even been a birthday card on his birthday. Who the hell do they think they are? I don't want him over here but I couldn't say anything because Manz was breathing down my neck. What am I going to do, Mena, tell me, what am I going to do?'

Mena was as shocked as me. 'Mother and Manz are inviting your husband over?'

'Yes! Mena, I don't know him, I can't even remember what he looks like. I stayed with him for a few months, got pregnant, and came back to Scotland. All I remember is that he is a horrible person who hurt me. I don't believe we got married. I didn't take the vows. I didn't understand what the *molvi* was saying. He can't come over here, Mena, he just can't.'

'But, Sam, what are you going to do?'

'I don't know yet, but I'll think of something. There's no way I want him over here.'

We were both silent; I was waiting for Mena to say something that would help me, but instead she sighed and said, 'I don't know about you, but I'm hungry. Will you go and get me a bag of chips, please?'

I stared. Didn't she understand? Obviously not. 'Okay. Give me some money.'

I went to the chip shop, where I was standing in the queue when suddenly I felt a touch on my arm. Osghar was there, smiling at me; he'd been in front of me in the queue and had come to join me when – as I was lost in thought – I'd failed to see him waving me forward.

After we'd talked about what we were going to order, Osghar said, 'Manz told me what your appointment was about, and by the look on your face when you walked in, I don't think you're happy about it.'

Osghar knew my story from our conversation the day before, but I didn't know if I should tell him what was going through my mind, not then, so, as we left the shop, I said, 'I'll talk to you later. Manz must be waiting for his food. If he catches us together too often, he'll start watching me like a hawk, and I don't need that at the moment.'

Osghar nodded and went on his way; I went back and sat with Mena, where we ate in silence as my brain buzzed with half-formed thoughts and plans. I just couldn't see any way out that would actually work.

At home that evening, Mother came into the kitchen after dinner. 'You won't be going to the shop tomorrow,' she said. 'I'm going shopping with Tanvir and you will stay here with the children, to look after them.' And she walked out.

I was so excited – a day at home with Azmier, all to myself. Somehow the evening went by and even that night things didn't seem too bad, because I could be with my son. The next morning, after everyone else had gone and I'd washed up the breakfast dishes, Azmier and Sham and I played games. Hide-and-seek in the house, and tag in the garden. We'd stop and I'd sit Azmier on my lap, Sham beside me, and tell them a story, and then they'd jump up and we'd start again. I wished every day could be like this.

The boys were racing around in the garden when I went inside to prepare lunch. There was a knock at the door. I went to answer it and found the postman waiting on the doorstep, a large flat brown envelope in his hand.

'Letter for Sameem Aktar. Sign here, please,' he said. I signed for it and shut the door, staring at the envelope. A letter for me? What could it possibly be? I certainly wasn't expecting anything; no one ever sent me anything.

I tore open the envelope to find my passport and a letter from the Pakistani embassy stating that they were returning the passport after stamping it with a visa to Pakistan.

It wasn't enough for Mother and Manz to plot to bring that man over here – now it looked as if they were going to send me to Pakistan to collect him. I wanted to smash up the flat in my fury, I wanted to tear the place apart. Instead I calmly walked into the bedroom and hid the passport under my mattress, then went back and got the boys lunch. I went through the rest of the chores like a zombie, without feeling anything. I felt dead inside. How could they do this to me?

When Tanvir and Mother returned from their shopping trip, laden with bags of material to make new outfits with, they also brought in a new suitcase. I asked them why.

'I'm going to Pakistan,' Mother said. 'It's sort of an emergency trip. Do you want to come with me?' she asked before adding, 'I'm going next week.'

'No, not really,' I said, as casually as I could. 'Who would look after Azmier? Would you like your lunch now?'

I gave them their lunch and then returned to the kitchen to cook the dinner. I was glad, for a change, to have to do this, as it meant I could keep out of their way. I chopped and sliced slowly and carefully, imagining all sorts of horrible things as I did so.

When, I wondered, were they going to tell me? Would Mother have packed my bag for me, and come in the car with Manz as if we were going to the shop? Oh, look it's the airport, let's go away, shall we? How would they have managed it? Did they imagine I was so scared of them they could do as they wanted?

At six o'clock Mena came in, trailing behind Osghar and Manz. They ate the dinner I had prepared, and then Manz said he was going out and would be back in a few hours. Mother went to bed because she was tired from the shopping trip. Saber and Tanvir were out anyway, and Mena said she was having an early night and went to bed around seven thirty. Azmier fell asleep by eight.

I went to sit with Osghar in the living room. He looked questioningly at me, and I said, 'No, it's okay, they're all asleep.' I looked down at my hands folded in my lap for a while, and then I took a deep breath: 'They're sending me back to Pakistan, Osghar. Getting the papers signed by the immigration solicitor was for when he comes back with me. They sent my passport to the embassy to get a visa stamped in it, and Mother's going next week. She wants me to go with her. They don't know I've found out about their plan, though,' and I looked at him as I said this. 'The postman brought my passport back today while Mother was out, so she doesn't know I've got it and that I know what they're up to. I can't go, Osghar, I can't; and I don't want that, that man to come here, ever.' My rage stopped me from feeling sorry for myself, stopped me from crying; instead I was boiling inside.

Osghar was shocked and after repeating back to himself some of what I'd said, sat silently for a while. 'I can't believe it; how could they do this to someone like you, Sam?' And those words made me hold my breath, just for a moment.

'What are you going to do about it?' he continued.

'I don't know.' I twisted my fingers, round and round, as if searching for a solution. 'I want to take Azmier and run away somewhere where they'll never find us.'

A silence, which Osghar broke. 'I'm leaving in a few days. Come with me.'

16

I just stared at Osghar. Go away with him? Away from all this?

He continued, 'I'm going to Manchester to stay with some friends down there.'

'What?' I finally managed to splutter. 'You're joking!'

'You want to leave; I am leaving,' he said, as if it were the most logical thing in the world. 'I'll make sure you and Azmier are safe. Look, when I came here, I bought a one-way ticket to the furthest place I could think of and got on that plane. You've been to Pakistan, you've seen what it's like there, I don't want to go back to that right now. I won't pretend it's going to be easy, because it's not. But I've got some money I've saved and a will to work. I promise to look after you.'

As I listened to his calm voice, I wondered if this were the miracle I'd been praying for. Was this the answer to my problems?

'I'll have to think about it,' I said, standing up to go. He stood up, too. He kissed me softly on the forehead and took me gently in his arms. It was the first time someone had comforted me physically, touched me tenderly, other than Mena, since I'd left the children's home ten years before. I didn't want him to let me go. I felt safe and secure.

The next evening, after a routine day at the shop, I came home to find Mother packing her suitcase. 'I'm going to Pakistan tomorrow,' she began, when suddenly Manz interrupted her.

'What about Sam? Isn't she going with you?'

'Her passport hasn't arrived yet. But, Manz, you make sure you send her to Pakistan as soon as it comes.'

This sent a shudder down my spine and I couldn't help asking, 'Why do I have to go? I don't want to.'

There was a tremendous thud on my back. I screamed as my knees buckled and I fell to the floor. Manz's fist was poised to punch me again, when Osghar ran into the room. When he saw what was happening, he pulled Manz back.

'You're going to Pakistan to get your husband!' Manz shouted at the top of his voice. 'Do you hear me? Do you hear me?'

'Are you out of your mind?' shouted Osghar, shoving him away from me into the living room, standing in front of Manz and saying angrily, 'You should never hit your sister. Or any woman.'

The door shut behind them, muffling their argument so that I couldn't distinguish the words.

Mother looked down at me. 'You asked for that,' she said in a sour voice. 'It serves you right.'

I ignored her, because I had something else to think about. Instead of feeling bruised by Manz's blow, I felt surprised that Osghar protected me. Nobody ever had before; no one had ever stood up for me. No one had ever had the courage to stand up to Mother and especially not to my brother. But Osghar did and he did it for me. I felt humble; someone cared for me, actually cared enough to question and object to the way I was being treated. Suddenly I knew he was the answer to my prayers; I knew I wanted him to protect me for ever.

I rose to my feet, and pressed my hand against my lower back as I went into the kitchen, where Mena had taken Azmier to be out of the way. Osghar came in and looked at me closely.

'Are you all right?' he asked.

'That was nothing,' I said, managing a weak smile. 'Most times, that's just a warm-up.'

Osghar poured some water from the tap into a glass and handed it to me. He then poured another glass and took it through to Manz, who was still shouting.

'She is not going to Pakistan, huh? Yes, she fucking is, even if I have to kill her and send her in a fucking body bag.'

Mother was in too much of a rush that evening to notice anything around her, and she didn't see that I felt happy. I couldn't wait for her to leave. I was worried that ... might find my passport; it was good that she was leaving so soon as I couldn't have hidden the fact my passport was already in the house for another few weeks because Mother or Manz would have made enquiries.

That night I lay wide awake in bed, unable to sleep. I could hear Osghar and Manz talking in the living room until two in the morning. I made up my mind that I was going to leave with Osghar. I couldn't stand the beatings any more, or the thought that Azmier might suffer as I had done. I'd had enough. No, I'd had more than enough. It didn't matter what Osghar had planned or what we would do; anything was better than living this nightmare. I didn't know what the future held, I only knew that if I stayed here I would have no future. Osghar had a calm manner, and I felt comfortable with him; more than that, I couldn't think about. Anyway, after Manz's threat about putting me in a body bag, I no longer felt I had the option to stay. And if anything happened to me, who would look after Azmier?

The next morning, no one spoke on the drive to the shops. When we got to the veg shop, I went straight into the back and started to weigh and bag the potatoes until Manz called me.

'Get behind the till. I'm going to take Mother to the airport. Come on, Osghar, let's go.'

'I thought I'd go and buy some shoes today,' Osghar said. 'Could you drop me in town on the way to the airport?'

'Sure,' said Manz, and Osghar left. Mother reminded Manz to send me to Pakistan as soon as my passport arrived; I didn't let the look on my face give away what I was thinking – *never in a million years* – I just smiled at her and nodded my head. She'd lost her power over me; I was no longer the frightened little Sam I had once been, cowering from her attacks on me; I was a grown woman, whose life was her own business, and not something to be decided by her. I'd had enough of her, and it was so easy to stand there and let her speak, knowing all the while that nothing she said meant anything to me at all any more. I was going to be free of her!

Finally they drove away; I didn't watch them go, I turned my back and went into the shop. She was going away – but so was I.

I'd been alone in the shop for about twenty minutes when Osghar returned empty-handed.

'Where are your shoes?' I asked.

He shrugged and gave me a disarming grin. 'I couldn't find any I liked.'

'You couldn't have looked properly.' Despite the way I felt – shook up and anxious – I smiled at him. 'You haven't even been gone half an hour.'

His face turned abruptly serious. 'I came back because we have to talk. I'm not leaving you here on your own. I love you, Sam, and I want to take care of you. And Azmier, too.' He pulled a ring out of his pocket. 'This is what I went into town for, Sam. Will you marry me?'

Everything froze. Except my heart, which started thumping wildly. 'Have you forgotten? I'm already married.'

'No, you're not.' His voice was fervent. 'You were too young, you didn't realise what was happening. You didn't even know what the words meant. So is that a yes or no?'

It was as if someone were wiping away a stain; it seemed so right. Of course I wasn't properly married, I had had no idea what was going on. All my life I'd been kept in the dark; now here was Osghar, welcoming me into the light. Everything suddenly seemed brighter as hope rose in my heart – I had a future, I would be happy! 'Yes, of course I'll marry you!' I slid the gold band on my finger. 'I made up my mind last night that I was going with you. I can't take it any more. So what's the plan?'

'The plan? Well, your mother has gone. That leaves your sister-in-law in the house. We have to figure out how to get your suitcase out without anyone knowing.'

I only had to think for a moment. 'Oh! She's taking Sham to the doctor tomorrow because of his bad cough. I'll have to stay at home to look after Azmier while she's gone. We can leave as soon as she goes.' And now that everything was falling into place, my stomach filled with butterflies.

Osghar held my hand tightly in his. 'Are you sure you want to do this?'

I nodded. 'Yes, I'm sure. I've never been more sure of anything. But I am a bit nervous. And I do have to tell Mena. I can't leave without saying goodbye to her. She is going to miss Azmier.'

Osghar and I worked out the plan for the next day. Before he let my hand go, he leaned forward and kissed me on the lips, gently. I felt the touch of them on me for the rest of the day.

That night I took Mena aside in the kitchen, when no one else was around.

'Mena, I have to tell you. I can't stay here, not with what I know they're planning for me. Osghar has asked Azmier and me to go with him, he wants to marry me, I have to go. I'm leaving, tomorrow.'

'What?' she cried. 'No, no, no! You can't go!'

'Shh! Keep your voice down,' I warned. 'If anyone hears . . .'

'Oh, Sam, Manz will find you and kill you. Then who will look after Azmier?'

She was right about Manz, I knew it. If he found out what I was planning he'd probably hurt me so badly I wouldn't be able to walk. Or worse. But I also knew that this was probably going to be my one and only chance.

'Look,' I said, clasping Mena's hands firmly in mine. 'If anything happens to me, I want you to look after Azmier, all right?'

She nodded and broke into tears. That set me off, and we held each other tightly as we wept.

'You do understand, don't you, Mena? I have to do this. I can't watch Azmier go through this torture any more. He needs love and care, not a slap here and a punch there.'

'I know. And I do understand why you're doing it. I'm just scared that if Manz finds you . . . I don't want to imagine what he'd do to you.' We hugged and cried some more.

I knew Mena would be all right, that no harm would come to her. She knew how to take care of herself: when anyone shouted at her, she'd cry; if they asked her to do something by herself she'd cut her finger or something, to make sure she wasn't asked again. She was more worldly than me, and she knew that she'd never be given any credit for anything so it was best just to keep her head down and let things go on around her. She knew ignorance was bliss, and she kept with it. I was the one who didn't know; or, rather, knew otherwise, as I had learned from Auntie Peggy. I was the one looking to please my family, the one always looking for a substitute for Auntie Peggy's love. As I held her thin body tightly in my grasp, I knew they wouldn't pick on her once I was gone.

Finally we pulled apart. As we dried our tears, Mena said, 'You take care and look after my favourite nephew. And try to keep in touch.' She paused. 'No, don't. Just look after yourself.' She looked at me, and tears started to her eyes again. 'I don't believe this is happening.'

'I love you, Mena.'

'I love you, too.'

The next morning I got up and made everyone breakfast. Mena came into the kitchen before leaving, gave me a hug, and whispered, 'I'm going to miss you. I love you.' Then she picked up Azmier and held him tightly to her. 'I want you to come back when you're older. And don't you dare forget me. I love you more than anyone in this world.'

I tried to swallow down the lump that rose in my throat as she stopped in the kitchen doorway and turned back for a last look. 'Goodbye,' I mouthed. 'I love you.'

And she was gone.

I listened for Manz's van to drive away. So far, so good. I took Azmier to my room with me, needing to make sure he didn't repeat anything Mena had just said to him where Tanvir might hear. I told him a story using both of my hands as characters, being sure to tickle him and make him laugh.

Finally, Tanvir came in. 'I'm going now. I should be back in an hour.'

'Okay,' I said, trying to keep my voice steady. 'I hope Sham feels better.'

A few moments later, the front door slammed shut. I raced to the window and peeked out, waiting until Tanvir and Sham were well away. When I was sure they wouldn't come back in, I raced to the other room to get a suitcase.

This one case would have to hold everything I wanted to take with me, so I packed carefully, even though in my haste, I was tempted just to throw things in. Several shalwar-kameez for me, an old bra, two extra pairs of shoes and a few bits of jewellery; my passport with its unwanted and now unneeded visa to Pakistan. I filled the rest of the case with Azmier's clothes.

Azmier decided this was a fun new game, and he kept taking things out almost as soon as I put them in. Normally, I would've played along with him, but there just wasn't time today. 'Azmier, no, not now, sweetie, I need to pack this case,' I scolded him, but not too harshly. 'Just sit quietly and watch Mummy do this. We're going to go on a train today, won't that be fun!' I kept my voice bright, trying not to sound as nervous as I felt.

Finally, the case was packed. I zipped it closed and put it near the front door. I walked around the rest of the flat; Osghar's case was in his room and I set it next to mine. I didn't feel sad at all to be leaving the flat behind; as a home, it didn't mean anything to me. Next I went into the kitchen and made some toast for Azmier. A snack would be good in case it was a while before I could feed him again.

I'd just wiped the last of the crumbs from his face when a knock came on the door. Even though I expected it to be Osghar, my heart pounded in my ears as I went to it. A quick look through the peephole proved it was. And though I breathed a sigh of relief, my heart didn't slow down. After all, I was running away. I hadn't said those words to myself before now, and saying them made my palms sweat. I realised that I was more scared than I had ever been before.

I opened the door. Our eyes met, but we were both too tense to smile. 'Are you ready?' asked Osghar.

'Yes. Here are the cases. Can you put them in the taxi while I get Azmier?'

While he did that, I picked up my son and carried him to the front door. Osghar was back by then and held the door open while I walked out.

'Have you got everything?' he asked.

I nodded, and he closed the door. I didn't look back as I walked down the path to the taxi. It was 17 November 1987, and I was leaving home at last.

'Central Station, please,' Osghar told the driver. To me he said, 'I bought the tickets before I came to pick you up. The train leaves in twenty minutes.'

I couldn't speak. Azmier sat on my lap, looking out of the window and pointing things out as we drove. I trembled as we walked into the station. I kept a firm grip on Azmier's hand while Osghar wheeled my large suitcase and his own small one towards the trains.

'It's platform eight,' said Osghar.

We walked quickly on to the platform, Azmier trotting along beside us. I picked up Azmier carried him on to the train, and found seats while Osghar stowed our luggage. I peered out of the window as we sat down, looking for Manz or anyone else I knew and willing the train to leave. Ten minutes to go. Anything could happen in those ten minutes. My fear drove me to imagine all sorts of things, all of which I knew were foolish, which is why I didn't mention them to Osghar.

What if Tanvir had come home, found that we weren't there, and contacted Manz? He could be on his way.

He could be in the station.

He could be on the train right now coming to grab me by the hair and pull me away. My heart beat so fast and loud I could hear it.

'Where are we going, Mummy?' Azmier asked.

'We're going on a journey on the choo-choo train, darling,' I said, pulling him closer to me. 'Shh. Look out of the window and tell me when we start moving.'

'Everything's going to be all right,' Osghar said, trying to reassure me as he sat in the opposite seat. 'It should take us four hours to get to Manchester. I'll phone my friend when we get there.'

Then I jerked in my seat.

'We're moving, Mummy!' Azmier was right. The train had finally started to move.

'Yes, we are,' I said, hugging him. My mind began to calm as the train pulled out of the station. My shoulders relaxed and my heart stopped racing.

Manz couldn't catch us now. He couldn't harm us any more. We were safe.

For much of the journey, we kept Azmier entertained. Osghar laughed along with Azmier at the silly story I told about two naughty boys who played tricks on passengers as they rode on a train. I made up more stories about Cannock Chase, and the goblins in the woods.

Azmier looked up at me, innocently enquiring, 'Was your mother there?'

An image jumped into my mind; not Mother, no, but Auntie Peggy. 'No, no, she wasn't,' I said to Azmier, and he turned and looked back out of the window, cheerfully telling us what he could see flashing past. I gripped Osghar's hand tightly as I realised what I must always have known: that Mother, while she might have borne me, showed me little care and even less love; and that if I thought of the woman who brought me up, showed me that love, taught me to be strong, gave me the values I lived by, it was Auntie Peggy, and it was her face that came before my eyes. She was not my mother, yet she was more of a mother to me than my own. My throat was dry, and Osghar went and got me a drink.

'Did you pack any of his toys?' Osghar asked. 'I can get something out of the case for him to play with.'

I swallowed. 'He doesn't have any toys.'

'You forgot to pack them?' Osghar asked in surprise.

'No, I mean he doesn't own any toys. The ones in the house are all Sham's.'

Osghar stared at me for a moment, then shook his head.

Not long after that, Azmier fell asleep with his head in my lap. Osghar told me that his friend would help us find a place to live and he would find work wherever he could to support us, while I could stay at home to look after Azmier. I didn't talk much. I still couldn't believe I had run away, that I was sitting on a train headed south and my family didn't even know it. Surely Manz would try to find me, and what would that mean for us? For all three of us. I could no longer think of just myself and Azmier, because Manz would try to hurt Osghar too if he caught up with us. I shut that thought out of my mind.

I looked at Osghar and smiled. Here we were on the road to nowhere, with no money, no food and no roof over our heads. And it didn't seem to matter. For the first time in ages, I knew what it meant to feel free, and to be happy with someone. I barely knew this man, but I did know he was kind and gentle, and I knew I would be safe with him. That we'd both be safe.

We arrived in Manchester at three in the afternoon. Osghar phoned his friend, Iqbal, who arrived within fifteen minutes.

'I can only put you up for a few weeks,' he said. 'I've just bought a house and haven't handed in the keys to the council house where I used to live yet. You can stay there for a while.'

Iqbal drove us straight to the house and handed over the keys.

'This is the front door key and this is the back door key,' he said as he led us into the house.

It smelled damp and was quite dirty. The living room was furnished with a three-seater black couch, and there was a small table in the corner of the room. The walls were grubby, it was cold, the gas fire looked broken. The floor was covered in a shabby grey carpet. The kitchen, at the back of the house, had a window over the sink and a bare concrete floor, and a four-burner cooker that looked as if it had never been cleaned. The only other item was a clean saucepan in the sink.

We went upstairs and looked at the bedrooms. They were in better condition than downstairs. The first room had a double bed with a bare mattress. The carpet was clean and the window in the corner looked over the back garden. The next room also had a bed and was decorated with teddy-bear wallpaper and had a brightly coloured carpet. The bathroom was filthy. Osghar looked at me, and I could see that he was worried about what I was going to say.

'Well, it's going to need a lot of cleaning,' I said. Then, watching Osghar again, added, 'But I'm used to that and it won't be too much trouble for me – after all the years of practice I've had I'm not worried about that!' I didn't add, because Iqbal was there, that it felt like a palace because my family wasn't there. Instead I was with Osghar and Azmier. I'd be cleaning for myself and those I loved – what a difference!

We made our way downstairs. 'Where are the nearest shops?' Osghar asked. 'I'll have to buy some bed linen and food.'

'I'll take you in the car. Sam can stay here with the baby,' said Iqbal.

Osghar gave me a quick hug. 'I'll be back soon.'

I sat on the sofa and Azmier came and sat next to me.

'I like it here,' he said. 'Is that my room? The one with the teddies on the walls?'

'Yes, it is. Your very own room, all to yourself.' I hugged him.

He wriggled out of my arms and ran off shouting, 'I'm going to play in my room.' I smiled. Azmier sounded like a normal three-year-old. Cheerful and lively, without a care in the world. Whatever happened next, it was worth it to hear that happy tone in his voice and to know that he was safe.

I sat there and a vision of my mother came before me. I knew she'd be angry, angrier than she'd even been before, when she realised that all her plans for me were over. I didn't care; she was too far away for me to fear any more. I lay down on the settee and listened to my son's happy giggling as I drifted off to sleep.

Two hours later Osghar returned with bags of shopping. He had got a couple of blankets and some food. Azmier ran downstairs shouting Osghar's name, and Osghar gave him one of the bags. 'That's for you,' he said.

'What's inside?' asked Azmier.

'Open it and find out,' Osghar said, catching my eye and giving me an impish grin.

Rahin opened it and pulled out a toy car, some crayons and a colouring book. At the bottom were some sweets and crisps.

'What do you say to Osghar, Azmier?' I prompted.

'I'm going to play in my room!' he shouted again, running back upstairs.

I laughed and didn't bother to correct him, while wiping away some happy tears from my eyes. 'Thanks,' I said to Osghar. 'From both of us.'

'You must be hungry,' Osghar said. He went into the kitchen and put the bag of groceries on the worktop. 'I got some paper plates and cutlery,' he called to me. 'I didn't get a saucepan because I noticed there was one here.' He opened a can of vegetable soup, heated it in the pan, and poured it into the bowls he had bought. Then he set it on the table in the living room with some bread.

'Come on, eat,' he said to me.

'You eat. I'm not really that hungry.'

'What are you thinking?' he asked.

I sighed, trying to compose my thoughts. 'I feel happy but lost. I don't know what to think. I know I'm on the first stepping-stone and there's a long way before I reach the end. Things can only get better, but it's scary.'

He came over to where I sat and took one of my hands in his. 'You're not going to be alone. I'm right here. We're lost together. It's going to be hard, but I promise you we'll get there, wherever 'there' is. Come on now, you have to eat.' He tugged my hand and pulled me to my feet.

I went to the hall and called for Azmier to come down and have some food. We all ate, not realising until then how hungry we were. The soup was gone in no time, and we wolfed down the whole loaf of bread.

After the meal, I put the sheets on the beds and gave Azmier a blanket. It was getting late, so I told Azmier to go to bed, which he did without a fuss but insisted on sleeping with his new toy car.

'Goodnight, sweetheart. Sweet dreams.' I kissed him.

'Are we going to stay here?' asked Azmier. 'I like it here.'

'Yes. We'll have to find a new house soon, but we're not going back to Glasgow again. And we'll go and find you a nursery tomorrow so you can make some friends.' I kissed him again and sat with him, stroking his hair and humming lullabies to him. Once he was asleep I tiptoed downstairs to where Osghar was sitting on the sofa.

'I thought I would go out and look for work tomorrow,' said Osghar. 'Iqbal said he's sure he can find me a job working in a clothes factory.' He shrugged and smiled. 'It's better than nothing.' He stood up and, moving towards me, took me in his arms. I knew I should feel embarrassed – perhaps even a bit awkward – but I didn't. It felt right to me, and so I leaned in towards him and turned my head up to look into his eyes. He kissed me. 'How are you feeling now?'

His lips were soft and gentle. 'I'm fine,' I murmured as he kissed me once more. 'Very fine.' All I wanted, right then, was for him to kiss me again.

'Shall we go upstairs where it's more cosy?' said Osghar.

I nodded.

We got into bed and cuddled up to each other. I felt comfortable and safe in his arms. I felt, for the first time I could remember, that I was cherished for who I was and not for some service I could provide. Lying there with him, memories of being happy as a small girl flooded back to me, and I wept a bit as I thought how seldom I had been happy in my life. Osghar just held me, and I realised that the love I felt for Azmier wasn't all the love I had, that I could love Osghar too, and that the years of burying feelings inside me were all over. Suddenly my life was like a dream and I didn't want to wake up.

We didn't make love, but Osghar stroked my face gently until I fell asleep.

17

In the morning, the sun shone through the net curtains and I wondered what time it was. I thought I had slept in and cursed Mena for not waking me up before she left for the shop.

'Good morning. What's the time?' asked Osghar, rolling over to face me.

How could I have forgotten where I was? And how strange and wonderful to wake up in a strange house, next to the man of my dreams! A giddy feeling swept over me.

When I didn't answer him, Osghar asked, 'How do you feel this morning?'

'Alive and on top of the world,' I replied.

'Love does that,' he said, winking at me and reaching for his watch on the windowsill. It was eight o'clock.

We were wondering whether to get up or not when we heard Azmier shout, 'Mummy, where are you?'

'I think we should get up,' we both said at the same time.

I made a simple breakfast and it was ready just as Osghar came downstairs, and we all ate together. Iqbal picked up Osghar at ten to go and look for work. I stayed at home with Azmier. I cleaned up and got ready to go out exploring the neighbourhood. I wanted to get to know where we lived. I took Azmier by the hand, and we went for a walk.

It was very quiet. The avenue was lined with trees, and I could hear birds singing all around. But I didn't go far because I didn't want to lose my way. When we got home, I sat with Azmier and we coloured in his colouring book. I prayed that Osghar would find work.

When he returned two hours later, it was with the good news that he had found a job.

'Let's go out, and I'll show you where the shops are and the bus stops into town,' he said.

We walked out of the avenue and down the road. 'All the buses from here go into town,' he said, 'and there are a few shops around the corner.'

On the main road there was a school.

'Oh!' I exclaimed in delight. 'We have to go in and ask if they have any nursery places.'

I led the way to the entrance. The school seemed quite small, and the walls in the hall were decorated with pictures of Jesus and Bible scenes drawn by the children. I was struck by a sudden pang of nostalgia for my own nursery school; it seemed to me to be just like this one, only in my mind a lot bigger.

At the office, I asked if they had any nursery places, and the woman said I'd have to talk to the nursery teacher and pointed me towards a door. I knocked on the door and it was opened by a tall woman who looked first at me and Osghar and then, catching sight of Azmier, smiled.

'Can I help you?' she asked.

'I was wondering if you have a nursery place for my son. We've just moved into the neighbourhood.'

After asking a few questions, she said they had a few places left and Azmier could start on Monday the following week. He'd only be there for the mornings but at least he could start playing with other children and make friends.

As we walked back to our house, I finally began to feel that this was all real. Osghar had a job, Azmier would be going to nursery, we even had a house to make into a home. My prayers really had been answered.

Our wedding took place six weeks later, just a few days before Christmas. It was a quick ceremony, and the only guests were two of Osghar's friends acting as witnesses. Osghar went back to work the same afternoon. We couldn't afford to go out for a meal to celebrate our marriage, so I put Azmier to bed early and had a candle-lit meal ready when Osghar came home that evening.

Although we'd slept in the same bed each night, we hadn't made love; we had talked about this and agreed to wait until we were married, so when, after the meal, we went upstairs and got into bed, we didn't hesitate. I no longer feared intimacy, and, when Osghar reached for me, real passion took over. The bad memories I'd carried with me for so long were swept away in a flood of pleasure.

'I love you,' he said as I lay in his arms afterwards.

'I love you, too.'

The next morning I was awakened by Osghar saying he was off to work. The sun poured through the open curtains.

'Do you *have* to go to work today?' I asked.

'Yes, I do.' He leaned over and gave me a passionate kiss that didn't change my opinion. 'And you have to get up and take Azmier to nursery. But I wish I could stay home.'

'Well, tonight then,' I said with a smile.

That day was the first day of the rest of our lives.

Over the next few months, we settled into our new life. Osghar worked six days a week and earned enough to get us on our feet. We bought a fridge, a television, plates, dishes and cutlery. We developed a routine. I took Azmier to nursery, had a quiet cup of tea while I read – the bliss of having time to read, with no one to tell me I was being idle or to snatch the book out of my hand – then cleaned the house. At midday I made lunch, then went to get Azmier.

One evening, Osghar came home at the usual time, we had supper, and I put Azmier to bed. We were cuddling on the sofa when there was a knock at the door. It was Iqbal, who needed to talk to Osghar. I went upstairs to do some ironing.

For the most part, I just heard the rumble of their voices, though at one point I heard Osghar say, 'Where will we go? We haven't a place lined up yet. Give us a few more weeks.' My stomach dropped. That could mean only one thing.

Soon after that, the door shut and Osghar came upstairs. He sat on the bed, his shoulders hunched, almost as if he were deflated. 'He said we've got to leave first thing tomorrow. We can put our things at his house until we find a place to live. He'll help me move them tomorrow.'

Fear rose up in me, but I didn't want Osghar to know. He'd done so much, and I hated the way he looked defeated at this first obstacle. After all, so many things could have gone wrong, but none of them had. 'Don't worry, Osghar. We'll find somewhere,' I said, trying to make my voice sound as reassuring as possible.

But I couldn't sleep that night. I kept thinking about where we'd move to. We had no money saved for a deposit for rented accommodation, as we'd had to spend everything Osghar earned on buying the necessities. I turned to the only one I knew who could help. I prayed and finally fell asleep.

The next day, matters didn't seem quite so daunting. I just knew somehow that things were going to be okay. Iqbal helped put our belongings in his garage and then he went to work.

'Let's go to the council,' I said. 'I'm sure they'll give us a place. We have nowhere to go.'

18

In the reception area of the housing office, there was another couple with two children waiting. We went and sat in the far corner, and Azmier ran off to play with some toys in another corner. After fifteen minutes a lady came from around the back and sat behind the desk marked Enquiries. 'Next, please,' she called.

I looked at the couple who were already waiting, but they said, 'Go ahead. We're already being seen.'

Osghar and I moved over to the desk and sat down.

'Can I help you?'

I hope so, I thought. 'We have nowhere to live,' I said.

The housing officer, called Linda, started by asking us a lot of questions. 'How long have you been in Manchester? Where have you lived for the past few months? Is this your husband? Why is he not working?'

I explained how we came to be in Manchester. I couldn't tell her Osghar was working, because he didn't have a work permit. Of course, I couldn't mention that either. As a matter of fact, his visa was due to expire in a few months, and we hadn't had a chance even to begin taking care of that. I couldn't worry about that now. First, we had to find a place to stay; we'd sort out everything else afterwards. I told her that I'd run away from home, that we'd come south to stay at a friend's house but he'd kicked us out and we needed somewhere to live. Linda listened sympathetically and told us to wait while she saw what she could do for us.

We returned to our seats and waited. And waited. We had got there at ten and it was now two. We were hungry and our anxiety was growing. It would be dark in just a few hours; if the council couldn't place us, where would we stay? The other family had left an hour ago. They had been given shelter until the council could house them properly. Surely they could do the same for us, couldn't they?

To pass the time, I told Azmier more stories about the woods at Cannock Chase, stories that reminded me of a time when I was happy. When he grew too restless, he ran off to play with the toys again. Osghar looked down at me in surprise as I leaned into him and let the tears fall down my face. 'It's okay,' I said, 'I'm just tired.' I smiled at him. 'I'm glad I'm here with you. Not here, I mean,' I said, looking around the office, 'but here, now, with you. We'll be okay, I'm sure; someone is looking out for us, and we'll be all right.'

Finally, Linda came out and said she had good news. 'There's a flat we could offer you,' she said with a smile. Osghar and I exchanged relieved glances. 'It's in a homeless complex, and you could stay there until we can find permanent accommodation for you.' She gave us the address, showed us where it was on a map, and said that the security guard would be expecting us.

The flat wasn't far from the house we'd been living in. We bought some chips on the way, and Azmier ate them hungrily. When we arrived at the building, the security guard explained the rules.

'You have to be in before ten p.m. or you won't be allowed in, and if you have friends or family coming, they have to report to me first,' he said sternly. He led us up to the first floor and opened the door to the flat on the right. Then he handed us the keys and walked away.

The flat had two rooms, a bedroom and a sitting room, with a very small kitchen. The bedroom looked bare with only three single beds lined up on the back wall. The sitting room had a two-seater settee, badly stained, and a small and scuffed dining table in the corner in front of the window. The kitchen barely had room to turn around in. There was an electric cooker on one side and a small worktop and cabinet on the other, and under the window opposite the doorway was the sink. It was somewhere to sleep, but it wasn't a home, not yet. But it was ours – the first place that I could call my own, where no one could come and tell us to leave, or, worse, order me about or hurt me. Not even my mother. I went back into the bedroom and lay down, dizzy but also energised; here was a place we could all be together, at last. Azmier lay down beside me.

Osghar came into the room. 'You've been on your feet all day,' he said. 'You and Azmier have a rest, and I'll go out and get something to eat for tonight.'

I nodded, closed my eyes, and fell asleep. I dreamed that I was floating in the air with Azmier and Osghar by my side. Then I was being shaken awake, and I groggily opened my eyes to find Osghar leaning over the bed, saying that there were police officers at the door asking for me.

My sleep had been heavy, and as I stumbled to the door, I felt disoriented, as if I were still in a dream.

There were two police, a man and a woman, standing in the hallway. 'Are you Sameem Aktar?' asked one of them, the woman. 'Yes.'

'Could we come in? We need to talk to you.' I hesitated a moment as my heart leaped to my throat, then held the door wide to let them in. Azmier, standing in the hall, ran into his bedroom as soon as he saw their uniforms. I led them into the sitting room.

'What do you want?' After my doze, my mouth was dry and the words came out as a squeak.

'We need to see that you and your son are all right. Where is your son? Can we see him, please?' asked the policewoman.

Puzzled, I went to the bedroom to get Azmier. I didn't see him anywhere at first and realised he must be under the bed. 'I haven't done anything wrong!' he cried out when I looked. 'Mummy, please tell them not to take me away. I promise to be good. Please, Mummy, please!' My heart broke as I recalled Mother threatening him that the police would take him away if he was naughty.

I crouched next to the bed. 'Shh, Azmier love, shh. They haven't come to take you away, silly. They have come to see if you are all right. Come on out,' I said softly as I put my hand out for him to hold. He slowly crawled from under the bed and grabbed my hand. I picked him up, and he clung tightly to me. He was shaking with fear as I carried him into the sitting room. I explained to the police why he was so afraid.

The policewoman shook her head and something like anger flashed across her face, as if these words of my mother hurt her as much as they had hurt me.

The policeman smiled gently at Azmier and said, 'Oh, no, young man. We don't take children away. That would make their parents very sad. We like to help people. We're here to help your Mummy. Is that okay? Can we help Mummy?' Azmier gave him the tiniest of nods. 'That's grand. You're a brave boy to take such good care of your Mummy. Would you like to come with me and see the police car?'

Azmier shook his head, but he was no longer clinging tightly to me.

I, on the other hand, was growing more and more tense. 'Could you tell me what all this is about, now?' I asked.

'Do you know anyone called Manz?' asked the policeman.

'Yes, he's my brother,' I replied. I looked around for Osghar but he had gone out of the room to close the front door.

The policeman's eyebrows shot up in surprise, but his voice remained calm as he spoke. 'Three men were arrested just outside Manchester this afternoon. When we searched their car, we found your name and an address and some equipment that they were going to use to restrain you and your son. They have made full confessions, and have told us that they were under instruction from Manz to return the pair of you to Glasgow, in any way possible. No matter what it took. If they couldn't bring you back, they had other plans.'

At this, I felt the blood drain from my face and sank down on to the settee, clutching Azmier even more tightly to my chest.

'Are you all right, Sameem?' asked the policewoman.

Osghar came in just then. The policeman told him what he'd just told me, spelling out the address, saying that the men had been there, looking for us. Osghar sat next to me and put an arm protectively around my shoulders.

'I don't believe it,' I said, shaking. 'That address was where we were staying until this morning. We moved into here today.' Tears started to pour down my face. 'Just this afternoon!' What if we had still been there? What if Iqbal hadn't asked us to move out that morning? 'Where did they get the address from?' I asked.

The officers shook their heads. 'They said that your brother gave it to them.'

Osghar gasped. 'I threw my old address book away the day before we left. I'd copied everything into the new one I had bought. He must have got it out of the bin when we left.'

The policeman nodded. 'That might be it. Sameem, could we ask you to come down to the station and make a statement?'

A knock on the door startled me, but the policewoman said, 'That must be DC Blackly. I'll let him in.' A moment later another officer came into the sitting room and introduced himself to us.

'It's a relief to see you're all right, Sameem,' he said. 'We have arrested Manz in Scotland and are bringing him down here.'

'I don't want to see him!' I blurted out.

'You won't have to,' DC Blackly assured me. 'All we need is for you to come down to the station to make a statement.'

I finally snapped. Losing our house, waiting in that office, moving into this small place, police arriving to drag me out of my sleep – all that had sapped my energy to the point where I couldn't stand up any more. I was tired to my very core, and I had almost no strength left to deal with the world today. And now this; I had run away from my family, and the hatred and fear they inspired in me, yet it seemed that I could not run away far enough. 'What statement? I shouted. 'All I want is for everyone just to leave me alone and let me live my life the way I want to. Why can't they understand that?' This outburst made Azmier cry. Osghar extracted him from my arms and took him out of the room, closing the door as he went.

The policewoman sat where Osghar had been, took my hand and held it as I struggled to calm myself. When I stopped crying, the policewoman handed me a handkerchief, which I used to dry my eyes. 'Sameem,' she said, 'we'll look after you. You won't have to see anyone you don't want to see at the station, but we do need you to come down to help us understand what's going on. It's better we go there because it'll upset your son less. Okay?' And she smiled at me, encouraging me.

Dabbing at my face, I nodded, and stood up. 'I'll just let them know I'm coming with you,' I said to the three officers.

I went to check on my son. Osghar had given him a biscuit and he was playing happily with a teddy bear and a truck. Osghar looked at me expectantly.

'I have to go and make this statement. I'll be back soon. Take care of Azmier.'

'No,' said Osghar. 'We're coming with you.'

'I don't want to take Azmier down to the station,' I said. 'He's happy here playing with his toys. He's been through enough today. You'll do fine taking care of him. You always do.'

Osghar reluctantly agreed.

DC Blackly walked me to an unmarked police car. The two uniformed officers returned to their car. I was silent on the way to the police station, turning over everything in my mind. How could Manz do this to us all? What was he thinking of? What would Mother say when she found out? What would happen to them now – if Manz was in trouble, who would run the shops?

We arrived at the police station. As we got out of the car, DC Blackly asked, 'Do you know why your brother did this?'

'He wants me to go back to Pakistan,' I said. 'If I wouldn't go willingly, he probably would've drugged me and put me on a plane, and I would have woken up in the middle of nowhere in Pakistan.'

'But why? You're eighteen. You're old enough to make your own decisions about your own life.'

I shrugged. 'That's what he was planning before I ran away from home,' I said. I saw he wanted to ask me more but he knew that it was best to wait until we were sitting down in an interview room. I looked at my feet, keeping my head down as he led me along a corridor; I didn't want to see, even accidentally, the men who had been sent for me.

He showed me through a door. 'I'll get a police officer to take a statement from you,' said DC Blackly as he left the room.

I sat on one of two chairs; the only other piece of furniture in the room was a small table. The room had no window and the walls were covered in dreary grey paint. A few minutes later a policewoman, carrying a file, entered the room.

'Hello, Sameem. My name is Theresa. How are you?' she asked in a friendly voice.

'I'm fine,' I lied.

'I need to take a statement from you, but first I'll tell you what's happened. A colleague and I stopped three men on the motorway for a routine search and found nunchucks, baseball bats and some knives in the boot of their car.'

I couldn't help but gasp when she told me this.

'We arrested them and brought them to the station,' she continued. 'After interviewing them, we found out that they were being paid to kidnap you and the baby and take you back to Scotland. Afterwards they would be paid more money. During the interview they gave Manz's name as the person who gave them the money. One of them had your name and address and the name of your son in his pocket. They told me that if they couldn't get you to come home with them, then they were to deal with you and bring the boy back.'

I shook as she told me this, thinking about what might have happened, of the weapons in the car that might have been used on me if they'd found us. Because I would never have let them take Azmier, and I would never have gone back.

'Are you all right?' she asked sympathetically. 'Could I get you a drink?'

'We just moved out of that house this morning,' I said, trembling. I looked upward. Someone surely was watching over us.

'Are you sure you are ready to make a statement? Let me get you some water before we start.' Theresa left the room and came back a moment later with a glass of water.

'Okay. Shall we get started?' she asked.

'I don't know what you want to know. I can only tell you why he may have done what he did. As I told DC Blackly, he wanted me to go back to Pakistan and I didn't want to go.'

I thought that giving my statement would be a short process, but it ended up taking two hours. Theresa went over every little detail and wrote everything down carefully for me to check and sign. I was exhausted afterwards and didn't say a word in the police car on the way back.

Azmier was asleep when I got home, but I lay down on the bed and hugged him tightly anyway. After a while I tucked him in and went back into the front room, where I told Osghar everything that had happened.

'Are you okay?' Osghar asked when I'd finished, taking me in his arms and holding me. 'It must have been hard talking about it for two hours. I was worried sick about you. I love you. And you're right; someone is watching over us and I hope he always will.'

19

I awoke the next morning feeling unwell. My head was heavy and I felt sick. It didn't seem such a surprise after the events of the previous day, but Osghar was worried and took me to the doctor.

After asking me about my symptoms, the doctor asked me to lie down on the bed behind a movable screen. Osghar waited on the other side. She felt my stomach, and then said, 'Did you know you are pregnant?'

'What?' Osghar and I both exclaimed together.

She laughed. 'I guess that answers my question. I'll have to run some tests to be sure, but it feels like you're about three months along.' Osghar came around the screen and hugged me. 'So I can't give you any medication. Besides, all your symptoms are just the normal signs of pregnancy.'

'We're going to have another baby,' he said, grinning. I hugged him back, feeling scared and happy at the same time, but right then I loved him even more. Another baby, he'd said, and although I'd never ever doubted his love for Azmier, this was proof, if ever I needed it.

Over the next few months we had a lot of planning to do. I was worried that we didn't have a proper house to raise Azmier in, never mind another baby. Meanwhile, I got bigger and bigger. My feet began to swell and I started to have nose bleeds.

When I was pregnant with Azmier, Mother had told me not to take the tablets the doctor gave me because she said the baby would grow too big and I would have trouble when I gave birth. Her command hung over me and so although my doctor gave me iron tablets, I didn't take them because of Mother. In spite of everything, I still believed that what she said was right. However I went to all of my ante-natal appointments and Osghar usually came with me, though sometimes he stayed at home and looked after Azmier.

Being pregnant a second time was different because I didn't feel that the nurses were judging me; instead, they treated me like all the other Mums there. Osghar fussed over me, which I found hard to take; if I felt unwell, he would make me put my feet up and he wouldn't let me do housework which, instead of being a treat, made me feel a little insecure. I hadn't had anyone fuss over me before and I wanted him to stop; I felt I was losing control in some weird way. I told him I was fine when I wasn't: I would push myself to do all the housework, fetch Azmier from nursery and make him some tea and then flop on to the settee feeling exhausted. I was so used to doing things for other people I didn't, I couldn't, slow down and think about myself. I wanted to be strong enough to deal with everything, or, rather, I felt I *had* to be strong enough to deal with everything. I had to go to the various offices and make sure we got a house to live in; I had to apply for Osghar's visa to remain in the UK; I had to look after my family's needs.

Every week, I'd walk into town – because I couldn't afford the bus fare – just to ask the council if they'd found us a council house. It was always the same answer: 'No, I'm sorry, nothing is available yet.'

It was frustrating to hear the same thing every time; Osghar needed a permanent address to give to the immigration office, because he had applied for a permanent visa to stay in the UK on the grounds that he was married to a British citizen. I kept worrying about whether he was going to be allowed to stay here with me. What if they sent him back? How would I cope on my own with two children, no home, and barely enough money to make ends meet? I prayed every day that things would improve. All I wanted was a house and for Osghar to get a visa to stay there with me. Was that really so much to ask for?

Then two weeks before the baby was due, we finally got the call we had been waiting for.

'A house has become available. Not far from where you are now. There will be a housing officer waiting there for you at eleven o'clock, to see if you think it is suitable,' the woman said.

'I'll take it!' I said, trying not to whoop for joy. 'I don't care where it is as long as it has four walls and a roof!'

I was so eager for a place I could call home, that by ten thirty we were outside the house in Moss Side waiting for the housing officer to arrive. It was a small terraced building with no front garden, the front door opening straight on to the pavement. We looked through the window into the lounge, which was quite small and had black and white wallpaper. It looked very clean and as soon as we saw it inside we knew we'd be happy there. It had two bedrooms upstairs – a big one for a double bed and a smaller one, just right for a young boy – and a kitchen/dining room that was big enough to fit in a dining table and settee.

Finally, a place to live that wouldn't be temporary; somewhere to bring the baby home. But the house had no furniture. Everywhere we'd stayed so far had been furnished. 'Where are we going to sleep?' I asked.

'I'm getting paid today,' said Osghar. 'I'll go and buy a second-hand bed. Besides, we don't have to move out of the homeless complex straight away. I'm sure we have at least a few days to get ourselves sorted.'

We went back to the flat that night and were getting ready for bed when I noticed that I felt more tired than usual.

The next day Osghar went to work but promised to be home around lunchtime. Azmier put his toys into bags and I packed our clothes into a suitcase. I hadn't done much, but I felt exhausted, as if I had been working hard all morning. When Osghar came home at lunch, I was lying on the bed and told him I didn't feel well – I was feeling some cramping.

'It's all the excitement of moving house,' said Osghar.

I wasn't so sure. I recognised the contractions. I timed them, and they were about seven minutes apart. At twelve thirty, I told Osghar that I thought the baby was coming.

'Are you sure?' His usually calm face took on the first signs of panic. 'Are you really going to have the baby soon?'

I thought back to my labour with Azmier. 'No, it'll be a while yet, I think,' I told him.

But Osghar started to fuss and called a taxi from the phone booth. It arrived within a couple of minutes, which was a good job because if it hadn't, I would have had the baby at home. The contractions became stronger as we approached the hospital. When we arrived, at twelve forty-five, I was barely upright as we went to reception.

'I think the baby is coming,' I puffed out to the woman. 'The contractions are bearable but getting stronger.'

'Can you walk?' asked a nurse who came running up to me. Without waiting for an answer she said, 'I'll be right back.' She disappeared and returned a few seconds later with a wheelchair. 'Have a seat, love, and I'll take you to maternity right away.'

I sat in the chair, and Osghar and Azmier walked by my side looking a bit worried. I explained to Azmier on the way to the unit that he'd soon have a little brother or sister to play with. He smiled and his face lit up at the thought of having a little brother or sister. Just before the nurse wheeled me into the labour room, Azmier whispered to me, 'I hope it's a brother.' I smiled at him.

In the labour room, another nurse handed me a gown. Two other nurses were plugging in machines and pulling wires. Once I'd changed into the gown, one nurse helped me on to the bed and another wired me up to the machine. The contractions were very strong at this point and I felt the sensation of wanting to push.

'You can't be ready yet!' said the nurse. 'I haven't checked if you're fully dilated. Wait, wait!'

'I can't wait!' I cried.

The other nurse ran out to get the midwife. Just then, my waters broke. That's when the contractions turned into excruciating pain. It was as if something had grabbed hold of my backbone and was twisting it round and round, the contractions pulled at me so much. I didn't remember anything like this from Azmier's birth. 'It hurts!' I screamed. 'I want something for the pain. Give me something for the pain!'

'It's too late for that. The baby is coming. Push, Sam, push!'

The midwife came in and took her place. She glanced between my legs then at me and said, 'Were you planning on having the baby at home?'

'No, I said. I felt my insides ripping apart.

'I can see the head,' said the midwife. 'Just a few more pushes.'

I pushed and pushed, and then I heard a scream – was that me? – and a little cry.

'It's a boy!'

Asim was in my arms by ten past one; the nurses had barely had time to get me to the delivery room. I was drained, and I'd imagined before that I only had a certain amount of love to give. But that wasn't the case; as I held this little bundle, love flowed through me and although I'd expected to divide my love between my precious boys I found this new joy let me feel I was brimming with love for Azmier, Asim and Osghar equally. It was amazing.

After a few moments, Osghar came in, tears streaming down his face. 'The nurse told me it's a boy,' he said, hugging me close.

I just nodded. It was such a relief, such a comfort, to have someone with me this time.

Azmier popped up next to him. 'Can I see? Can I see?' he asked eagerly.

'Yes. Come here,' I said, holding my arms out. 'Give me a hug. You got your wish. You have a baby brother.'

After we'd all hugged and kissed some more, one of the nurses placed a hand on Osghar's shoulder. 'Could you wait outside now while we clean her up? We'll take her to the ward when we've finished. You can go and wait there.'

'We love you,' said Osghar as they waved to me, and Azmier blew me a kiss.

I waved back. 'See you in a bit.'

When I got to the ward, Osghar and Azmier were waiting for me. The baby, Asim, was asleep in his cot at the foot of the bed. I kissed him and got into bed.

'You look tired,' said Osghar, gently brushing a strand of hair back from my cheek. 'You rest now. We'll go into town to get clothes for the baby, then we'll come back later on this evening to visit you.'

I managed to nod and fell into a deep sleep. I was awakened by the nurse telling me the baby was crying. 'Have you decided if you're going to breast- or bottle-feed? He seems hungry.'

'Definitely breast-feed,' I said.

The nurse handed Asim to me and closed the curtain.

Osghar and Azmier visited me every day while I was in hospital. I was allowed to go home on the fourth day, and Osghar had a taxi waiting outside to take us home.

When we got to the new house, I found that Osghar had furnished the rooms. There was a second-hand settee he had bought for twenty pounds. There was an old camping bed for Azmier. For our bedroom, he had bought a new mattress and placed it on the floor in the corner of the room.

'I couldn't afford much, but at least we have the basics,' he said.

'And I got Asim some clothes, Mummy,' Azmier said proudly. 'Look!' And he pulled everything out of a bag.

'They're lovely, sweetie. You did a good job choosing.'

We stood in the living room, Asim asleep in my arms. Osghar put an arm around my waist and held me close. Azmier hugged my knees as he grinned up at his new baby brother. My own, loving family.

I had had nothing for Azmier when he was born which had bothered me, but now, with Asim, I didn't have to worry as Osghar would take care of practicalities. Best of all, I wasn't on my own, which was the most wonderful feeling I'd ever known. I snuggled closer into Osghar, kissed his cheek, and said, 'Everything is wonderful.'

I had to go through one more trauma: Manz's trial was scheduled to start two months after Asim's birth. I stayed away from all of it, except for the day when I had to give evidence. The policeman taking me in to the courtroom came to visit me the day before and said, 'We know that some of your family are attending the trial, and they'll probably be there tomorrow – they've been there throughout. When we go in, just keep your head down, don't speak to them, don't look over at them. Is that okay?'

I just nodded, and made my own plans.

The next morning, I put on my smartest, newest outfit, clothes they'd never have bought for me, and, when we walked into the courthouse, made sure I looked over to see Mother was looking at me. I knew she'd be there; and she just stared at me. I stared back.

Head held high, I walked on with my escort into the waiting room, proud of myself, proud to be there that day, and proud I'd stood up to her – to all of them – and had my own, loving family waiting for me at home.

Manz was found guilty of conspiracy to kidnap, and sentenced to four years in jail in Manchester's notorious Strangeways Prison.

20

I loved being a Mum, and the closeness I felt with my boys meant so much to me. In the months and years that followed, when I went to collect Azmier from his nursery, some of the other Mums would be standing outside the school talking. I'd nod at them when I passed and a few of them would comment, pointing at Asim as he sat in his pushchair, 'I bet you can't wait until he starts school, you'll be free then,' and they'd giggle. I would smile and nod back politely, but inside I'd be thinking, I'm in no hurry for him to start nursery, I want to spend all the time I can with him.

One Manz was safely locked away from me, and once I'd had the chance to look at my mother as a free woman, that day in court, I felt more settled. Azmier made friends and would talk about school and what he did that day when I asked him. I always spent time with him in the evenings, helping him with his homework. After a while, I started talking to the other Mums. They would chat about general stuff like what they were going to do when they got home, what the children did last night, and what they got up to when they went out to the pub. I didn't think we had much in common but stood with them anyway, and gradually joined in the conversations, which was how I got to know some of them really well. I gradually started to feel part of the community, and definitely started to feel a sense of place. I belonged somewhere, at last.

Osghar and I worked hard to build the best life we could for our family. He learned English and eventually became a citizen. We managed to save enough money to buy a house near a huge park where the boys could play the same sorts of games as Amanda and I had in Cannock Chase. Azmier and Asim did well in school and always brought me great joy. There have been hard times, but my adult life has never been the nightmare that most of my childhood was.

One day when Asim was around five, the phone rang and I answered it.

A strong Scottish voice spoke. 'Hello, is that Sam?'

I said yes; I didn't recognise the caller.

'Sam, it's me, Saber.'

My hands started to shake and my eyes filled with tears. I didn't know my own brother's voice. I smiled through my tears.

'How are you?' I gasped. 'Where did you get my number from?'

'Tanvir got it from Osghar's family in Pakistan,' he said. 'I'm ringing about Dad.'

Oh, no, I thought. There could be only one reason my family would call me about Dad.

'He's very ill,' Saber went on. 'He was in Glasgow, fell ill, and now he's in hospital and was asking about you. I think you should come and see him.'

'Yes, of course. Which hospital?'

'Victoria, ward four.'

'Is he really bad?' I could hardly speak over the lump in my throat.

'Come quickly.' And then he put the phone down without even saying goodbye.

When Osghar came home that evening, I told him that I had to go to Glasgow in the morning and explained why.

'Why are you going? What if Manz is there or, worse, your mother?'

I shuddered at that, but I was determined. 'I don't care. I have to see Dad before it's too late. If I bump into anyone I'll just face it.'

I caught the 6.07 train the following morning. As the train made its way north, my mind began to imagine the worst. What if I actually bumped into Manz? He'd served a prison sentence for attempted kidnap, and even though I hadn't seen him or anyone else from the family, I knew he blamed me for it. After all, that's the sort of man he was. And what about Mother? What would I do if I saw her? Or anyone else in the family? Would they curse me, drag me into a back street, beat me up and leave me for dead? I was frightening myself, so I went to the snack cart at the rear of the train and bought a cup of coffee. Back in my seat, I pulled a magazine out of my bag and tried to read, only the words blurred on the page in front of me and I sat fidgeting all the way.

When the train arrived in Glasgow, I took a taxi to the hospital. Saber had said ward four, and it seemed to take years to walk through the corridors and up the stairs to get there. I stood outside the ward door for a few moments, gathering my courage. Then I pushed open the door, walked to the nurses' station and asked where my father was.

'Second bed from the end,' said a nurse, pointing and giving me an encouraging smile.

I went past four beds in which elderly people slept. And then I stood at the foot of the bed the nurse had indicated. This didn't look like my father; this was an old, frail-looking man, a drip attached to his arm, on the verge of death. I almost went back to the nurses' station to double-check. But then his eyes opened and his face broke out in that bright smile I always loved.

'I knew you would come,' Dad said in a quiet voice I could hardly hear.

I moved to his bedside and we hugged each other for a long time. Neither of us spoke. Tears rose in my eyes, but I didn't want him to see me cry, so I blinked them away. Finally, we let go.

'You look so ill, Dad. What happened?' He looked worse than ill; he looked as if he were eighty-five instead of the fifty-five I knew him to be.

He gave a weak shake of his head. 'No, I'm getting better now. You should have seen me last week.' He paused as he studied my face closely. 'You look the same as ever, Sam. Are you happy?'

'Yes, Dad,' I said, wishing I had thought to bring photos of Azmier and Asim for him to see. Unlike my own childhood, I made sure there were masses of photos of the boys, at every stage of their young lives; I'd look at them, sometimes, when the boys were at school, and wish I could see myself at that age too. 'I'm very happy now.'

We talked for hours, reminiscing about all the things we'd done together, the times he sneaked us off to the zoo or the fair or the library and how he'd get into trouble afterwards.

'Pass me that radio out of there,' he said as he pointed to his bedside cabinet. I opened the small door and pulled out a small blue radio. I handed it to him.

'No, you keep it,' he said. 'Give it to my favourite grandson.'

I put it in my bag and tears filled my eyes. It felt like a going-away present. I wanted to stay longer but Dad mentioned that Manz came to see him in the afternoons and he didn't want me to bump into him. So I hugged and kissed him before saying goodbye. I kept looking back and waving as I walked out of the ward.

I saw my dad more when I lived in the children's home than I ever did later in life; and in the children's home I was happiest. I knew this was no coincidence.

Exactly as I expected, Saber didn't ring me again until Dad had died.

'The funeral is on Tuesday,' he told me. 'We wanted to have it tomorrow but the hospital won't release him.'

'I'll get the earliest train on Tuesday,' I managed to say over the lump in my throat. 'I should be there around ten.'

'Yeah, I think that's best. And you should leave the same day. Everyone's going to be upset and you don't want to upset them even more by staying any longer than necessary.' And he hung up.

My hand shook as I replaced the receiver, and I broke into uncontrollable sobs. Osghar held me, rocking me the same way I did when one of the boys was upset. We agreed it wasn't a good idea for him to go to the funeral because he thought it would just make tempers flare. He knew that Manz wouldn't be happy to see him, and he didn't want to be the cause of a scene on such an occasion.

I arrived in Glasgow alone, and climbed into a taxi. Mother had moved out of the area she called 'Little Pakistan' after I'd run away and Manz had gone to prison; Saber had told me she'd felt too embarrassed to stay there, where people knew what had happened. I walked into the house to find Saber waiting in the hallway. I reached out to hug him, but he stepped away. I swallowed down a sob, but he just looked at his feet and pointed towards a door.

'The women are in there,' he said.

I wrapped my scarf tightly around my head and walked in the room. There were a dozen women sitting on the floor chanting prayers and crying. Tara, Hanif and Mena sat in the middle of the room. My heart leaped at the sight of Mena, and I walked towards them, tears streaming down my face. Tara looked up at me. An ache rose up inside me, wanting her to hug me. We'd never been close, but we were sisters and our dad had just died. I wanted to grieve with them, to share this one thing we had in common at that moment.

'Don't sit here,' she said. 'Sit over there.' She pointed to the empty corner next to the fireplace.

I stared at her for a moment, and she glared back. Then I gave one slow nod and sat where she'd indicated. The other women shifted uncomfortably and bowed their heads when I glanced around at them.

But whatever Tara thought she could do to me, she couldn't stop me from grieving for my father, praying that he was in a better place, that he was happy now.

The men of the family – Manz, Saber, Salim, Bashir and a few others I didn't recognise – walked in with Dad's coffin and placed it in the room for us to say our farewells; as women, we weren't allowed to go to the cemetery. None of them looked my way. Tara, Hanif and Mena supported each other as they gathered around the coffin and wept loudly.

I kept my head down and I could only see Manz's chin. I didn't want to make eye contact with him at all. I thought his temper might flare up and I certainly didn't want that; I was scared as I didn't know what he might do but there were so many people there, Mother's friends and the like, that I thought he wouldn't make a scene in front of them.

I stood up, trembling, and walked towards the coffin. My father's face looked so peaceful, and tears began to trickle down my cheeks. He looked younger than he had in hospital. All I could think was how quickly ten years had passed and how stupid it was that we hadn't kept in touch until it was too late.

The women put their arms around Tara and Mena, comforting them. Then we all began to chant prayers. As we did, the men carried the coffin out; I looked away, so as not to catch sight of Manz's face.

'Bye, Dad,' I whispered as he was taken out of the room.

Tanvir came over to me a few minutes later. 'I think you should leave now,' she said.

My breath caught in my throat. 'But I want to stay for the three-day prayer ceremony.'

'There's nowhere for you to stay.'

I summoned all my courage and speaking as sincerely as I could, I said, 'Thanks for letting me know about Dad and giving me the chance to say goodbye.'

And I left.

I visited Glasgow a few times after Dad died. I felt like a stranger among my family but I wanted to make an effort to get to know Mother and my brothers and sisters as an equal, not as someone to be kicked about. After Dad died, Mother had contacted me and asked me to visit her. It took a while to find out why: it wasn't just that she feared her own death, and wanted to get to know her grandchildren before she died. During our first visit, about six months after Dad's funeral, she told me her reason: she wanted me to leave Osghar. She thought she could persuade me to return. She would say things like, 'We have forgiven you for what's happened. Just come back and go to Pakistan, to your husband.'

I was incredulous. 'Forgiven me – for what?'

'For running away.'

'I didn't do anything wrong.'

I would get upset, and return home disappointed after these visits because Mother still thought I was no good, I was still letting her down. Osghar was very good at dealing with me when I came home; he knew what they'd been saying, and how to calm me down.

Mother lived with Salim, his wife and their two children. He owned a butcher's shop and was doing well. The first couple of times I visited, it was awkward because the atmosphere between myself and Mother was very tense. She wouldn't talk to me much: she would just ask me how I was and then go to her room complaining of a headache.

Shahad, Salim's wife, was a distant cousin from Pakistan. She was a kind young woman who always smiled when I came to visit. On my third visit, when everyone else was off at work or school one day, and Mother was in bed as usual, she sat down next to me in the living room and asked what had happened between us – between my family and me – and the reason why they were so cold towards me.

'Surely they've told you the story,' I said.

'Yes, their version.' She looked down into her teacup. 'But you don't seem like the kind of person they say you are.'

I swallowed. 'What have they said about me?'

'That you're not a nice person and you're not worth knowing.' Shahad looked straight into my eyes. 'But you seem like a good person to me.'

I put a finger to my lips. 'Shh. You'll get into trouble if Mother hears you saying that.'

We giggled, and in that instant became friends.

I told her about being raised in the children's home, which she hadn't been told about, and how I was married at thirteen and a mother at fourteen. It didn't surprise me that they had conveniently omitted to mention that to her.

When I finished the story, she said, 'You're very brave, coming back.'

'I wanted to give them a second chance, to get to know me and my children. But if they don't want to, then that's fine – that's their loss, not mine.'

Later on that visit, when Mother was with us, Shahad said something about Manz, and Mother surprised me by saying, 'Well, you know what Manz is like: he acts first and thinks later.' She looked at me as she said it and I felt that this was the closest I would get to an explanation of what had happened before the trial; Manz would have said, 'I'll get her back even if it's in a body bag,' and no one would have been able to tell him otherwise.

When Mother was out of the room, Shahad said, 'Your mother's very ill. She doesn't spend much time here in Glasgow, her asthma's too bad, so she stays in Pakistan most of the year and only comes back during the hottest months.'

I had always known that Mother was ill; goodness knows she'd made us all aware of it with her spitting and headaches, but I'd never known what she was actually diagnosed with. She had developed diabetes and would eat bars of chocolate because she craved sweets sometimes. Her health had deteriorated so much that she had an oxygen cylinder by her bed, and would take oxygen when she needed it.

Shahad sighed. 'I do think she should let bygones be bygones. If she makes an effort to get on with you then everyone will.'

That did happen, gradually, over the next three years. I went up to visit Mother in Glasgow when she came in the summer months, and sometimes I even stayed overnight. I felt seeing her now, when I was confident in who I was, and had the security of knowing Osghar and my boys back at home loved me, gave me a new strength. Being able to look her in the eye – even though she averted her gaze, as always, when I did so – was, to me, a measure of what I'd been able to do for myself. And as I did so, I felt the fear, and the hatred, seep away from me.

I saw Mena when I went to Glasgow. She'd bought a house opposite where Mother lived. At first, she was hesitant about talking to me, even though we were alone, as if she were scared to tell me everything in her heart. So instead, I said it to her, 'I really missed you. So did Azmier.'

She looked at me and whispered as if someone were listening in. 'I missed you, too.' Then she told me how everyone had changed after I left. Mother had become much calmer, and because I'd run away, they hadn't forced her into an early arranged marriage. 'I got married when I was twenty-one,' she said proudly.

I smiled as I realised I *had* made a difference.

Eventually, the time came to take Azmier to see Mother. But before I could do that, I had to tell Azmier about his real father. Osghar had raised Azmier as his own son, but now that he was in his early teens I judged that it was time to tell him the truth. Somehow, I knew that Mother would make a point of mentioning it, and I wanted Azmier to hear it from me.

So, shortly before our scheduled trip to Glasgow, on an afternoon when Osghar was working and Asim was out playing with his friends, I told Azmier we needed to talk.

As he sat looking at me expectantly, I wondered how I could tell him that his biological father was a man in Pakistan who had never made any effort at all to contact him. Then I took a deep breath and plunged into the story. He didn't seem surprised when I told him I'd been married and got pregnant so young, but then he was old enough to have already figured out the maths. Then I told him that he was the angel who rescued me, that because of him I stopped wanting to commit suicide. And that it was he who'd given me the strength to get away from my family.

'I'm sorry I haven't told you all this before,' I ended. 'I'll understand if you want to go and see him.'

He looked at me and smiled. 'Nah. Why would I want to do that?' He shrugged. 'In the future if I feel the need to, maybe.' And he hugged me tightly and went out to play football with the neighbourhood boys.

When we went to see Mother a few weeks later, I'd hardly introduced Azmier when she blurted out, 'Your real father is in Pakistan.'

Azmier just shrugged his shoulders and said, 'Yeah, I know. And?'

I almost burst with pride. And with suppressed laughter. Mother's face was a picture – robbed of the opportunity to be horrible, she didn't know what to do.

Mother tried to talk to me about Afzal, too: 'He has got married now; you have missed your chance, but if we persuade him he'll still have you back.' I wouldn't even acknowledge what she'd said, so she tried again: 'He's only got daughters, you know, he hasn't got a son yet.' But I paid no attention to this and she soon stopped.

I kept on returning. Azmier came with me now and again, but it was just the two of us as Mother made it clear that she didn't want anything to do with Osghar and Asim. I don't know why I kept going back, but I did, still feeling the same, that Mother was still not accepting me for who I was, for who I'd become.

When he was nearly twelve, I took Asim to see Mother because he wanted to know who my mother was and what we did when we went to Glasgow to visit her. I didn't have the heart to tell him he couldn't go too, so off the three of us – Azmier as well – went together. We took some flowers, and all the way up on the train I was worried, although I didn't let it show. I didn't know what to expect from Mother, I didn't know how she would react because I hadn't told her that Asim was coming – I knew she'd say no if I asked her. I knew no matter what, I would be there if Mother rejected him. I would protect him, I would stick up for him like a mother should.

Mother, though, surprised me. We walked in and I introduced him, looking at her nervously as I said, 'This is your grandson, Asim.'

She looked at him for a few moments and suddenly said, 'Come here, then, aren't you going to give your grandma a hug?' She hugged him and as she did so looked at me over his shoulder, her eyes saying everything while she didn't speak a word. There was acceptance, there was acknowledgement, which meant everything to me.

I felt satisfied, I felt a sense of accomplishment, I felt I had achieved everything I'd wanted. Deep inside, the reason why I returned again and again was because I wanted a pat on the back from Mother, I knew that now. I wanted her acknowledgement and to know that she was proud of something I had done in my life. I felt that I could do anything I put my mind to after that.

I continued to visit my family occasionally. I even managed to learn to love Mother, in a way. Not in the way of usual mother–daughter relationships, but we did settle into a sort of peace. I realised that if Mother needed to let bygones be bygones, so did I. If not for that cruel sham of a marriage, I wouldn't have my lovely son Azmier. And, as the sequence of events worked out, I probably wouldn't have married Osghar and we wouldn't have Asim. Perhaps I wouldn't have had any happiness at all.

★   ★   ★

It was Tara who telephoned me, in January 2001, to tell me of Mother's death, out in Pakistan, although she could hardly speak through her tears when I answered; instead she handed the phone over to her eldest daughter, who told me Mother had died and everyone was going to her funeral. 'You must come too,' she said.

After I hung up, I wept. I felt a real sense of loss that surprised me. I thought about a saying I'd once read, that if someone doesn't love you the way you want them to, it doesn't mean they don't love you with all they have. In that moment, I realised the truth, that Mother was simply someone who hadn't had a lot of love to give.

I told Osghar the news, and we agreed I should go; he said to me, 'Go over, pay your last respects. It's the right thing to do.' As well as the sorrow I felt, I was also concerned; I knew I should go, indeed I wanted to go, but I was scared. I was going back to the place where nightmares dwelled.

Osghar spoke to his brother and arranged things with him. 'I've organised for you to stay at my brother's house and he will get a car and a driver to take you to your mother's house every day, wait there for you, and bring you back again. That way we'll all know where you are, and you can always get away if you feel uncomfortable.'

I managed to get an emergency visa to Pakistan and a flight the same day. Manz was already there; he'd been with Mother when she died. Mena, Tara, Saber and Salim arrived in time for her funeral, as everyone chipped in and helped each other out; except for me, of course, as I was left to organise my own trip. I spent the time on the plane listening to some self-help CDs, to give me strength to get through what was to come. Just before we landed, I finished one about facing your fears – it really helped over the next few days.

I arrived at my brother-in-law's house in the evening and rested the first day. I wished in a way I hadn't because it gave me time to reflect, to think about what I was doing there. What if Azmier's dad was there, and he wanted to talk to me? I hadn't seen him for two decades; I never thought about him as I had no connection with him. My thoughts were just running away from me. After a few bleak hours, I told myself I would have to be strong and face my fears, deal with things when they happened – *if* they happened.

For Muslims, the earlier the body is buried the better, but the funeral ceremonies go on for a month, so although I didn't make it for Mother's burial I was there for the ceremonies afterwards, which began the next day. The main mourning period is for the three days after the body is buried, which is for family, and then for other relatives and friends – who have further to travel – it is the ten days that follow. This is when everyone who knew Mother would sit outside on the floor and pray for her, the men inside (with the fans on) while the women sat outside. Mostly, the women would chat rather than pray.

Osghar's sister came to spend the night with me, and she kept my mind off things as she filled me in on what everyone was doing. I was so tired I fell asleep as she was talking.

The next day I was about to leave when my sister-in-law came running up to me and said, 'Don't go alone. Take Nura, the housemaid, with you. You need someone with you, you know, to raise the alarm if there's any trouble.'

I thanked her, and Nura and I went out to the car. The driver had also been told he was to watch over me, but my throat was too dry to speak, from my being so nervous, so it was as well he needed no encouragement to talk.

'Don't worry about anything, sister, I know where I'm going and if you need anything I'll be waiting there at all times. Shall we get some rose petals and incense sticks on the way?'

'What?' I asked.

'Do you want to go to your mother's graveside first? Don't worry, I'll be there with you.'

'Yes.'

'Then we will get some petals on the way; you people from England don't know the customs, but don't worry, I'm here to help.'

I didn't know what he was talking about, so I just nodded my head.

We drove through a bazaar and he stopped at a couple of stalls and bought some rose petals and incense sticks. We drove for about twenty minutes and all the time I was looking through the window as the driver was being the tour guide. I tried to recognise the surroundings.

'That's your mother's house,' he said, pointing to a building as he turned into a street, as he kept driving, 'Your mother is buried just down here.' We drove for a couple more minutes and he stopped the car. I looked out of the window and I could see farmland to my left and a small amount of cleared land, with three mounds on it.

'This one is freshly buried, this one must be your mother,' he said as he handed me the petals. 'You can scatter them over her, this side is her feet, that side is her face,' he said, pointing.

It all suddenly became real. This heap of earth, here, this is my mother. I didn't feel anything up to that point, only numbness. I though, I hope you go to heaven, I really do. I thought of how overpowering she was when she lived and yet here, now, she was nothing. Truly ashes to ashes, dust to dust. I didn't cry, I just felt sorry for her as I scattered the rose petals on the mound of what looked to me like nothing, and yet here lay my mother. I lit the incense and placed it next to my mother's body. The driver and servant girl left me alone for a few minutes and went and stood by the car. After seeing her grave I felt stronger. I thought, I am ready to face whatever is waiting for me at Mother's house; I will stick up for myself.

With these thoughts I walked up to the car and we drove over to join the others. As I walked into the village in the mid-afternoon sun and looked around, I thought that it seemed smaller than I remembered and it didn't feel quite as intimidating as it had twenty years before. I opened the gates to Mother's house and walked through. I didn't recognise any of the women who were sitting on the floor chanting prayers. The drooping tree was still there, standing taller than I remembered. The yard looked the same except for a building that had been added at the side of the house. I walked inside, where, just like outside, everything looked exactly the same. There were still two beds and a lamp in the corner.

Tara and Mena were sitting on one of the beds. They looked at me and started to cry. I didn't know whether to hug them or not but then Tara stood up and put her arms out so I stepped forward and hugged her. I couldn't cry, I felt sad, really, really sad, but I didn't cry. After hugging Mena I sat on the bed next to them. I asked where Manz was and Tara said he was around somewhere. I was nervous about meeting him but I knew I was safe because Saber was there, and I had Nura with me and the driver outside. I didn't speak much; Tara and Mena didn't either; they asked how my flight was and where I would be staying and that kind of stuff. But it wasn't uncomfortable, just not the time for chatting.

A few hours later Manz walked in and looked at me. I rose to my feet, unsure what to do or say. He came up to me and I flinched inside, thinking, What is he going to do? But all he said was, 'I'm glad you made it. Mother died in my arms and before she did she said to me that she wanted us to get along with each other. You can stay here for as long as you like.' He took a step nearer and gave me an awkward hug.

I nodded. I knew we could never be friends, but at least we could be civilised when we saw each other and I no longer needed to fear him.

Just then Saber and Salim walked in.

'Hey, you made it.' They were pleased to see me. Saber even called me Sid. I nodded once again.

Not a lot of women turned up to prayer that day but it was going to be different the next day because it was the third day ceremony, which is usually the big event of the mourning period. Before I left Tara told me to come as early as possible, around eight thirty in the morning. It was dusk on the way home and the sun was just setting; people were walking home slowly from a hard day's work, the horse and carts plodding along at their own pace. I felt as exhausted as any of them.

The next day some women were already sitting in the yard praying when I arrived at eight fifteen. There were three chairs set out at the end of the yard, and I thought we were going to be sitting there, but I carried on into the house. Tara was sitting on the bed, looking tired. She looked up, and said, 'I like what you're wearing; we'll be sitting outside all day, so that'll keep you warm.'

I was wearing a blue shalwar-kameez, a cardigan and a wrap-around black shawl. I wasn't expecting her to say anything like that, so I only managed to mutter, 'Thanks.'

After breakfast the yard looked a bit fuller so we put our scarves around our head and sat on the chairs. I sat at one end, Mena in the middle and then Tara. I looked around and saw these women staring back at me, which made me feel uneasy, so I leaned in and whispered to Mena, 'They're staring at us as if we're alien or something, what's going on?'

'Shut up, don't make me laugh,' she said.

'What's she saying?' Tara asked.

'She said they are staring at us like aliens,' Mena told her.

Tara leaned behind Mena so no one could see our faces, smiled and said, 'I know, you're right.'

Then someone came up to me. 'Your mother said we could see the boy.'

I looked up at her and saw an elderly woman.

'You know who I am, I'm Fozia, Afzal's sister.' I was going to say, 'No, I don't recognise you,' but I didn't; instead I said, 'Pardon?'

'Your mother said we could see the boy,' she repeated coldly.

'What boy?' I was puzzled.

'Our boy.'

And then it clicked, she was talking about Azmier. I looked at Tara, who just shrugged her shoulders. I said, 'Please don't do this now.'

She ignored me, and carried on, 'We want to see the boy.'

I sighed. 'Okay, you want to cause a scene, do you?' My voice was getting louder. 'You want to upset everyone here? Now? I don't think so.'

She looked at me in surprise and backed away. Perhaps she didn't think I'd oppose her. 'My boy's name is Azmier,' I whispered as she walked away.

I stayed for two weeks, going to Mother's house and leaving before dusk every day.

When I got back to England, I slept for ages as I was so drained by the whole experience; but I was pleased and surprised that I had gone. I made peace with Mother before she died and that was good. I know the hole – unconditional love from a mother – inside me is never going to be filled; it took me a long time to figure out why and what the void is, but it's getting easier and easier to live with.

For all that, though, she was a piece of me, and I a piece of her, and that's why I went back to Pakistan. I wanted to say goodbye to her. It meant I'd finished with something that was never going to bother me in my life again. My mother knew what she was doing to me when she hit me, because never once did she strike me on the face. Was she evil? I don't think so; she was ill, very ill, and because she never bonded with me when I was a baby, then I suppose she never felt there was anything to stop her from treating me like a disobedient slave. I was an annoyance; an inconvenience. I was not loved.

Did I hate her? No. Do I hate her, now, for what she did to me? Not really, she's dead, and she can't hurt me any more. Did I love her? No, not really, not in the way I love my sons, as a mother should; I wanted to love her, but she wouldn't let me. But I did fear her.

One last horrible surprise awaited me. I learned from Tara – who, of course, said it spitefully – that my marriage in Pakistan had not just been something arranged by Mother; my uncle had lost money in gambling, a lot of money, and he'd promised his debtor a nice, English-born Pakistani girl as a way of avoiding the debt. My mother had wanted to help her brother more than look after me. I suppose I should have expected that.

21

The scars on my body, though nothing like the ones inside me, are with me still. For me they are a map, a guide to the past that shows the journey I've taken to get where I am now. I am stronger because of all that's happened to me; I've learned to push for what I want now. And that's why I challenged myself to write my story, although I haven't had any schooling since the age of twelve.

I learned to love with Osghar; I learned to trust again with the new friends I made, in Manchester. A dear friend made sure that I was welcomed back into the Pakistani community there, and that I should have nothing to fear from it; and I have made something of my life.

I was lucky to have spent the first seven years of my life in the children's home; the strong foundation of love I received there enabled me to cope with everything that was thrown at me in the years afterwards. I was taught to love, not to hate, to forgive and move on with life. I'm glad for what happened to me, even if not for the way it happened. I feel now my father would have given me more freedom and treated me like the child I was, but Mother knew if that happened she wouldn't have any control over me and she didn't want that. In her view, you had to control your child and make them follow traditions whether the child likes it or not. This is why there are tight-knit Asian communities who will not let the western world in; in the past organisations such as the police, social and health services have tiptoed around them, but this is changing. I believe it should have been done earlier. I mean how can they know the needs of a community if they aren't going to get inside it?

Forced marriage still happens today and people are being killed in the name of honour. I am one of the lucky ones who ran away and survived to tell the story. The government has helped people become aware of forced marriage but I believe more has to happen within the communities who think it is okay to do this.

In 1990 I got my first paid job, working in a local immigration office; and by the end of that decade I'd gone back to study for the first time since I was twelve, and obtained a GNVQ in Travel and Tourism. With this qualification, I worked at Manchester Airport as a check-in agent. More recently, I set up a local residents association in the area in which I live, and, as a result, got to know most of the councillors and council executives. My involvement with the council has led us to secure millions of pounds to give the area a facelift.

In May 2007 I stood as the Labour Party candidate for Moss Side in the local council elections, and I was elected with twice the number of votes of all the other candidates put together. I don't say this to boast, but just to record how far I've come.

Sometimes I comb my hair over my ears, and then suddenly recall that this is what Mother wanted me to do – she always said my hair was like hers, and that I should wear it as she did – and I'll quickly pull it back behind my ears. I don't want to catch sight of my reflection in a shop window, and be reminded of her like that.

In my social services file, one line hit me hard. The anonymous writer was compiling a report on both me and Mena, and he or she referred to the social worker, who I don't know for sure but believe to be Auntie Peggy, and said: 'The social worker is concerned because the children are becoming more Anglicised and if rehabilitation is attempted in future this will be very difficult.'

I was about three when this was written; I didn't return to my family, for 'rehabilitation', for another four years. To call this time in my life 'difficult' initially seemed like an insult to me; but being who I am now, with my husband and two sons, means that I look back on that time and feel that I have come through it, safely, happily, triumphantly.

A few weeks ago, Osghar and the boys and I went for a walk near where we live, and, while the boys played football, the two of us climbed a small hill standing in the centre of the park. As I stood up at the top, remembering all the times I'd sought the refuge of a place like this, whether it was the isolation of the monkey hills in Walsall, or the trees in Pakistan, I thought about the little, frightened girl, lonely and unhappy, that I used to be. And I turned to Osghar, and leaned into him, listening to the sounds of my sons laughing as they chased each other about with the ball, and I laughed with them, happy at last.

Acknowledgements

I would like to give special thanks to Aunty Peggy, Amina Khan, Sarah, Terie Garrison, Judith Jury, Denis Pelletier, South Manchester Writers Group, Broo Doherty, Humphrey Price, Eleanor Birne, Helen Hawksfield and Nikki Barrow.

Thank you for giving me all the encouragement and support I needed to write my story.